MREXCEL

XL

Bill Jelen and Szilvia Juhasz

Holy Macro! Books
PO Box 82
Uniontown OH 44685

D0793000

MrExcel XL — 40 Greatest Excel Tips of All Time

Printed in USA by Hess Print Solutions

First Printing: July 2015

Authors: Bill Jelen & Szilvia Juhasz

Copy Editor: Kitty Wilson

Tech Editor: Bob Umlas

Indexer: Nellie Jay

Layout Consulting: Anne Marie Concepcion with David Blattner and Dawn Kosmakos

Cover Design: Shannon Mattiza, 6Ft4 Productions

Illustrations: Scott Adams, Cartoon Bob D'Amico, George Berlin, Chelsea Besse, Chank Diesel, Sarah Lucia Jones, Walter Moore, Libby Norcross, Chad Thomas, Michelle Routt

Photography: Sean Carruthers, Karen Eonta, Freddy Fuentes, Mary Ellen Jelen, Kenny Spain,

Photography Post Processing: Michael Seeley & Jared Haworth

Production Assistance: Mary Ellen Jelen

Cocktail recipe development by Eric Ho

Cocktail photography by BurkleHagen Studios with creative direction by Sustainable Love Corporation

Cocktail graphic illustration by designprovaction

Published by: Holy Macro! Books, PO Box 82, Uniontown OH 44685

Distributed by Independent Publishers Group, Chicago, IL

ISBN 978-1-61547-004-2 (Print) 978-1-61547-227-7

Library of Congress Control Number: 2015907320^

Table of Contents

Dedication

Bill:

For Anne Troy. Thank you for dragging me through Book #1. I never would have gotten to Book #40 if you hadn't forced me to finish Book #1.

Szilvia:

To my dad, John Juhasz. It was your tireless devotion to my early education in science and math that ultimately shaped my appreciation of the art of good spreadsheet design. Additionally, your many predictions that my being a smart aleck would only result in my own peril have all proven completely accurate.

Acknowledgments

This book was funded through an IndieGogo campaign. I wanted to produce a color book, and I am grateful for the response and preorders.

My sincere thanks to everyone who participated: Access Analytic (Jeff Robson), Christopher Akina, Alumni Ryan & Matthew Albern, Peter Albert data2impact, Areef Ali, Belinda L Allen, Addie Allison, Matt Allington - ExceleratorBI.com.au, Scott St. Amant, Brian Høg Andersen, Amy Andrae, Rod Apfelbeck, Frank Arendt-Theilen, Ron Armstrong - XL GURU Inc., Myles Arnott Clarity Consultancy Services Ltd, Association for Computers & Taxation, ateebit

Julie Babcock-Hyde, Jo Ann Babin, Alnis Bajars, Freddy Barahona, Salvador M Barreiros, Zack Barresse, Jeremy Bartz, Andrew Basey, Suvojit Basu, Christopher Battiston, Dave Baylis, Prem Beejan, Vladimir Belikov, Tarquin Bell, Aaron Bembry, Simon Z Benninga, Oliver Berghaus, Michael V. Bernot, Carsten Bieker, Blockhead Data Consultants (Julie Quick), Max Martin Blum, Marcus Bolton, Caroline Bonner, Lyne Borbe-Navarra, Lan Boughton, Sid Bowman, Eric Boyer, Andrew Brad, Jeff Bradbury , Melanie Breden, Robert Breedlove, Walt Breuninger, Sheri Brewer, Quentin Brooke, Steve A Brooks UK, Derek Brown from Basingstoke (UK), Sam Bruce, Sean R. Buck, Lisa Burkett, Daniel Burleigh, Michael Byrne

Siva C, Tami Calleia, Anita Campbell CEO of Small Business Trends, Gregory R Canda, Brian D Canes, Dave Carlson DynoTech Software, Jose Castaneda, Guy-Francois Castella, Mike Cawley, Tony Chaouch, Petros Chatzipantazis (RibbonCommander.com), John Chis, SJ Choi, Patty Cisneros, Khalif John Clark, Luann Clark, Conn Clissmann, Marion Coblentz, Cynthia Cockburn, John Cockerill, Christopher C. Cole, Arend Collen, Rob Collie, Randy Collier, David Colman, Steve Comer, Jessica Commins @renewabelle, Lee Conner, Ed Corell, Nick Corrie, Jeffrey P. Coulson, CPASelfstudy.com, Crystal (strive4peace), CTROY, Aaron D Culbertson, David Cullipher, Nuno Cunha, Ricky Curioso

Amey Dabholkar (Exploring Excel), Brad Dancer, Kwame Davis, Karen Davison, Bryan J Delfs, Will DeLoach, Vicki Denny, Edwin Deo, Dethmer, Mike Dietterick , Karlheinz Dölger, Mark Domeyer, Heather Drake, Larry Duko, John Durran

Eileen Eckes, Brad Edgar, Snorre Eikeland, Ian Elsum, Elizabeth Elswick, Peter Ennis, Ron Esposito, Melissa Esquibel, Excel Strategies LLC (Blog.ExcelStrategiesLLC.com), The Excel4apps Team, ExcelSmart.com (Dennis Plum), www.exceltricks.de, EZBOE

John Fairlie, Tammy Farmer, Edward Feder, Roger Fisher, Mike Dolan Fliss, D Floyd, Michael Foran, Mark Ford, Jerid C. Fortney, Brian Fox, Derek Fraley (Row 6 in Springfield), Nick Freeman, Thomas Fries, Fuchsi, Freddy, Nancy and Elena Fuentes, Dan Fylstra

David Gainer, Mario Garcia, Yesenia Garcia, Alexa Gardner, Tim and Debbie Garlak, Lianna Gerrish, Tony Giannotti, Wim Gielis, Dawn Gilbert, Stephen Gilmer, Mike excelisfun Girvin, Judy A. Glaser, Anand Goel, Jordan Goldmeier, Hernán González, Susan Goodreau, Alex Gordon, Ryan Gottesman, Roger Govier, Rick Grantham, Joni Graves AICP, Bob Greenblatt, Olen L. Greer, Donovan Grimett, Frédéric Le Guen, James Gunther

David Haggarty, Patty Hahn, Paul Hannelly, Sabine Hanschitz, Arly Hansen, David Hansen, Jason Hanson, Matt Hard, Roy Harrill, Matt Harris, Be'eri Gurtler Har-Tuv, Hartville MarketPlace and Flea Market, Peter Harvest Harvest Consulting (Melbourne Australia), Mark Hauser, Steven Havelock, Alex Havermans (Belgium), Bill Hazlett, Michael D Hecht, Heiko Heimrath, Jean-Yves Hemlin, John Henning, Jonathan Hepplewhite, George Hepworth, Jon von der Heyden, Jon Higbed, Greg Hill, Grace P. Hinrichs, Don and Patty Hitt, Carl Hjortsjö, Chad Hobson, Helen Hoefele, Mr D C Hoey, Brad Hoffer www.xlyourfinances.com, Robert Holleran, Carl R Hooker, Jeneta Hot, Timb Hours, Simon Hughes (Morpeth UK), John Hughes, Paul Humphris, Jacqui Hunter, Gary Hutson

Nazeerul H M Ihthisham, INDZARA, Christopher Ivester

Bruce J, J.Ty., Kathy Jacobs, Dennis P Jancsy, Johanna Jaramillo, Jaumier , Robert F Jelen, Robert Karl Jelen, Zeke Jelen, JEVS Human Services, JH Training Services, Excel by Joe, Torstein S. Johnsen (Norway), James N Johnson, Al Johnston, Barbara Johnston (How To Excel At Excel.Com), Jackilyn Jones

Masaru Kaji, Gary Kane, Ryan Kane, Wayne Kao, Greg Karl, Michael Karpfen, Ryan Awesome McAwesomepants Kauffman, Gordon A. Kendall, "Dr Frank" Kendralla, Kathy Key, Jeannette Kight, Don Knowles, Sergey Kochergan, Dawn Kosmakos, Arne Kotowski, Martin 'Ulf' Kreitmair, Martin Kreitmair, Stephen J Krisel, Olga Kryuchkova

LaFrenier Sons Septic, Lake Local School District, Esko Lakso, Dan Langer, Richard B Lanza, David F. Lawson, S Leavitt, DeLisa Lee, G Lee, Kevin Lehrbass www.youtube.com/user/MySpreadsheetLab, The Leitz/ Stutzman Families, Todd A Lesko, Thomas Leung, Mindy Lewis, Geoff Lilley, Daryl Lim, Ria Lee Shue Ling, Craig Little, Anthony J. LoBello Jr., Jeff Long, Celine Loos, Ronald J. Lopez Sr., Mourad Louha, Martin Lucas, Michelle Lucchese, Ruth Ludeman, Lugh Information Services Consulting, John A Luff, Mark Luhdorff, John T Lutz, Mike Lygas, Audrey Lynn

Jack Madden, Karen Madigan, Muhammed Ashfaq Ashraf Makda, Ana V Maldonado-Molina, Dawnita Malevris, Christin Malmquist, Jean-Philippe Maltais, Mike Mann, Peter Mantell, Alex De Marco, Thiago Cerqueira Marcos, Keith Marshall, Bob Martinez, Isaac Matarasso, Emily Mathews, James Mathews, Robert Matthews, Shannon Mattiza, Stacey Matula, Allen Matz, Lynda Maynard, Dan Mayoh, Stephanie (Sam) McAtee, Patricia McCarthy, Bob McClellan, Steve McCready, Diana McGunigale, McGunigale/Ringling/Liles, The McGunigales, Wyatt McNabb, Dan Means, Claire Medland, Micah Melnyk, Carlo Melone, Beth Melton, Leo Menard, Mary Middleton, Robert P Mika, MikeAsHimself, Jade Miller, Saw Kyaw Htike Moe, James E. Moede CPA, Bob Moffatt, Jamil Mohammad, Chris "moomoo" Moore, Ryan Moore, Jeffrey Morgan, Steve and Linda Morosko, Bradford Myers, myexcelonline.com

Hiroshi Nakanishi, German Nande, Rafael I. Farfán Navarro, Kevin Nee, Justin Newsom, nidzela, Kim Nir, Robert Nix, Anthony Nixon, Augustin Nizery, Martin Nolan SurtenExcel.com, Kevin Norris, Simon Nuss

Wendall F Oakes, Mark O'Brien, officetrain.co.uk, Richard Oldcorn, Sam O'Leary, Tim O'Mara, Aizhan Omarbekova, Nate Ondricek, Jacqueline L Oneil, Victor Ooi, Michael Ortenberg

Donald Parish, Catherine Parkinson, Keyur Rahul Patel, JoAnn Paules, Susan Payton Egg Marketing & Communications, Michele M. Pearce, Lynette Pebernat, Avidan Pell, Michael Pennington, Raul Perez, Ian Perry, Rob Phillips, Keith Pieper, Mr Joseph Pierre, Alex Pilar, Kimberlie Pilar, Tony Pitakpaivan, Peter Polakovic, Shlomi Postelnik, Sherry Prindle, ProfitSpreadsheet.com, Profology.com, Ken Puls, Julie Quick (Blockhead Data Consultants)

Sam Radakovitz, John Raffin, Mohammed Altaf Ur Rahman India, Peter Raiff, Shishir Ranjan, Jake C. Rau. Mary Raya, Chris Raymundo, Palakodeti Bangaru Rayudu, Ahsan Raza S., Nigel Reardon, Bruce Reynolds, Micheal Reynolds, Rhodri., Cecelia Rieb, Will Riley, Darwin & Darla Ringling, David Ringstrom CPA, Mark Risner, Julie Rohmann, Mark Rosenkrantz, Jürgen Rösing, Richard Rost, Mike Rottenborn, Tony Rozwadowski, Rub5ter, Rylewski

Aiman Sadeq, The Salem Historical Society Salem Ohio, Edward Salinas, Ion Saliu, John W Salmons, Jon Sanderson, Sandy Sandmeyer, Victor E. Scelba II, Gail Scheuer, Morten Schjoldager, Tom Scullion, Robert D. Seals, Michael Seeley, Francesca Seidita, Serving Brevard Realty, Stephen Shay, Thomas Sherrouse, Joseph Shivers, Madeline Patton Shivers, David N Short, Linda Shrewsbury, Joanne Siegla, Sergio.Silva77, Letty

Silva, Ian Silver, Ute Simon, Jim Simons, Denise Simpson, David Sisson, Susan Slinkman, Sean Smith, Chris "Smitty" Smith, Ambjörn Snickars, Jerry Solares, Oz du Soleil, Humberto Soto, Andrew Spain, Jon Spain, Mark Spencer, Stan, Cindy Stark-Jones, Graham Stent, Edward Stephen, Ken Stern, Tsuneaki Sugawa, Kathryn Sullivan , Kevin J Sullivan, Sam Suppe, SurtenExcel.com, Peter Susen, Ben Sutton (Brookson LTD), Erik Svensen, Rick Symons, Tracy Syrstad

Eros Tagliabue, John Takacs, Ryo Takagi, Joe Takher-Smith, James Tallman, David Tan, Michael Tarzia, Dean Taunton, Angelina Teneva, Andreas Thehos, Robert Thorne, thrivebookstore.com, Tom Thususka of Brampton ON, Raymond K Gota Toudji, Shannon Travise (Creative Correspondence), Mynda Treacy, Anne Troy, TWeegels

Mike Ulrich, Bob Umlas, Tom Urtis, Larry Vance, Jose Varas, Siva Prasad Vempali, Stephen Venables, Dr. Gerard M. Verschuuren, Khushnood Viccaji, Darrell Wade, Clay B. Wagner, Ian Wainwright, Anne Walsh MCT, Mark Walter CPA, Rickard Warnelid, Alex Waterton MCT, Trevor Weaver UK, Adam Weaver, Russ Webster, Stephan van Well, Martha K Wendel, Jonathan Wernick, Michele Whaley, Steven White, Roy Wilkinson, Jenna Williams, Jim Williams, Rich Williams, Kitty Wilson, Ryan Wilson, Jeff "DrSynthetic"Wilson, Alan J. Wind, Anneliese Wirth, Patrick Wirz, John C. Wisse, Jon Wittwer, Bob Wright, Linar Yafarov, Melody Yang, www.yourgoodk9.com, Steve Yun, Nathan Zelany, D. Zureski

About the Authors

Bill Jelen is the host of MrExcel.com and the author of 40 books about Microsoft Excel including *Excel Gurus Gone Wild*, *Pivot Table Data Crunching*, and *Power Pivot Alchemy*. He has made over 80 guest appearances on TV's *The Lab with Leo / Call for Help with Leo Laporte* and was voted guest of the year on the *Computer America* radio show. He writes the Excel column for *Strategic Finance* magazine. He has produced over 1900 episodes of his daily video podcast Learn Excel from MrExcel.

Los Angeles based, Ohio-born consultant **Szilvia Juhasz**, aka XSzil is a true story of spreadsheet-love at first sight. Szilvia first cut her teeth on Excel in Budapest, Hungary, as a staff auditor at a consulting firm where she got hooked on pivot tables. Now she runs her own consulting business, helping clients leverage and integrate Excel with other systems and designing customized Excel training programs and workshops for their employees. She originally stumbled upon her first big claim to Excel-fame in Ohio, where she met MrExcel at one of his seminars and stumped him on a pivot table trick. Off-spreadsheet, Szilvia enjoys wise cracking on Twitter and creating, singing, and recording Excel-inspired parody music.

About the Contributors

Peter Albert runs the Excel-for-Consultants blog and operates data2impact - a boutique specialized in building Excel, Access, SQL Server and data centric web solutions for consultants and professionals.

Mike Alexander is the host of DataPigTechnologies.com and the author of more than a dozen books on Excel and Access.

Zack Barresse is a Microsoft MVP in Excel and Excel ninja. He is the coauthor of *Excel Tables*. He provides Excel consulting and training.

Rob Collie is the host of PowerPivotPro.com and the author of *DAX Formulas for Power Pivot* and *Power Pivot Alchemy*. He is a former software engineer on Excel at Microsoft.

Debra Dalgleish is an Excel MVP and runs the popular Contextures web site. Her Pivot Power add-in and Excel Theatre blog are two of our favorite things about Excel.

Jordan Goldmeier is a producer and co-host of Excel.TV, author of *Advanced Excel Essentials*, blogger at OptionExplicitVBA.com, and owner of CambiaFactor.com. He has been an Excel MVP since 2013.

Andrew Spain is the owner of Spain Enterprise located in Huntsville, Alabama. He provides consulting services to companies and trains individuals and groups in Excel and the Office suite.

Sam Radakovitz is a program manager on the Excel team at Microsoft. He has designed many features while there including sort and filter, sparklines, and the ribbon interface. And, more than anyone else on the team, he's done the best job of bringing the sloths, LOL cats, and the cast of twilight deeper into everyone's lives.

Chris Smith is an Excel MVP, author of *Excel 2010 Business Basics and Beyond*, Excel Trainer and Consultant.

Katie Sullivan is a program manager on the Word team at Microsoft. GO, WORD!!!!! WOOOOO!!!!!

Mynda Treacy is an Excel MVP and creator of the amazing Excel Dashboarding course. Find her at MyOnlineTrainingHub.com

Excel4apps is a leading provider of real-time, Excel-based reporting solutions for 20,000+ Oracle and SAP users worldwide.

About the Illustrators

Cartoonist **Bob D'Amico** creates custom cartoons for business and more. See www.cartoonbob.com for more about his work.

George Berlin is all about delight and wonder! He puts a smile on the world's faces with illustration, animation, and interactive projection art. See more at www.georgeberlin.com

Chelsea Besse has been drawing all her life. She graduated with her bachelors in art and loves all things creative. She can be found at www.chelseabesse.com

Chank Diesel is an alphabetician & builder of fonts. He designed the MrExcel.com font years ago. Find him at www.Chank.com

Emily Jones is a graphic designer and painter in Chicago with a passion for innovative and intuitive design. Her work can be found at www.emilyjones.com

Sarah Lucia Jones is a children's book author and illustrator living and working in Cincinnati. She creates her bright and cheery work in watercolor, cut paper, and digital. Her fine art and illustration can be seen at www.SarahLuciaJones.com.

Em DeMarco is seamstress-carpenter-baker turned journalist. She broke a national story about shale gas wastewater and has investigated amusement park safety. These days she is doing comics journalism, which merges nonfiction storytelling with illustration. View her work at www.emdemarco.com.

Walter Moore is famous for his ape cartoons. If you need an illustration of the monkey business at your work, search Bing for Walter Moore Apes.

By day, **Libby Norcross** is a space science educator; by night, she is the quirky artist & founder of Libbydoodle. She loves to spread inspiration and encouragement with her hand-doodled artwork. You can find more at www.libbydoodle.com.

Bobby Rosenstock is a printmaker who specializes in woodcut & letterpress printing. He is owner of the letterpress & design studio in Marietta, Ohio, Just A Jar Design Press. Find his amazing letterpress posters at www.justAjar.com.

Michelle Routt is a freelance multimedia artist, and has been drawing her whole life. Her portfolio is available at www.routtstanding.com where she does everything from illustrations to animation and video game development.

Chad Thomas is an illustrator who showcases his artwork on his website at www.whiterabbitart.com. His colorful and detailed artwork ranges anywhere from pet and people portraits to illustrating children's books.

Foreword

Microsoft Excel debuted 30 years ago in 1985. It wasn't the first spreadsheet program – VisiCalc had debuted in 1979. It certainly wasn't the most popular spreadsheet program – Lotus 1-2-3 had 89% market share by the late 1980s. But Microsoft had one thing in its favor – it was based on a graphical interface from the beginning. There was never a DOS-style text-based version of Excel.

If you had a long view in 1985, going with a GUI from the beginning was brilliant. But it had to be painful in 1985, originally on the Mac and then in early versions of Windows. The computing power was not fast enough to repaint the screen. In many cases, Lotus 1-2-3 would calculate ten times faster than Excel.

It wasn't until the mid-1990s, when computing power caught up, that Excel became a viable contender. 1993 to 1997 were some golden years in spreadsheet development. Every new version of Lotus 1-2-3 and Excel introduced some killer features. Pivot tables, subtotals, new functions and VBA macros all debuted in Excel during this period.

As Excel battled for market share, Microsoft had to make sure that they were 100% compatible with Lotus 1-2-3. That meant making the same mistakes as Lotus (there was no February 29 in 1900) and replicating all of the less-than-useful functions used in Lotus.

In the course of writing *Special Edition Using Excel 2007*, I had to research and document every single function in Excel. There were some that were hard to explain (FACTDOUBLE and SQRTPI) and some that were easy to explain but left you scratching your head. For example, who in real life could use the =ROMAN() function? I guess the Vatican could use =ROMAN in naming future popes. Movie production companies could use =ROMAN() to put the copyright at the end of the movie credits. And the NFL folks could use =ROMAN() to figure out the names of the upcoming Super Bowls. That is not a big audience of Excellers who could find a use for =ROMAN().

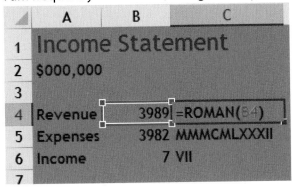

I am frequently on the road, doing half-day or all-day Power Excel seminars for groups like the Institute of Managerial Accountants or the Institute of Internal Auditors. I love these live seminars. The right tip will help someone save an hour a week – 50 hours a year. I often interject some humor. I have a variety of spreadsheet quips and gags that get added to the seminar. One that I used many years ago: "If you have to present bad financial news, Excel has a function for you: Hide column B, and you can escape the president's office before he figures out what is going on." It brings laughter every time.

I keep a spreadsheet listing the books I've authored. It was a few years ago that I realized I would soon be writing book #40, and that the =ROMAN(40) is XL.

	A	B	C	D	E
1	Book #	Roman	Date	From	Title
2	1	I	8/1/2002	HMB	Holy Macro! It's 1,600 Excel VBA Examples
3	2	II	9/1/2002	HMB	Guerilla Data Analysis Using Microsoft Excel
39	38	XXXVIII	2014	HMB	PowerPivot Alchemy
40	39	XXXIX	2015	HMB	GDA II
41	40	XL	2015	HMB	MrExcel XL
42	41	XLI	2015	HMB	Power Excel with MrExcel

Illustration: Chank Diesel

I figured this would be a milestone – and thus this book was born. My 40 favorite Excel tips. Some good Excel stories. Szilvia Juhasz added 30 more Excel tips to coincide with the 30th birthday of Excel. There are some Excel jokes from Jordan Goldmeier, some tweets collected by Debra Dalgleish, and an awesome collection of Excel-themed cocktails from Szilvia Juhasz.

The spreadsheet in 2015 has a promising future. Yes, Excel is again facing competition from Google Docs and Tableau. But that competition brings innovation. Look at the amazing new features like Power Pivot, the feature formerly known as Power Query, and 3D Maps that have debuted since 2010. It is another golden age for spreadsheet development.

Introduction

This book is broken into these sections.

Part 1 – Bill's Top 40 Tips - my favorite 40 tips that I cover in my Power Excel seminars.

Part 2 – 40 Keyboard Shortcuts - so many of the votes from the readers were for keyboard shortcuts that they are all provided together.

Part 3 – 30 More Tips for the 30th Anniversary of Excel. Szilvia Juhasz adds her favorite tips and tips from readers.

Part 4 – Excel Fun - Excel cocktails, jokes, tweets, and stories.

The files used in this book are available for download from mrx.cl/40bookfiles.

You will see a number of shortlinks in this book in the format of mrx.cl/short. The idea is that it will be easier for you to type mrx.cl than a long URL. (Thanks Felix Jelen in Chile for securing the .cl suffix for me.)

Bill will do videos to go with each of his 40 tips. Search at http://mrx.cl/billonyoutube.

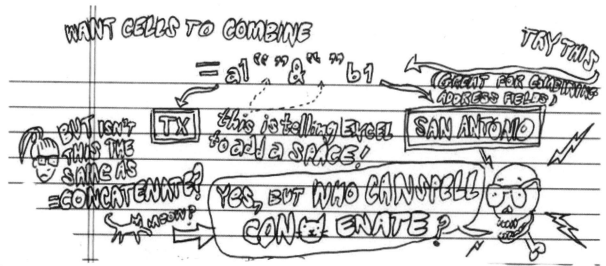

Illustration: Em DeMarco

Part 1 - Bill's Top 40 Tips

#1 Double-Click the Fill Handle to Copy a Formula

You have thousands of rows of data. You've added a new formula in the top row of your data set, some-thing like this =PROPER(A2&" "&B2), as shown below. You now need to copy the formula down to all of the rows of your data set.

C2	▼ :	× ✓ f_x	=PROPER(A2&" "&B2)

	A	B	C
1	First Name	Last Name	Name
2	PETER	ALBERT	Peter Albert
3	AMY	ANDRAE	
4	FRANK	ARENDT-THEILEN	
5	FR. TONY	AZZARTO	
6	LORNA	BANUILOS	
7	ZACK	BARRESSE	
8	JEREMY	BARTZ	
9	SIMON	BENNINGA	

Many people will grab the Fill Handle and start to drag down. But as you drag down, Excel starts going faster and faster. Starting in Excel 2010, there is a 200-microsec-ond pause at the last row of data. 200 microseconds is long enough for you to notice the pause but not long enough for you to react and let go of the mouse button. Before you know it, you've dragged the Fill Handle way too far.

110	RYAN	WILSON
111	PATRICK	WIRZ
112	JOHN C.	WISSE
113		
114	Excel 2010 does pause here - not long enough for anyone to react, though.	
115		
116		
117		
118		
119		
120		

Drag the Fill Handle... You inevitably go too far...

+

The solution is to double-click the Fill Handle! Go to exactly the same spot where you start to drag the Fill Handle. The mouse pointer changes to a black plus sign. Double-click.

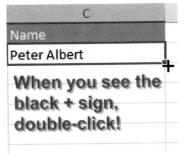

Excel looks at the surrounding data, finds the last row with data today, and copies the formula down to the last row of the data set.

In the past, empty cells in the column to the left would cause the "double-click the Fill Handle" trick to stop working just before the empty cell. But as you can see below, names like Madonna, Cher, or Pele will not cause problems. Provided that there is at least a diagonal path (for example, via B76-A77-B78), Excel will find the true bottom of the data set.

	A	B	C
73	ROBERT	MIKA	Robert Mika
74	JADE	MILLER	Jade Miller
75	SIMON	NUSS	Simon Nuss
76	RICHARD	OLDCORN	Richard Oldcorn
77	PELE	**Blank cells used to**	Pele
78	ROBERT	**be a problem. Fixed in 2010.** PHILLIPS	Robert Phillips
79	PETER	POLAKOVIC	Peter Polakovic
80	SHLOMI	POSTELNIK	Shlomi Postelnik
81	SAM	RADAKOVITZ	Sam Radakovitz

In my live Power Excel seminars, this trick always elicits a gasp from half the people in the room. It is my number-one time-saving trick.

Alternatives to Double-Clicking the Fill Handle

This trick is an awesome trick if all you've done to this point is drag the Fill Handle to the bottom of the data set. But there are even faster ways to solve this problem:

- Use Tables. If you would select one cell in A1:B112 and press Ctrl+T, Excel will format the range as a table. Once you have a table, simply enter the formula in C2. When you press Enter, it will be copied to the bottom.

- Use a complex but effective keyboard shortcut. This shortcut requires the adjacent column to have no empty cells. While it seems complicated to explain, the people who tell me about this shortcut can do the entire thing in the blink of an eye.

Here are the steps:

1. From your newly entered formula in C2, press the Left Arrow key to move to cell B2.

2. Press Ctrl+Down Arrow to move to the last row with data. In this case, B112.

3. Press the Right Arrow key to return to the bottom of the mostly empty column C.

C2	▼ :	✕ ✓	fx	=PROPER(A2&" "&B2)

	A	B	C	D
1	First Name	Last Name	Name	
2	PETER	ALBERT	Peter Albert	
3	AMY	ANDRAE		
97	TRACY	SYRSTAD		
98	SEREN KAUR	TAKHER-SMITH		
99	JAMES	TALLMAN		
100	ANDREAS	THEHOS		
101	ANNE	TROY		
102	LARRY	VANCE		
103	RICKARD	WARNELID		
104	ALEX	WATERTON		
105	ADAM	WEAVER		
106	RUSSELL	WEBSTER		
107	MARTHA K.	WENDEL		
108	JONATHAN	WERNICK		
109	JAMES	WILLIAMS		
110	RYAN	WILSON		
111	PATRICK	WIRZ		
112	JOHN C.	WISSE		
113				
114				

1. Left
2. Ctrl+Down
3. Right
4. Ctrl+Shift+Up
5. Ctrl+D

1   2   3

4. From cell C112, press Ctrl+Shift+Up Arrow. This selects all of the blank cells next to your data, plus the formula in C2.

5. Press Ctrl+D to fill the formula in C2 to all of the blanks in the selection. (Note that Ctrl+R fills right, which might be useful in other situations.)

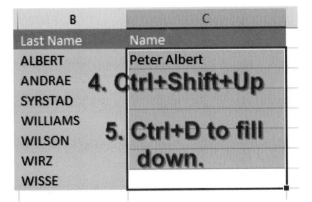

As an alternative, you can get the same results by pressing Ctrl+C before step 1 and replacing step 5 with Ctrl+V.

Thanks to the following people who suggested this tip: D. Carmichael, Shelley Fishel, Dawn Gilbert, @Knutsford_admi, Francis Logan, Michael Ortenberg, Jon Paterson, Mike Sullivan and Greg Lambert Lane suggested Ctrl+D. Bill Hazlett, author of *Excel for the Math Classroom,* pointed out Ctrl+R. It was Em DeMarco's cartoon posted on Twitter that was the inspiration for hiring illustrators for this book.

#2 Filter by Selection

The filter dropdowns have been in Excel for decades, but there is a much faster way to filter. Normally, you select a cell in your data, choose Data, Filter, open the dropdown menu on a column heading, uncheck Select All, then scroll through a long list of values, trying to find the desired item.

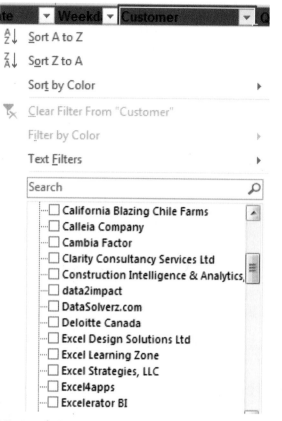

Microsoft Access invented a concept called Filter by Selection. It is simple. Find a cell that contains the value you want. Click Filter by Selection. The filter dropdowns are turned on, and the data is filtered to the selected value.

Nothing could be simpler.

Guess what? The Filter by Selection trick is also built into Excel, but it is hidden and mislabeled.

Here is how you can add this feature to your Quick Access Toolbar. Look at the top left of your Excel screen for the tiny row of icons with Save, Undo, and Redo. Right-click any of those icons and choose Customize Quick Access Toolbar.

There are two large listboxes in the dialog. Above the left listbox, open the dropdown and change from Popular Commands to Commands Not In the Ribbon.

In the left listbox, scroll to the command called AutoFilter and choose that command. That's right – the icon that does Filter by Selection is mislabeled as AutoFilter.

In the center of the dialog, click the Add>> button. The AutoFilter icon will move to the right listbox. Click OK to close the dialog.

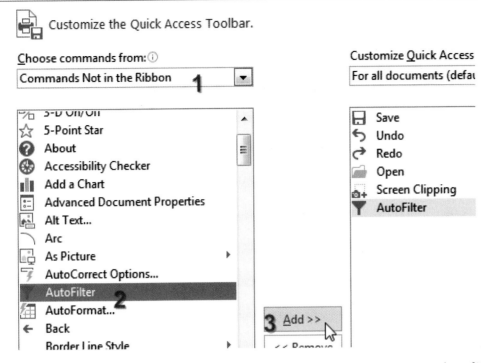

Here is how to use the command. Say that you want to see all West region sales of Widgets. First, choose any cell in column B that contains West. Click the AutoFilter icon in the Quick Access Toolbar.

Excel turns on the filter dropdowns and automatically chooses only West from column B.

Next, choose any cell in column E that contains Widget. Click the AutoFilter icon again.

You could continue this process. For example, choose a Utilities cell in the Sector column and click AutoFilter.

> **Caution**: It would be cool if you could multi-select cells before clicking the AutoFilter icon, but this does not work. If you need to see sales of Widgets and Gadgets, you could use Filter by Selection to get Widgets, but then you have to use the Filter dropdown to add Gadgets. Also. Filter by Selection does not work if you are in a Ctrl+T table.

How can it be that this cool feature has been in Excel since Excel 2003, but Microsoft does not document it? It was never really an official feature. The story is that one of the developers added the feature for internal use. Back in Excel 2003, there was already a Filter icon on the Standard toolbar, so no one would bother to add the apparently redundant AutoFilter icon.

Of course, this feature was added to Excel 2007's right-click menu, but three clicks deep: Right-click a value, choose Filter, then choose Filter by Selected Cell's Value.

Bonus Tip: Total Visible

After you've applied a filter, it would be great to see the total of the visible cells.

Select the blank cell below each of your numeric columns. Click the AutoSum button.

Instead of inserting SUM formulas, Excel inserts =SUBTOTAL(9,…) formulas. The formula below shows you the total of only the visible cells.

=SUBTOTAL(9,I2:I564)

Customer	Quant	Reven	Pro	C
cel4apps	600	11628	5082	6546
rtex42	900	17964	7623	10341
cel4apps	200	4158	1694	2464
rtex42	400	6860	3388	3472
cel4apps	400	8164	3388	4776
rtex42	800	15104	6776	8328
cel4apps	300	5847	2541	3306
	3600	69725	30492	39233

Insert a few blank rows above your data. Cut the formulas from below the data and paste to row 1 with the label of Total Visible.

I1   fx   =SUBTOTAL(9,I4:I566)

	E	F	G	H	I	J	K	L	M
1				Total Visible:	10200	196791	86394	110397	
2									
3	Produ	Date	Weekd	Customer	Quant	Reven	Pro	C	
20	Widget	1/24/2018	Wed	Excel Strategies, LLC	600	12606	5082	7524	
30	Widget	2/7/2018	Wed	All Systems Go Consult	1000	19890	8470	11420	
52	Widget	3/7/2018	Wed	Spain Enterprise	500	10155	4235	5920	
63	Widget	3/23/2018	Fri	Calleia Company	300	5355	2541	2814	
93	Widget	5/1/2018	Tue	NetCom Computer	200	3802	1694	2108	
129	Widget	6/13/2018	Wed	Wilde XL Solutions Ltd.	1000	19630	8470	11160	
133	Widget	6/23/2018	Sat	NetCom Computer	500	10330	4235	6095	
190	Widget	9/1/2018	Sat	Excel Strategies, LLC	100	2012	847	1165	
244	Widget	11/15/2018	Thu	Spain Enterprise	900	15255	7623	7632	
262	Widget	12/5/2018	Wed	Spain Enterprise	900	18243	7623	10620	

Now, as you change the filters, even if the data fills up more than one full screen of data, you will see the totals at the top of your worksheet.

Thanks to Sam Radakovitz on the Excel team for Filter by Selection – not for suggesting Filter by Selection, but for formalizing Filter by Selection!

#3 The Fill Handle Does Know 1, 2, 3...

Why does the Excel Fill Handle pretend it does not know how to count 1, 2, 3?

The Fill Handle is great for filling months, weekdays, quarters and dates. Why doesn't it know that 2 comes after 1?

In case you've never used the Fill Handle, try this: Type a month name in a cell. Select that cell. In the lower-right corner of the cell is a square dot. Click the dot and drag right or drag down. The tooltip increments to show the last month in the range.

When you let go of the mouse button, the months will fill. An icon appears giving you additional options.

The Fill Handle works great with months, days…

January	JAN	Monday	mon
February	FEB	Tuesday	tue
March	MAR	Wednesday	wed
April	APR	Thursday	thu
May	MAY	Friday	fri
June		Saturday	sat
July		Sunday	
August		Monday	

The fill handle works with quarters in many formats:

To do both quarters and years, you have to start with a number, then Q, then any punctuation (period, space, apostrophe, dash) before the year.

Q1	Qtr 1	1st Quarter	1Q-2018
Q2	Qtr 2	2nd Quarter	2Q-2018
Q3	Qtr 3	3rd Quarter	3Q-2018
Q4	Qtr 4	4th Quarter	4Q-2018
Q1	Qtr 1	1st Quarter	1Q-2019
Q2		2nd Quarter	2Q-2019

But when you type in 1 and grab the Fill Handle, Excel gives you 1, 1, 1, 1, 1, …. Many people tell me to enter the 1 and the 2, select them both, then drag the Fill Handle. But there is a faster way.

The secret trick is to hold down Ctrl! If you hold down Ctrl while dragging, Excel will fill 1, 2, 3.

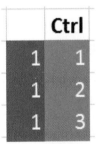

	Ctrl
1	1
1	2
1	3

Note: Huntsville Alabama's Andrew Spain of Spain Enterprise taught me a cool variation on this trick. If you start dragging without Ctrl, you can press Ctrl during the drag. A +icon appears at the bottom of the drag rectangle to indicate that you are going to fill instead of copy.

How were we supposed to figure out that Ctrl makes the Fill Handle count instead of copy? I have no idea. I picked up the tip from Row 6 at an IMA seminar in Kent, Ohio. It turns out that Ctrl seems to make the Fill Handle behave in the opposite way. If you Ctrl+drag a date, Excel will copy instead of Fill.

I've heard another trick: type 1 in A1. Select A1 and the blank B1. Drag. Excel fills instead of copies.

Right-Click the Fill Handle for More Options

If you right-click and drag the Fill Handle, a menu appears with more options, like Weekdays, Months, and Years. This menu is great for dates.

Normal	Ctrl	Weekday	Months	Years
1/31/2018	1/31/2018	1/31/2018	1/31/2018	1/31/2018
2/1/2018	1/31/2018	2/1/2018	2/28/2018	1/31/2019
2/2/2018	1/31/2018	2/2/2018	3/31/2018	1/31/2020
2/3/2018	1/31/2018	2/5/2018	4/30/2018	1/31/2021

What if your payroll happens on the 15th and on the last day of the month? Put in both dates. Select them both. Right-click and drag the Fill Handle. When you finish dragging, choose Fill Months.

Payroll
1/15/2018
1/31/2018
2/15/2018
2/28/2018
3/15/2018

Payroll
1/15/2018
1/31/2018

Teach the Fill Handle a New List

The Fill Handle is a really handy tool. What if you could use it on all sorts of lists? You can teach Excel a new list, provided that you have anywhere from 2 to 240 items. Here is the easy way:

1. Type the list in a column in Excel.

2. Select the list.

3. Select File, Options, Advanced. Scroll almost to the bottom, and click Edit Custom Lists.

Excel Options

General	☐ Provide feedback with ~~a~~nimation
Formulas	☐ Ignore other applications that use Dynamic Data Exchange (DDE)
Proofing	☑ Ask to update automatic links
Save	☐ Show add-in user interface errors
Language	☑ Scale content for A4 or 8.5 x 11" paper sizes
	At startup, open all files in:
Advanced	
	Web Options...
Customize Ribbon	☑ Enable multi-threaded processing
Quick Access Toolbar	Create lists for use in sorts and fill sequences: Edit Custom Lists...
Add-Ins	

In the Custom Lists dialog, click Import.

Excel will now understand your list as well as it understands Sunday, Monday, Tuesday.

Type any item from the list (it does not have to be the first item).

Grab the Fill Handle and drag. Excel will fill from your list.

I use this trick for lists that should be in Excel, such as a list of the U.S. States and a list of the letters of the alphabet.

Bonus Tip: Fill 1 to 100,000 in a Flash

What if you have too many items to drag the Fill Handle? Follow these steps:

1. Type the number 1 in a cell.

2. Select that cell.

3. On the Home tab, toward the right, in the Editing group, open the Fill dropdown and choose Series.

4. Select Columns.

5. Enter a Stop Value of 100000.

6. Click OK.

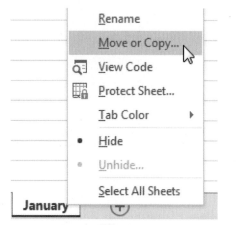

What if you have to fill 100,000 cells of bagel flavors?

1. Type the first bagel flavor in A1.

2. Select A1.

3. Type A100000 in the Name box and press Shift+Enter. This selects from the current cell to A100000.

4. Home, Fill, Series…. Click AutoFill in the Type box.

Thanks to the young lady in row 6 at the Meonske Conference in Kent, Ohio for suggesting this feature.

#4 Fast Worksheet Copy

Yes, you can right-click any sheet tab and choose Move or Copy to make a copy of your worksheet. But that is the very slow way to copy a worksheet.

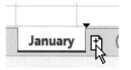

The fast way: Hold down the Ctrl key. Drag the worksheet tab to the right.

The downside of this trick is that the new sheet is called January (2) instead of February – but that is the case with the Move or Copy method as well. In either case, double-click the sheet name and type a new name.

January	**January (2)**

Ctrl+drag February to the right to create a sheet for March. Rename February (2) to March.

Select January. Shift-select March to select all worksheets. Hold down Ctrl and drag January to the right to create three more worksheets. Rename the three new sheets.

Select January. Shift-select June. Ctrl+Drag January to the right, and you've added the final six worksheets for the year. Rename those sheets.

Using this technique, you can quickly come up with 12 copies of the original worksheet.

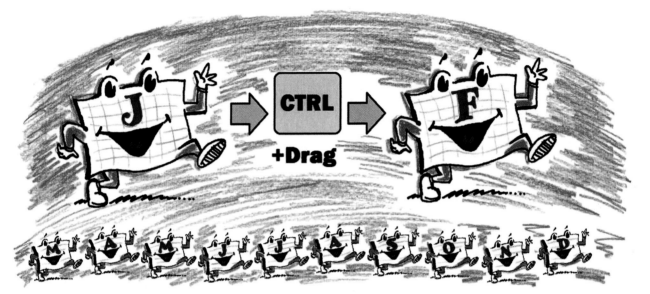

Illustration: Walter Moore

Bonus Tip: Worksheet Name in a Cell

If you want each report to have the name of the worksheet as a title, use

```
=TRIM(MID(CELL("filename",A1),FIND("]",CELL("filename",A1))+1,20)) &"
Report"
```

The CELL() function in this case returns the full path\[File Name]SheetName. By looking for the right square bracket, you can figure out where the sheet name occurs.

A1	▼	⋮	✕	✓	*fx*	=TRIM(MID(CELL("filename",A1),FIND("]",CELL("filename", A1))+1,20)) &" Report"	^

	A	B	C	D	E	F	G	H	I	
1	January Report									
2										
3	Flavor	Week 1	Week 2	Week 3	Week 4	Week 5	Total			
4	Asiago	288	132	144	240	264	1068			

◀ ▶ | **January** | February | March | April | May | Ju ... ⊕ ⋮ ◀ ▶

Now You Are Making Copies Too Quickly

You've heard of the Manager's 15 minute rule, right? Any time your manager asks you for something, he or she comes back 15 minutes later and asks for an odd twist that he or she did not specify the first time.

Now that you can create worksheet copies really quickly, there is more of a chance that you will have to make changes to all 12 sheets instead of just one sheet, when your manager comes back.

I will show you an amazingly powerful but incredibly dangerous tool called Group mode.

At this point, you have 12 worksheets that are mostly identical. You need to add totals to all 12 worksheets. To enter Group mode, right-click on the January tab and choose Select All Sheets.

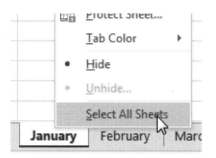

The name of the workbook in the title bar now indicates you are in Group mode.

Anything you do to the January worksheet will now happen to all the sheets in the workbook.

Why is this dangerous? Because if you get distracted and you forget that you are in group mode, you might start entering January data and overwriting data on the 11 other worksheets!

When you are done adding totals, don't forget to right-click a sheet tab and choose Ungroup Sheets.

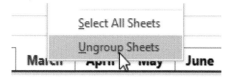

Bonus Tip: Create a SUM that Spears Through All Worksheets

So far, you have a workbook with 12 worksheets, one for each month. All of the worksheets have the same number of rows and columns. You want a Summary worksheet in order to total January through December.

The formula is =SUM(January:December!B4).

▲	A	B	C	D	E	F
1	Summary Report					
2						
3	Flavor	Week 1	Week 2	Week 3	Week 4	Week 5
4	Asiago	=sum(January:December!B4)				
5	Raisin					
6	Onion					
7	Garlic					

SUM   × ✓ *fx*   =sum(January:December!B4)

| B4 | | | f_x | =SUM(January:December!B4) | | | |

▲	A	B	C	D	E	F	G
1	Summary Report						
2							
3	Flavor	Week 1	Week 2	Week 3	Week 4	Week 5	Total
4	Asiago	2400	2040	2004	2388	2688	11520
5	Raisin	2220	2244	2076	2160	1968	10668
6	Onion	2484	2256	2388	1848	2208	11184
7	Garlic	2292	2172	2412	2292	2460	11628
8	Tomato	2328	2256	2340	2412	2460	11796
9	Blueberry	2328	2172	1848	2220	2268	10836

Caution: I make sure to never put spaces in my worksheet names. If you do use spaces, the formula would have to include apostrophes around the sheet names: =SUM('Jan 2018:Mar 2018'!B4)

Thanks to Othneil Denis for suggesting 3D formula and Olga Kryuchkova for suggesting Group mode.

#5 Compare Sheets Side by Side with Synchronous Scrolling

This feature appeared in Excel 2003 with very little fanfare. Say that you have two workbooks that you

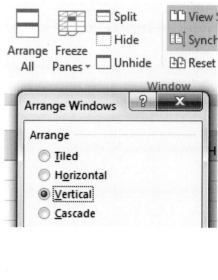

want to compare side by side. You aren't looking for a VLOOKUP, but just want to "eyeball" the two workbooks. Open both workbooks. On the View tab, choose View Side by Side.

For whatever reason, Excel defaults to arranging the first workbook in the top half of the screen and the second workbook in the bottom half of the screen, which

clearly means that someone on the Excel team does not know the meaning of "Side by Side."

The command doesn't say, "View One Above the Other," does it? While this choice annoys me, it is easy enough to truly get them side by side: Just select View, Arrange All, Vertical, OK.

At this point, one workbook is on the left half of your monitor, and the other workbook is on the right half. I have this monster 1080p monitor, which means that each workbook is only taking up a quarter of the screen real estate. So, for those of you with monitors more than twice as wide as your worksheet, hover over the right edge of the left workbook. You will see the mouse pointer below. Click and drag left.

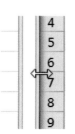

Then drag the left edge of the right workbook to the left.

You end up with this arrangement of the two workbooks:

	A	B	C	D
1	Company	Bluefeather8989	INDZARA	MikeAsHimself
2	Access Analytic	2	3	2
3	adaept information management		5	6
4	Analytic Minds	1	1	5
5	Areef Ali & Associates	4	6	2
6	Association for Computers & Taxation	6	4	8
7	Berghaus Corporation	2	3	6
8	Bits of Confetti	3	2	4

	A	B
1	Company	Bluefeather8989
2	Access Analytic	1
3	adaept information management	
4	Analytic Minds	
5	Areef Ali & Associates	2
6	Association for Computers & Taxation	1
7	Berghaus Corporation	
8	Bits of Confetti	1

But this is nothing new. Excel 97 offered Arrange All Vertical. There is the big difference, though:

Grab the scrollbar and scroll the right workbook down so it starts at row 8. Miraculously, the left workbook scrolls at the same rate, and both workbooks are showing row 8 through 17.

	A
1	Company
8	Bits of Confetti
9	Blockhead Data Consultants
10	bradedgar.com
11	Budget Wand
12	CPASelfStudy.com
13	Excel-Translator.de
14	Fintega Financial Modelling
15	F-Keys Ltd
16	Frontline Systems
17	GL Wand

	A
1	Company
8	Bits of Confetti
9	Blockhead Data Consultants
10	bradedgar.com
11	Budget Wand
12	CPASelfStudy.com
13	Excel-Translator.de
14	Fintega Financial Modelling
15	F-Keys Ltd
16	Frontline Systems
17	GL Wand

This is great, until one workbook adds or deletes a row.

Then, things are out of sync. The Harlem Globetrotters were added on the left, so now we need row 19 on the left and row 18 on the right to scroll together.

	A
1	Company
17	GL Wand
18	Harlem Globetrotters
19	Hartville Marketplace & Flea Market
20	Harvest Consulting
21	How To Excel At Excel.Com
22	Hybrid Software
23	IMA Houston Chapter
24	JEVS Human Services
25	Juliet Babcock-Hyde CPA, PLLC

	A
1	Company
17	GL Wand
18	Hartville Marketplace & Flea Market
19	Harvest Consulting
20	How To Excel At Excel.Com
21	Hybrid Software
22	IMA Houston Chapter
23	JEVS Human Services
24	Juliet Babcock-Hyde CPA, PLLC
25	LaFrenier Sons Septic

The key is to temporarily turn off Synchronous Scrolling. This was turned on when you used View Side by Side. It is in the View tab, in the Window group, but these three icons collapse when the Excel window narrows, so you are likely to only see the icons, and not the words.

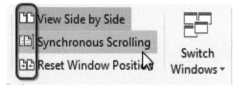

Turn off Synchronous Scrolling. Get the two workbooks lined up again. Turn on Synchronous Scrolling. As shown below, row 26 on the left is matched with row 25 on the right.

1	Company	1	Company
26	LaFrenier Sons Septic	25	LaFrenier Sons Septic
27	Lake Local School District	26	Lake Local School District
28	leanexcelbooks.com	27	leanexcelbooks.com
29	Mary Maids	28	Mary Maids
30	MAU Workforce Solutions	29	MAU Workforce Solutions
31	MN Excel Consulting	30	MN Excel Consulting
32	MrExcel.com	31	MrExcel.com
33	myexcelonline.com	32	myexcelonline.com
34	MyOnlineTrainingHub.com	33	MyOnlineTrainingHub.com
35	MySpreadsheetLab	34	MySpreadsheetLab
36	New Hope Laundry	35	New Hope Laundry
37	Open Sky Martial Arts	36	Open Sky Martial Arts

As you continue to scroll, the rows will remain lined up.

	A		A
1	Company	1	Company
54	The Lab with Leo Crew	53	The Lab with Leo Crew
55	The Salem Historical Society, Salem, Oh	54	The Salem Historical Society, Salem, Ohio
56	University of North Carolina	55	University of North Carolina
57	Wag More Dog Store, San Antonio	56	Wag More Dog Store, San Antonio
58	Wilde XL Solutions Ltd.	57	Wilde XL Solutions Ltd.
59	WM Squared Inc.	58	WM Squared Inc.
60	WSLCB	59	WSLCB
61	www.ExcelTricks.de	60	www.ExcelTricks.de
62	XLYOURFINANCES, LLC	61	XLYOURFINANCES, LLC
63	Yesenita	62	Yesenita

Can I Compare Sheet1 and Sheet2 of the Same Workbook?

Yes. Make sure you only have one workbook open. From the View tab, select New Window. It now appears that you have two workbooks open. One has :1 in the title bar, and one has :2 in the title bar. Select Sheet1 in :1 and Sheet2 in :2. Follow the View Side by Side steps from above. You will now be able to see both worksheets of the workbook side by side. When you are done, go to the :2 version of the file and click the X in the top right to close that window.

Note: You have not opened a second copy of the workbook. Think of the :2 as a second camera pointed at a different section of the workbook.

Thanks to Anne Walsh, author of *Your Excel Survival Kit*, for suggesting this feature.

#6 Turning Data Sideways with a Formula

Someone built this lookup table sideways, stretching across C1:N2. I realize that I could use HLOOKUP instead of VLOOKUP, but I prefer to turn the data back to a vertical orientation.

Copy C1:N2. Right-click in A4 and choose the Transpose option from the Paste Options. Transpose is the fancy Excel word for "turn the data sideways."

Illustration: Emily Jones

I transpose a lot. But I use Alt+E,S,E,Enter to transpose instead of the right-click.

There is a problem, though. Transpose is a one-time snapshot of the data. What if you have formulas in the horizontal data? Is there a way to transpose with a formula?

The first way is a bit bizarre. If you are trying to transpose 12 horizontal cells, you need to select 12 vertical cells in a single selection. Start typing a formula such as =TRANSPOSE(C2:N2) in the active cell but do not press Enter. Instead, hold down Ctrl+Shift with your left hand and then press Enter. This puts a single array formula in the selected cells. This TRANSPOSE formula is going to return 12 answers, and they will appear in the 12 selected cells.

As the data in the horizontal table changes, the same values will appear in your vertical table.

But array formulas are not well known. Some spreadsheet rookie might try to edit your formula and forget to press Ctrl+Shift+Enter.

| B4 | | ▼ | ⋮ | ✕ | ✓ | f_x | {=TRANSPOSE(C2:N2)} |

◢	A	B	C	D	E	F	G	H	I	J	K	L	M	N
1			Jan	Feb	Mar	Apr	May	Jun	Jul	Aug	Sep	Oct	Nov	Dec
2			5%	4%	5%	5%	3%	4%	5%	3%	2%	2%	3%	2%
3														
4	Jan	5%												
5	Feb	4%												
6	Mar	5%												
7	Apr	5%												
8	May	3%												
9	Jun	4%												
10	Jul	5%												
11	Aug	3%												

To avoid using the array formula, use a combination of INDEX and ROW, as shown below. =ROW(1:1) is a clever way of writing the number 1. As you copy this formula down, the row reference changes to 2:2 and returns a 2.

The INDEX function says you are getting the answers from C2:N2, and you want the nth item from the range.

◢	A	B	C	D	E	F	G	H	I
1			Jan	Feb	Mar	Apr	May	Jun	Jul
2			1%	1%	4%	4%	1%	2%	2%
3									
4	Jan	1%	=INDEX($C$2:$N$2,ROW(1:1))						
5	Feb								
6	Mar								

In the figure below, =FORMULATEXT in column C shows how the formula changes when you copy down.

◢	A	B	C	D	E	F	G	H	I	J	K	L	M	N
1			Jan	Feb	Mar	Apr	May	Jun	Jul	Aug	Sep	Oct	Nov	Dec
2			4%	1%	1%	1%	5%	2%	3%	4%	2%	2%	4%	5%
3														
4	Jan	4%	=INDEX($C$2:$N$2,ROW(1:1))											
5	Feb	1%	=INDEX($C$2:$N$2,ROW(2:2))											
6	Mar	1%	=INDEX($C$2:$N$2,ROW(3:3))											
7	Apr	1%	=INDEX($C$2:$N$2,ROW(4:4))											
8	May	5%	=INDEX($C$2:$N$2,ROW(5:5))											
9	Jun	2%	=INDEX($C$2:$N$2,ROW(6:6))											
10	Jul	3%	=INDEX($C$2:$N$2,ROW(7:7))											
11	Aug	4%	=INDEX($C$2:$N$2,ROW(8:8))											

Thanks to Excel Ace and Tracia Williams for suggesting this feature.

#7 Default Settings for All Future Workbooks

Do you have favorite worksheet settings in Excel? I do. There are things I do to every new workbook I create.

In a few minutes, you can teach Excel your favorite settings. Then, every time you create a new workbook with Ctrl+N or insert a new worksheet, the worksheet will inherit all of your favorite settings.

The key step is to save the workbook as a template into a specific folder with two specific names.

Start with a blank workbook with a single worksheet.

Apply all your favorite settings. There are dozens of possibilities. Here are a few that I use:

On the Page Layout tab, change the Scale to Fit so the Width is 1 page. Leave the Height set to Automatic and width set to 1 Page.

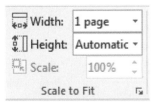

Create a custom header or footer. Use the dialog launcher in the bottom right of the Page Setup group. Go to the Header/Footer tab. Choose Custom Footer. Type whatever is your company standard is in the footer.

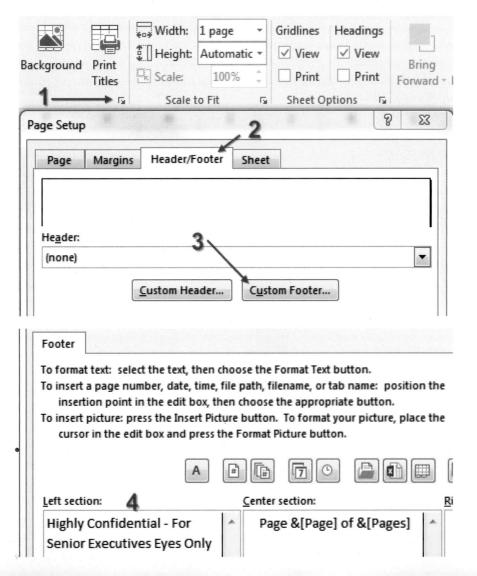

Create custom margins. I like narrow margins – even more narrow than the built-in Narrow margin settings. I've been using 0.25-inch margins since the 1990s, and they're automatically set for me because I've added that to my template.

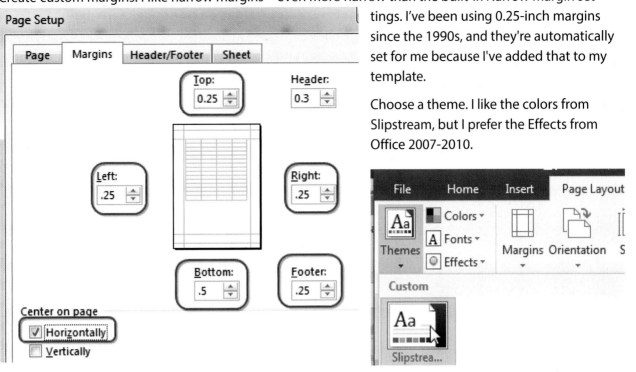

Choose a theme. I like the colors from Slipstream, but I prefer the Effects from Office 2007-2010.

The next settings seems a little over the top. When you set a pivot table default theme, it only applies to the current workbook. Excel never saves your preference. Create a tiny two-cell data set. Create a pivot table. Change the default formatting. Delete the pivot table and the data set. The template will remember the setting.

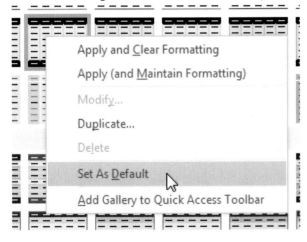

Would you use Cell Styles more often if they weren't so ugly? Do you hate that input cells are orange? Go to Cell Styles, right-click Input and choose Modify. Click the Format button and choose a different input color.

I've just shown you some of my habitual settings. I'm sure you have your own favorites. Maybe you always set up a name to define the tax rate. Add it to your template, and you will never have to set this up again. Turn off gridlines. Do whatever you always do.

Once you've finished customizing your workbook, you need to figure out which file type you use most often. For people who never use macros, this is often XLSX. But I always use macros, so my default file type is XLSM. Maybe you want workbooks to open faster, and you use XLSB. There is a template format related to each of these file types – just change the extension as needed. So, for me, I save the workbook as XLTM. You might save it as XLTX.

As soon as you choose one of these file types, the Save As dialog box moves to a templates folder. You need to save the workbook in a different folder.

> C:\Users\Bill\AppData\Roaming\Microsoft\Excel\XLSTART

In the folder bar, type %AppData% and press Enter to get to the AppData\Roaming\ folder on your computer. From there, navigate to Microsoft\Excel\XLSTART.

Save the workbook with the reserved name Book plus the appropriate extension.

Save As again and save the workbook in the same folder but use Sheet (plus the same extension) as the name.

Of course, you only have to set this up once. After you do it, any time you use Ctrl+N to create a new workbook, the new workbook will inherit all of the settings from your template named Book.

Why did you have to also save templates named both Book and Sheet? Any time you insert a new worksheet into an existing workbook, Excel uses the Sheet template.

My Rant About New and New...

I've been using Book.xltm for 20 years. Back in all versions of Excel from Excel 95 up through Excel 2003, the Excel Standard toolbar had an icon called "New". Click that icon, and Excel load the Book template. Everything was great.

The File menu offered a different icon called "New…". Hardly anyone used "New…" because it was half as many clicks to simply click the "New" icon on the Standard toolbar. "New" respects your custom settings in the Book template. "New…" does not.

Things fell apart in Excel 2007. When Microsoft moved to the ribbon, the good "New" icon was missing from the ribbon. People had to open the Office icon and choose the evil "New…". Microsoft allegedly studied the Excel 2003 SQM (pronounced skwim, the result of the Customer Experience Improvement Program) data to figure out what belonged in the ribbon. But somehow, they massively screwed up and left "New" out of the Ribbon. The problem remained in Excel 2010.

Then, in Excel 2013, someone on the Office team decided that Excel should start by showing you a pane that has recent files and a bunch of templates. This is called the Start screen. Now, for the first time, Microsoft is shoving the Blank Workbook template in your face every time you open Excel. This is the evil Blank Workbook template that you would have had to use File, New… to get to in the past.

This stupid template does not inherit settings from Book.xltx and Sheet.xltx. This stupid template is built in. There is no way to change it. Microsoft had a great but obscure feature, and they've made it harder to use by shoving this useless Blank Workbook template down your throat when you open Excel 2013 or Excel 2016.

If you've set up custom Book and Sheet templates, do not click the Blank Workbook template. Simply dismiss this opening screen by using the Esc key, and your custom Book template will load.

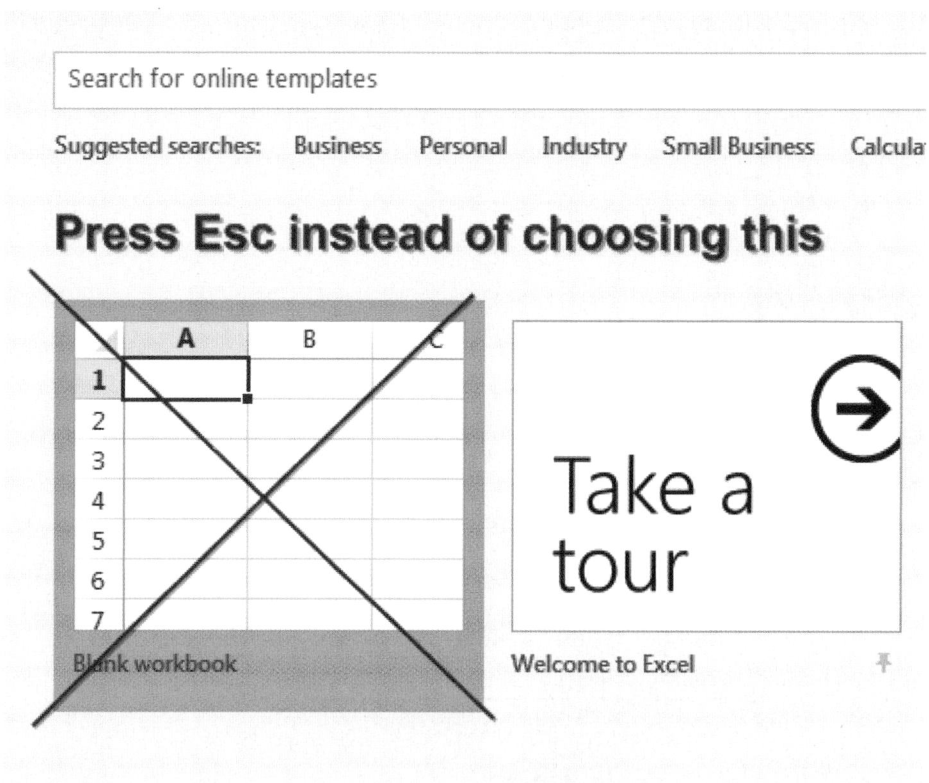

Search for online templates

Suggested searches: Business   Personal   Industry   Small Business   Calcula

Press Esc instead of choosing this

If you get tired of pressing Esc, go to File, Options, General. Uncheck Show the Start Screen When This Application Starts.

Start up options

Choose the extensions you want Excel to open by default

☑ Tell me if Microsoft Excel isn't the default progam for

☐ Show the Start screen when this application starts

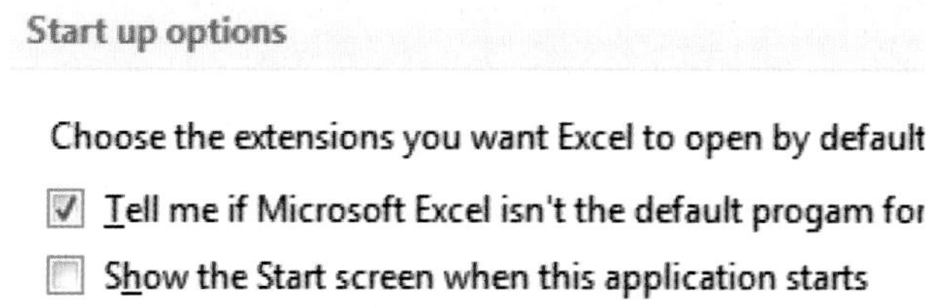

Thanks to Jo Ann Babin for an idea similar to this one.

#8 Recover Unsaved Workbooks

The Auto Recover feature is a lifesaver. It is turned on automatically in Excel 2010 and newer.

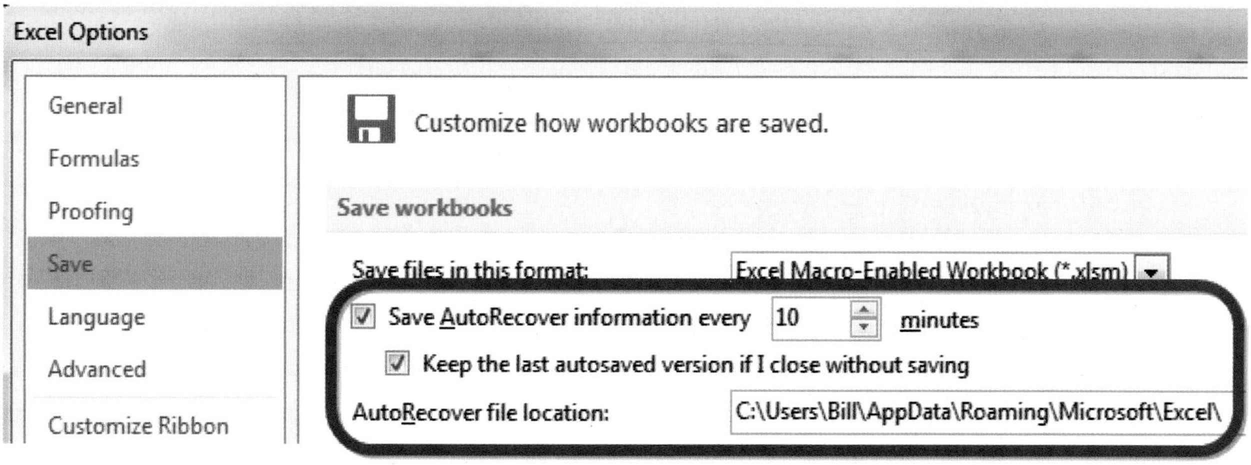

Say it is 4:59 PM on Friday, and you are trying to get the heck out of work. You have a bunch of files open in Excel and issue the Alt+F+X command to exit Excel.

Illustrator: Sarah Lucia Jones

Standing between you and the after-work PowerPivotini happy hour are a bunch of dialogs like this one:

Microsoft Excel	✕
⚠ Want to save your changes to 'Book3'?	
Save	Save All	Don't Save	Cancel

There is no need to save this file, so you click Don't Save.

Next file? Don't Save.

Next file? Don't Save.

Now you are in a rhythm, clicking Don't Save in perfect synchronization with Excel presenting the message. Then, as you click Don't Save the last time, you realize that *this* workbook had a lot of unsaved changes. And you really needed to save it. You should have clicked Save.

You look at your watch. It will take two hours to re-create all of those changes. Your happy hour plans are sunk. But wait! Excel has your back. If the workbook was open for at least 10 minutes and went through an AutoSave, Excel kept a copy for you.

Walter Moore

Follow these steps to get it back:

1. Hold your breath.

2. Open Excel.

3. In the left panel, all the way at the bottom, choose Open Other Workbooks.

4. In the center panel, scroll all the way to the bottom of the recent files. At the very end, click Recover Unsaved Workbooks.

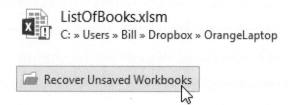

5. Excel shows you all the unsaved workbooks that it has saved for you recently.

Name	Date modified
Book2((Unsaved-3045080003942761400)).xlsb	6/11/2015 6:03 PM
Book1((Unsaved-3045078414461565691)).xlsb	6/11/2015 4:04 PM
Book2((Unsaved-3045078414461695698)).xlsb	6/11/2015 4:04 PM
Book1((Unsaved-3045077618222199421)).xlsb	6/11/2015 3:08 PM
Book1((Unsaved-3045076142805245598)).xlsb	6/11/2015 1:24 PM
Book1((Unsaved-3045075335635066691)).xlsb	6/11/2015 12:26 PM
Book1((Unsaved-3045073612640733015)).xlsb	6/11/2015 10:20 AM
Book1((Unsaved-3045031632324003525)).xlsb	6/9/2015 8:17 AM
Book6((Unsaved-3045011818164566846)).xlsb	6/8/2015 8:38 AM

6. Click one and choose Open.

7. If it is the wrong one, go back to File, Open and scroll to the bottom of the list.

8. When you find the right file, click the Save As button to save the workbook.

RECOVERED UNSAVED FILE   This is a recovered file that is temporarily stored on your computer.   Save As

Unsaved workbooks are saved for four days before they're automatically deleted.

Using AutoSave Versions to Recover Files Previously Saved

This might seem confusing, but Recover Unsaved Workbooks applies only to files that have never been saved. If your file has been saved, you will use AutoSave versions to get the file back.

If you close a previously saved workbook without saving recent changes, one single AutoSave version is kept until your next editing session. To access it, reopen the workbook. Use File, Info, Versions to open the last AutoSave version.

You can also search for the last AutoSave version using Windows Explorer. Excel Options specifies an AutoRecover File Location. (See the first screenshot in this topic). If your file was named Budget2018Data, look for a folder within the AutoRecover File folder that starts with Budget.

While you are editing a workbook, you can access up to the last five AutoSave versions of a previously saved workbook. These can be opened on the Info tab under the Versions section. You may make changes to a workbook and want to reference what you previously had. Instead of trying to Undo a bunch of revisions, or using Save As to save as a new file, you can open an AutoSave version. AutoSave versions will open in another window so you can reference, copy/paste, save it as a separate file, etc.

Note: An AutoSave version is created according to the AutoRecover interval AND only if there are changes. So if you leave a workbook open for two hours without making any changes, the last AutoSave version will contain the last revision.

Caution: Both the Save AutoRecover Information option and Keep The Last AutoSaved Version option must be selected in order to recover an AutoSave version.

Note: Under the Manage Version options on the Info tab is the ability to Delete All Unsaved Workbooks. This is an important option to know about if you work on public computers. You may want to make sure you don't leave copies of your work behind. Note that this option only appears if you're working on a file that has never been previously saved. The easiest way to access it is to create a new workbook.

Thanks to Beth Melton and Paul Seaman and for clarifying the differences between AutoRecover and Recover Unsaved Files.

#9 Perfect One-Click Charts

One-click charts are easy: Select the data. Press Alt+F1.

	A	B	C	D	E	F
1		Jan	Feb	Mar	Apr	May
2	East	25277482	26035938	27076169	26805884	26805477
3	Central	21256874	20831794	21248165	22098791	21877882
4	West	15915727	16597709	17909655	16727092	16902886

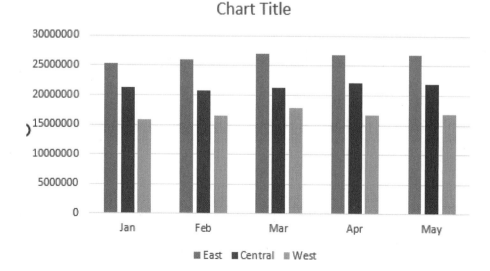

But one-click charts are rarely the type of chart you need to create day after day. To make your life easier, you can change the settings on a chart and then teach Excel to produce your favorite chart in response to Alt+F1.

Say that you want to clean up the chart above. All of those zeros on the left axis take up a lot of space without adding value. Double-click those numbers. Change Display Units from None to Millions.

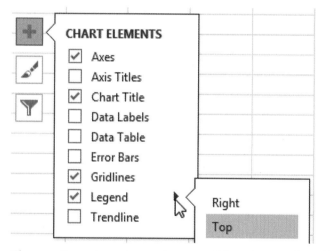

To move the legend to the top, click the+sign next to the chart, choose the arrow to the right of Legend, then choose Top.

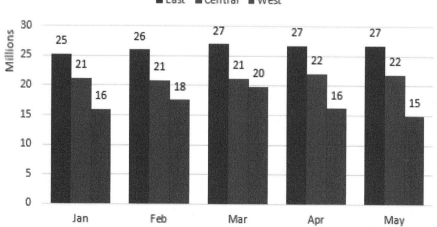

Change the color scheme to something that works with your company colors.

Right-click the chart and choose Save As Template. Then, give the template a name. (I called mine ClusteredColumn.)

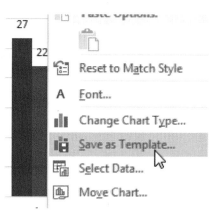

Select a chart. In the Design tab of the ribbon, choose Change Chart Type. Click on the Templates folder to see the template that you just created.

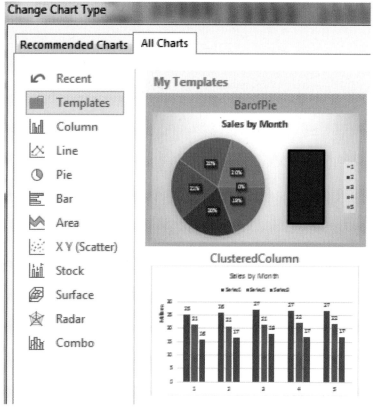

Right-click your template and choose Set As Default Chart.

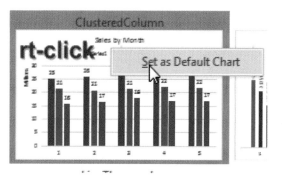

The next time you need to create a chart, select the data and press Alt+F1. All your favorite settings will appear in the chart.

	2013	2014	2015	2016
East	303,329,784	333,662,762	367,029,038	403,731,942
Central	255,082,488	280,590,737	308,649,811	339,514,792
West	190,988,724	210,087,596	231,096,356	254,205,992

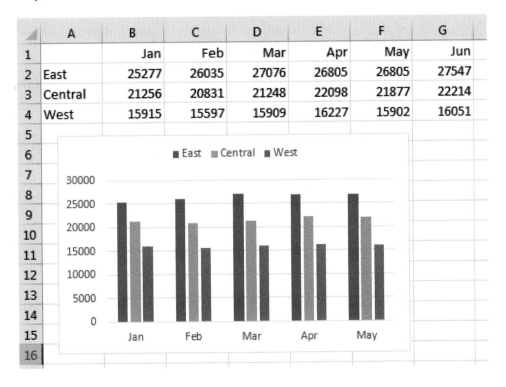

Thanks to Areef Ali, Olga Kryuchkova, and Wendy Sprakes for suggesting this feature.

#10 Paste New Data on a Chart

You might be responsible for updating charts every month, week, or day. For example, in my last job, a collection of charts were updated during the month-end close process. The charts would track progress throughout the year.

There is an easy way to add new data to an existing chart. Here, the chart shows data for January through May, and there is new data for June that is not on the chart.

	A	B	C	D	E	F	G
1		Jan	Feb	Mar	Apr	May	Jun
2	East	25277	26035	27076	26805	26805	27547
3	Central	21256	20831	21248	22098	21877	22214
4	West	15915	15597	15909	16227	15902	16051

Rather than re-create the chart, you can paste new data on the chart. Select the new data in the worksheet, including the heading. Press Ctrl+C to copy.

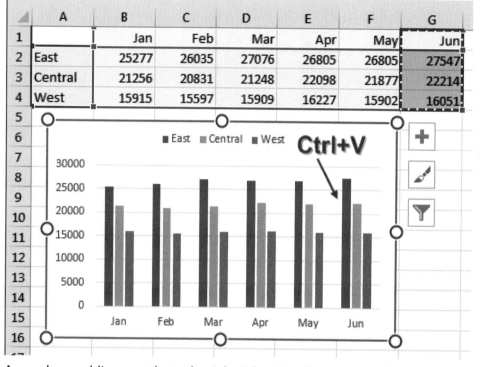

F	G
May	Jun
26805	27547
21877	22214
15902	16051

Ctrl+C

Click on the chart and press Ctrl+V to paste the data on the chart. As shown below, the new data is added to the existing chart.

	A	B	C	D	E	F	G
1		Jan	Feb	Mar	Apr	May	Jun
2	East	25277	26035	27076	26805	26805	27547
3	Central	21256	20831	21248	22098	21877	22214
4	West	15915	15597	15909	16227	15902	16051

Ctrl+V

As you keep adding months to the right side, what if you want to remove data from the left side? Is there any way to Ctrl+X that data off the chart?

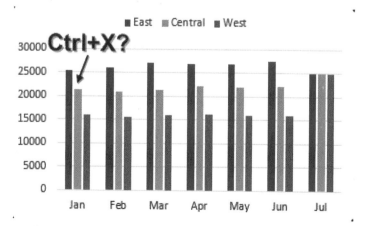

Ctrl+X?

No, but there is another way. Select the chart. Outlines appear around the charted data in the worksheet. A blue box surrounds the data points for the charts, and in each corner of the blue box is a square dot. The square dot is a resizing handle.

Click on the lower, left resizing handle in the blue box and drag to the right.

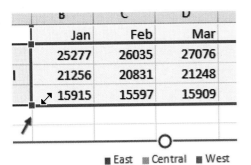

The data is removed from the left side of the chart.

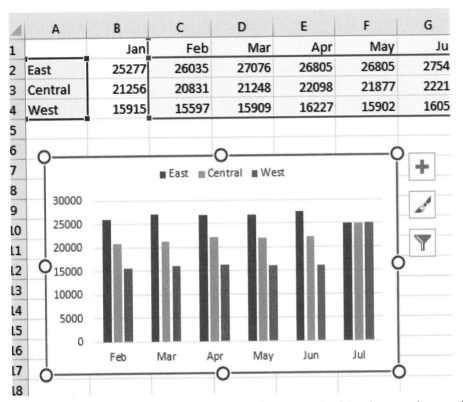

You can use these resizing handles to resize or drag the blue box to change the data that appears on the chart. Of course, you could have dragged the bottom, right resizing handle to add June to the chart in the first place, but it is good to know this copy and paste trick in case the chart and data are on different sheets in the workbook.

Tip: If you wanted to remove East from the chart, you could click on any East column and press Delete on your keyboard to remove that series. To temporarily hide a series, you can hide the row or column where the underlying data is stored..

Bonus Tip: Comparative Scatter Charts

The chart below is an X-Y scatter chart. Each blue dot represents a salaried employee. The numbers along the bottom of the chart are years of experience. The vertical position of the dot indicates salary.

There is a second group of employees: assembly line workers. There are more workers in this category than in the first category. Select the data for the second group, including the headings. Copy with Ctrl+C.

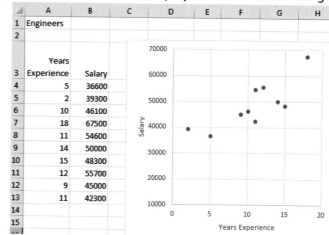

	A	B
1	Engineers	
2		
3	Years Experience	Salary
4	5	36600
5	2	39300
6	10	46100
7	18	67500
8	11	54600
9	14	50000
10	15	48300
11	12	55700
12	9	45000
13	11	42300
14		
15		

Assembly Line

Years Experience	Hourly
6	17778
8	17746

Click on the chart. In the Home tab, open the Paste Dropdown and choose Paste Special. In the Paste Special dialog, check the box Categories (X Values) in First Column. Click OK.

Paste Special

Add cells as
- ○ New point(s)
- ● New series

Values (Y) in
- ○ Rows
- ● Columns

- ☑ Series Names in First Row
- ☑ Categories (X Values) in First Column
- ☐ Replace existing categories

The result: You've added a new X-Y series to the chart. I changed the color of the second series and added a legend in this image.

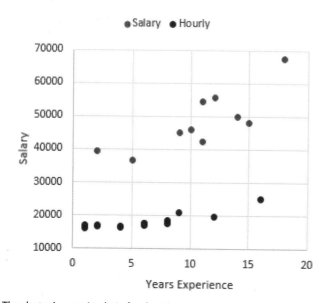

● Salary ● Hourly

Thanks to Access Analytic for the idea about pasting new data on a chart. Paul Seaman provided the Delete key tip.

#11 Sort East, Central, and West Using a Custom List

At my last day job, we had three sales regions: East, Central, and West. The company headquarters was in the East, and so the rule was that all reports were sorted with the East region first, then Central, then West. Well, there is no way to do this with a normal sort.

Region	Customer	Revenue
West	Access Analytic	956425
East	Budget Wand	692375
West	DataSolverz.com	332375
East	Deloitte Canada	805775
Central	Excel Design Solutions Ltd	810475

Sort AZ, and you will have Central at the top.

Region	Customer	Revenue
Central	Excel Design Solutions Ltd	810475
Central	Excelerator BI	243675
Central	WSLCB	1116175
East	Budget Wand	692375
East	Deloitte Canada	805775
East	New Hope Laundry	507200
East	SkyWire, Inc.	616200
West	Access Analytic	956425
West	DataSolverz.com	332375
West	Harvest Consulting	437600

Sort the data ZA, and you will have West at the top.

Region	Customer	Revenue
West	Access Analytic	956425
West	DataSolverz.com	332375
West	Harvest Consulting	437600
West	MySpreadsheetLab	651825
West	The Lab with Leo Crew	243925
East	Budget Wand	692375
East	Deloitte Canada	805775
East	New Hope Laundry	507200
East	SkyWire, Inc.	616200
Central	Excel Design Solutions Ltd	810475

I actually went to my manager to ask if he would rename the Central region. "To what?" he asked incredulously. I replied that I didn't care, as long as it started with F through V. Perhaps "Middle"? John shook his head no and went on with his day.

Illustration: Michelle Routt

So, over and over, I would sort the report, then Ctrl+X to cut the East region records and paste them before the Central region. If only I had known this trick.

The first thing to do is to set up a custom list with the regions in the correct order: East, Central, West. (See "#3 The Fill Handle Does Know 1, 2, 3…" on page 8 for instructions on setting up a custom list.)

Once the custom list is defined, open the Sort dialog using the Sort icon on the Data tab. Choose to sort by Region. Open the Order dropdown. You don't want A to Z. You don't want Z to A. You want Custom List….

Choose the East, Central, West custom list.

One you've chosen that custom list, you can either sort it East, Central, West or West, Central, East.

The result: an easy way to sort a list into a nonstandard sequence.

Region	Customer	Revenue
East	Deloitte Canada	805775
East	Budget Wand	692375
East	SkyWire, Inc.	616200
East	New Hope Laundry	507200
Central	WSLCB	1116175
Central	Excel Design Solutions Ltd	810475
Central	Excelerator BI	243675
West	Access Analytic	956425
West	MySpreadsheetLab	651825
West	Harvest Consulting	437600
West	DataSolverz.com	332375
West	The Lab with Leo Crew	243925

At that old day job, we also had a product list that refused to sort correctly. PTC-610, PTC-710, PTC-860, PTC-960, PTC-1100 was the desired order. But the PTC-1100 always fell first in a text sort. A custom list would solve this problem as well.

Thanks to @NeedForExcel for suggesting this tip.

#12 Sort Left to Right

Every day, your IT department sends you a file with the columns in the wrong sequence. It would take them two minutes to change the query, but they have a six-month backlog, so you are stuck rearranging the columns every day.

	A	B	C	D	E	F	G	H	I
1	Last Name	Apt	Street	Company	First Name	Middle	ST	Zip	City
2	Hooker		123 Pivot Drive	Phare View Concepts	Carl	R.	KY	40361	Paris
3	Cordell	#101	234 Excel Lane	Lake Local School District	Trace		OH	44685	Uniontown
4	Corrie		345 Precedent Trace	excelisfun	N		FL	32919	Melbourne
5	Gilbert	Apt 2	456 Analysis Ave	SlinkyRN Excel Instruction	Dawn		FL	32953	Merritt Island
6	McClellan		567 Fisher Way	Resource Optimizer	Robert	S.	OH	4440	Salem

You can reorder the columns with a left-to-right sort.

1. Add a new row above the data. Type numbers to represent the correct sequence for the columns.

2. Select Data, Sort. In the Sort dialog, click the Options… button and choose Sort Left to Right. Click OK.

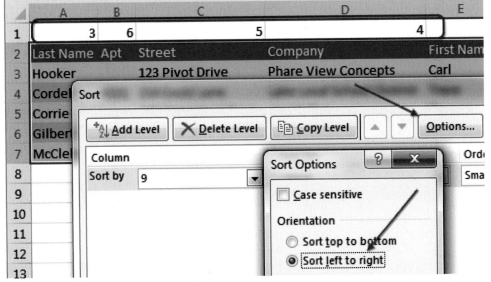

3. Specify Row 1 in the Sort By dropdown. Click OK.

Sort						
	⁺ᴬ↓ Add Level	✕ Delete Level	⧉ Copy Level	▲ ▼	Options…	☑ My data h
Row		Sort On		Order		
Sort by	Row 1 ▼	Values	▼	Smallest to Largest		

The problem: The column widths do not travel with the columns.

	A	B	C	D	E	F	G	H	I
1	1	2	3	4	5	6	7	8	9
2	First Name	Middl	Last Name	Company	Street	Apt	City	ST	Zip
3	Carl	R.	Hooker	Phare View Concepts	123 Pivot Drive		Paris	KY	40361

But it is easy to select the data and Press Alt+O, C, A or select Home, Format, Column, AutoFit.

Bonus: Another Way to Move columns

Select one cell in the column you want to move. (You can also do this with multiple columns.)

Press Ctrl+Space bar to select the whole column.

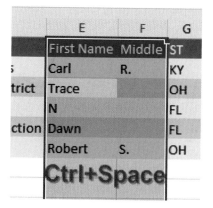

Shift+drag the edge of the selection to a new location. The columns move and get inserted where you drop them. The remaining data shifts over.

1	Last Name	Apt	Street	Company	First
2	Hooker		123 Pivot Drive	Phare View Concepts	Carl
3	Cordell	#101	234 Excel Lane	Lake Local School District	Trace
4	Corrie		345 Precedent Trace	excelisfun	N
5	Gilbert	Apt 2	456 Analysis Ave	SlinkyRN Excel Instruction	Daw
6	McClellan		567 Fisher Way	Resource Optimizer	Robe

Shift+Drag border

Tip: If you need to move rows, press Shift+Space bar to select the whole row. Follow with Shift+drag.

Bonus Tip: Use Power Query

If you really have to move columns every day, it would be better to use a macro or Power Query to solve the problem. Power Query will remember your steps. When you get a new file from IT tomorrow, you can simply ask Power Query to refresh the steps.

Power Query is built in to Excel 2016 (under Data, Load & Transform) and it's a free add-in for Excel 2013 and Excel 2010. There are two different Power Query examples in this book: "#38 Load a File List into Excel with Power Query" on page 127 and "#20 Data Shaping (Unpivot) with Power Query" on page 197.

From a blank workbook, specify a new query from a file. Point to the file created by IT. While you are editing the query, right-click each column and select Move, To Beginning. Or simply grab the field heading and drag it to the correct place.

After you finish, select Close & Load from the Power Query home tab. Tomorrow, when there is a new file available from IT, just open your query file and choose Data, Refresh All. Power Query replays all the steps, including rearranging the order of the columns.

#13 Sort Subtotals

This tip is from my friend Derek Fraley in Springfield, Missouri. I was doing a seminar in Springfield, and I was showing my favorite subtotal tricks.

For those of you who have never used subtotals, here is how to set them up.

Start by making sure your data is sorted. The data below is sorted by customers in column C.

	A	B	C	D	E	F	G	H
1	Sales Rep	Date	Customer	Quantity	Product	Revenue	Profit	Cost
424	Geoffrey G Lilley	12/1/2019	Open Sky Martial Arts	900	Gizmo	22887	9198	13689
425	Geoffrey G Lilley	12/2/2019	Open Sky Martial Arts	600	Gizmo	13290	6132	7158
426	Kevin J Sullivan	1/25/2018	Spain Enterprise	1000	Widget	20770	8470	12300
427	Kevin J Sullivan	2/8/2018	Spain Enterprise	100	Widget	1817	847	970
428	Kevin J Sullivan	2/28/2018	Spain Enterprise	900	Gizmo	21456	9198	12258
429	Kevin J Sullivan	4/13/2018	Spain Enterprise	600	Gadget	11598	5082	6516

From the Data tab, choose Subtotals. The Subtotal dialog box always wants to subtotal by the leftmost column. Open the At Each Change In dropdown and choose Customer. Make sure the Use Function box is set to Sum. Choose all of the numeric fields.

When you click OK, Excel inserts a subtotal below each group of customers. But, more importantly, it adds Group and Outline buttons to the left of column A.

1 2 3		A	B	C
	1	Sales Rep	Date	Customer
	223	Kevin J Sullivan	11/30/2019	CPASelfStudy.
	224	Kevin J Sullivan	12/7/2019	CPASelfStudy.
	225	Kevin J Sullivan	12/22/2019	CPASelfStudy.
−	226			CPASelfStudy.
	227	Michael Dietteric	1/9/2018	F-Keys Ltd
	228	Michael Dietteric	2/3/2018	F-Keys Ltd

When you click the #2 Group and Outline button, the detail rows are hidden, and you are left with only the subtotal rows and the grand total. This is a beautiful summary of a detailed data set. Of course, at this point, the customers appear in alphabetic sequence. Derek from Springfield showed me that when the data is collapsed in the #2 view, you can sort by any column. In the figure below, a Revenue column cell is selected, and you are about to click the ZA sort button.

=SUBTOTAL(9,F2:F37)

C	D	E	F	G	H
Customer	Quantity	Product	Revenue	Profit	Cost
Association for Computers & Taxation Total	20200		430540	190598	239942
Blockhead Data Consultants Total	21500		460086	206861	253225
BradEdgar.com Total	24700		546662	243117	303545
Clarity Consultancy Services Ltd Total	17400		369567	164599	204968
Construction Intelligence & Analytics, Inc. Total	17800		374497	169684	204813
CPASelfStudy.com Total	23400		505279	221591	283688
F-Keys Ltd Total	23100		490827	218470	272357
Hartville Marketplace & Flea Market Total	19000		410118	181689	228429

The top customer, Wag More Dog Store, comes to the top of the data set. But it does not come to row 2. Behind the hidden rows, Excel actually sorted a chunk of records. All of the Wag More detail rows moved along with the subtotal row.

	C	D	E	F	G	H
1	Customer	Quantity	Product	Revenue	Profit	Cost
49	Wag More Dog Store, San Antonio Total	28900		606128	273935	332193
91	BradEdgar.com Total	24700		546662	243117	303545
133	CPASelfStudy.com Total	23400		505279	221591	283688
172	F-Keys Ltd Total	23100		490827	218470	272357
222	Hybrid Software Total	23100		486697	215678	271019
259	Blockhead Data Consultants Total	21500		460086	206861	253225
295	Open Sky Martial Arts Total	20800		448241	196403	251838
332	Association for Computers & Taxation Total	20200		430540	190598	239942
371	Hartville Marketplace & Flea Market Total	19000		410118	181689	228429
408	SurtenExcel.com Total	17600		375472	164413	211059
439	Construction Intelligence & Analytics, Inc. Total	17800		374497	169684	204813
469	Spain Enterprise Total	17600		373852	163926	209926
505	Clarity Consultancy Services Ltd Total	17400		369567	164599	204968
533	The Salem Historical Society, Salem, Ohio Total	15000		329597	145571	184026
559	Juliet Babcock-Hyde CPA, PLLC Total	13900		295018	131416	163602
580	IMA Houston Chapter Total	9900		205231	90443	114788
581	Grand Total	313900		6707812	2978394	3729418

If you go back to the #3 view, you will see the detail records that came along. Excel did not sort the detail records but brought them in their original sequence.

3		C	D	E	F
	1	Customer	Quantity	Product	Revenue
	44	Wag More Dog Store, San Antonio	900	Widget	17289
	45	Wag More Dog Store, San Antonio	500	Gizmo	10940
	46	Wag More Dog Store, San Antonio	1000	Widget	21010
	47	Wag More Dog Store, San Antonio	600	Gizmo	13680
	48	Wag More Dog Store, San Antonio	800	Gadget	17136
	49	Wag More Dog Store, San Antonio Total	28900		606128

To me, this is astounding on two fronts. First, I am amazed that Excel handles this correctly. Second, it is amazing that anyone would ever try this. Who would have thought that Excel would handle this correctly? Clearly, Derek from Springfield.

Bonus Tip: Filling in a Text Field on the Subtotal Rows

Say that each customer in a data set is assigned to a single sales rep. It would be great if you could bring the sales rep name down to the subtotal row. Here are the steps:

1. Collapse the data to the #2 view.

2. Select all of the sales rep cells, from the first subtotal row to the last customer subtotal row. Don't include the Grand Total row. At this point, you have both the visible and hidden rows selected. You need just the blank rows or just the visible rows.

3. At the right side of the Home tab, open the Find & Select dropdown. Choose Go To Special. In the Go To Special dialog, choose Blanks. Click OK.

4. At this point, you've selected only the blank sales rep cells on the Subtotal rows. In my case, the active cell is A49. You need a formula here to point one cell up. So, as in the figure below, type =A48. Instead of pressing Enter, press Ctrl+Enter. This will enter a similar formula in all of the subtotal rows. In each case, it will bring the sales rep from the previous row down.

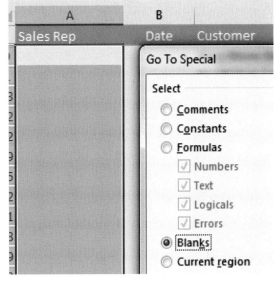

The results: The subtotal rows show the sales rep name in addition to the numeric totals.

	A	B	C
1	Sales Rep	Date	Customer
49	Geoffrey G Lilley		Wag More Dog Store, San Antonio Total
91	Geoffrey G Lilley		BradEdgar.com Total
133	Kevin J Sullivan		CPASelfStudy.com Total
172	Michael Dietterick		F-Keys Ltd Total
222	P B Rayudu		Hybrid Software Total
259	Peter Susen		Blockhead Data Consultants Total
295	Geoffrey G Lilley		Open Sky Martial Arts Total
332	David Ringstrom		Association for Computers & Taxation Total

Bonus Tip: Formatting the Subtotal Rows

It is a little odd that Subtotals only bolds the customer column and not anything else in the subtotal row. Follow these steps to format the subtotal rows:

1. Collapse the data to the #2 view.

2. Select all data from the first subtotal to the grand totals.

3. Press Alt+; (which is the shortcut for Go To Special, Visible Cells Only).

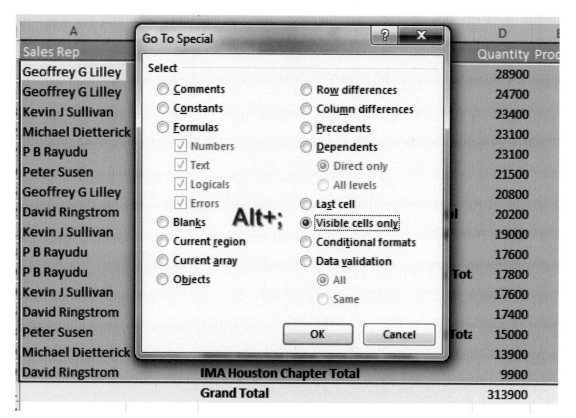

4. Click OK. Format the subtotal rowsby applying Bold and a fill color.

Now, when you go back to the #3 view, the subtotal rows will be easy to spot.

	A	B	C	D
1	Sales Rep	Date	Customer	Quantity
557	Michael Dietteric	8/25/2019	Juliet Babcock-Hyde CPA, PLLC	300
558	Michael Dietteric	10/22/2019	Juliet Babcock-Hyde CPA, PLLC	700
559	**Michael Dietterick**		**Juliet Babcock-Hyde CPA, PLLC**	**13900**
560	David Ringstrom	1/26/2018	IMA Houston Chapter	400
561	David Ringstrom	3/1/2018	IMA Houston Chapter	500
562	David Ringstrom	4/14/2018	IMA Houston Chapter	400

Bonus Tip: Copying the Subtotal Rows

Once you've collapsed the data down to the #2 view, you might want to copy the subtotals to a new worksheet. If so, select all the data. Press Alt+; to select only the visible cells. Press Ctrl+C to copy. Switch to a new workbook. Press Ctrl+V to paste. All the subtotal formulas are converted to values.

Thanks to Patricia McCarthy for suggesting to select visible cells. Thanks to Derek Fraley for his "row 6" suggestion.

#14 Easy Year-over-Year Report in a Pivot Table

Walter Moore

Let's say you have two years' worth of detail records. Each record has a daily date. When you build a pivot table from this report, you will have hundreds of rows of daily dates in the pivot table. This is not much of a summary.

Choose one of those date cells in the pivot table. From the Analyze tab in the ribbon, choose Group Field.

Because you are on a date field, you get *this* version of the Grouping dialog. In it, unselect Months and select Years.

The daily dates are rolled up to years. Move the Date field from ROWS to COLUMNS.

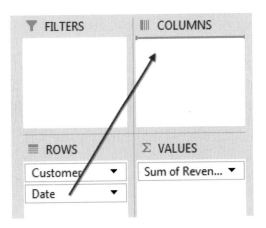

The result is almost perfect. But instead of a grand total in column D, you probably want a percentage variance.

To get rid of the Grand Total column, on the Design tab choose Grand Totals, On for Columns Only. (I agree, this is one of the more awkward wordings in Excel.)

To build the variance column, you need to write a formula outside the pivot table that points inside the pivot table. Do not touch the mouse or arrow keys while building the formula, or the nasty GETPIVOTDATA function will appear. Instead, simply type =C5/B5-1 and press Enter.

D5 f_x =C5/B5-1

	A	B	C	D
3	Sum of Revenue	Date		
4	Customer	2018	2019	% Change
5	Fintega Financial Modelling	283244	177286	-37.4%
6	Frontline Systems	319606	285579	-10.6%
7	Harlem Globetrotters	290940	359243	23.5%
8	JEVS Human Services	320340	383803	19.8%
9	MAU Workforce Solutions	306489	197928	-35.4%
10	Reports Wand	433045	335513	-22.5%
11	Serving Brevard Realty	239663	369485	54.2%
12	Tennessee Moon	228735	247500	8.2%
13	University of North Carolina	237031	199803	-15.7%
14	Wilde XL Solutions Ltd.	218750	177280	-19.0%
15	WM Squared Inc.	210623	313700	48.9%
16	www.ExcelTricks.de	319087	253139	-20.7%
17	Grand Total	3407553	3300259	-3.1%

Thanks to Александр Воробьев for suggesting this tip.

#15 True Top Five in a Pivot Table

Pivot tables offer a Top 10 filter. It is cool. It is flexible. But I hate it, and I will tell you why.

Here is a pivot table showing revenue by customer. The revenue total is $6.7 million.

Customer	Sum of Revenue
Orange County Health Department	448241
Phare View Concepts	375472
Profology.com	505279
Reports Wand	430540
Resource Optimizer	460086
Ribbon Commander Framework	490827
Roto-Rooter	606128
Safety Elements Ltd.	486697
Serving Brevard Realty	410118
SkyWire, Inc.	369567
SlinkyRN Excel Instruction and Consulting	329597
SpringBoard	295018
St. Peter's Prep	546662
Steve Comer	374497
Surten Excel	373852
Tennessee Moon	205231
Grand Total	6707812

What if my manager has the attention span of a goldfish and wants to see only the top five customers?

To start, open the dropdown in A3 and select Value Filters, Top 10.

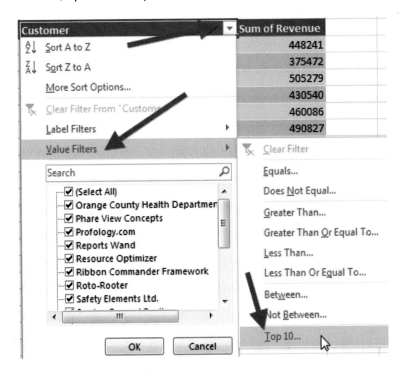

The super-flexible Top 10 Filter dialog allows Top/Bottom. It can do 10, 5, or any other number. You can ask for the top five items, top 80%, or enough customers to get to $5 million.

But here is the problem: The resulting report shows five customers and the total from those customers instead of the totals from everyone.

	A	B	C
1			
2			
3	Customer	Sum of Revenue	
4	Profology.com	505279	
5	Ribbon Commander Framework	490827	
6	Roto-Rooter	606128	
7	Safety Elements Ltd.	486697	
8	St. Peter's Prep	546662	
9	Grand Total	2635593	
10			

Total does not include all

But First, a Few Important Words About AutoFilter

I realize this seems like an off-the-wall question. If you want to turn on the Filter dropdowns on a regular data set, how do you do it? Here are three really common ways:

- Select one cell in your data and click the Filter icon on the Data tab.
- Select all of your data with Ctrl+* and click the Filter icon on the Data tab.
- Press Ctrl+T to format the data as a table.

These are three really good ways. As long as you know any of them, there is absolutely no need to know another way. But here's an incredibly obscure but magical way to turn on the filter:

- Go to your row of headers, go to the rightmost heading cell. Move one cell to the right. For some unknown reason, when you are in this cell and click the Filter icon, Excel filters the data set to your left. I have no idea why this works. It really isn't worth talking about because there are already three really good ways to turn on the Filter dropdowns. I call this cell the Magic cell.

And now, Back to Pivot Tables...

So, there is a rule that says you cannot use the AutoFilters when you are in a pivot table. See below? The Filter icon is grayed out because I've selected a cell in the pivot table.

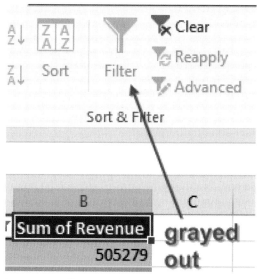

grayed out

1

I never really considered why Microsoft grays this out. It must be something internal that says AutoFilter and a Pivot Table can't coexist. So, there is someone on the Excel team who is in charge of graying out the Filter icon. That person has never heard of the Magic cell. Select a cell in the pivot table, and the Filter gets grayed out. Click outside of the pivot table, and Filter is enabled again.

But wait. What about the Magic cell I just told you about? If you click in the cell to the right of the last heading, Excel forgets to gray out the Filter icon!

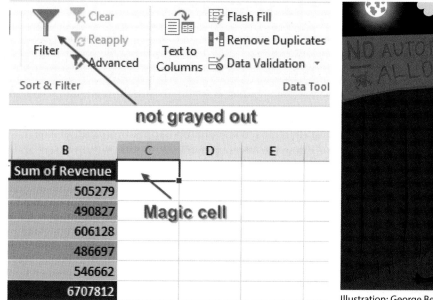

Illustration: George Berlin

Sure enough, Excel adds AutoFilter dropdowns to the top row of your pivot table. And the AutoFilter operates differently than pivot table filters. Go to the Revenue dropdown and choose Number Filters, Top 10….

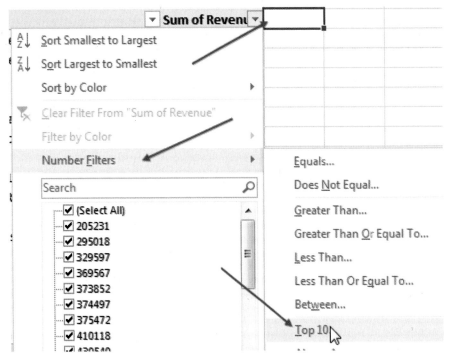

In the Top 10 AutoFilter dialog, choose Top 6 Items. That's not a typo…. If you want five customers, choose 6. If you want 10 customers, choose 11.

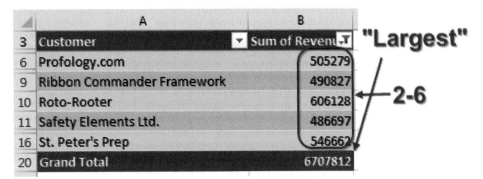

To AutoFilter, the grand total row is the largest item in the data. The top five customers are occupying positions 2 through 6 in the data.

	A	B	
3	Customer	Sum of Revenu	"Largest"
6	Profology.com	505279	
9	Ribbon Commander Framework	490827	
10	Roto-Rooter	606128	2-6
11	Safety Elements Ltd.	486697	
16	St. Peter's Prep	546662	
20	Grand Total	6707812	

Caution: Clearly, you are tearing a hole in the fabric of Excel with this trick. If you later change the underlying data and refresh your pivot table, Excel will not refresh the filter, because, as far as Microsoft knows, there is no way to apply a filter to a pivot table!

Note: Our goal is to keep this a secret from Microsoft, because it is a pretty cool feature. It has been "broken" for quite some time, so there are a lot of people who might be relying on it by now. I know that David Gainer from the Excel team preordered this book, so this box is my rationalization to David for why he should not take this out.

A Completely Legal Solution in Excel 2013+

If you want a pivot table showing you the top five customers but the total from all customers, you have to move your data outside of Excel. If you have Excel 2013 or 2016, there is a very convenient way to do this. To show you this, I've deleted the original pivot table. Choose Insert, Pivot Table. Before clicking OK, select the box that says Add This Data to the Data Model.

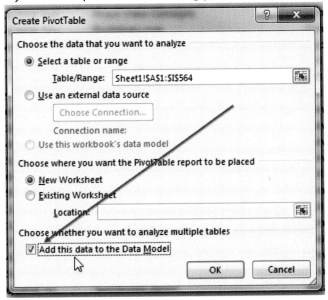

Build your pivot table as normal. Use the drop-down in A3 to select Value Filters, Top 10, and ask for the top five customers. With one cell in the pivot table selected, go to the Design tab in the ribbon and open the Subtotals dropdown. The final choice in the dropdown is Include Filtered Items in Totals. Normally, this choice is grayed out. But because the data is stored in the Data Model instead of a normal pivot cache, this option is now available.

		Sum of Revenue
		505279
		490827
6	Roto-Rooter	606128
7	Safety Elements Ltd.	486697
8	St. Peter's Prep	546662
9	Grand Total	2635593

Choose the Include Filtered Items in Total option, and your Grand Total now includes an asterisk and the total of all of the data.

3	Customer	Sum of Revenue
4	Profology.com	505279
5	Ribbon Commander Framework	490827
6	Roto-Rooter	606128
7	Safety Elements Ltd.	486697
8	St. Peter's Prep	546662
9	Grand Total *	6707812

This trick originally came to me from Dan in my seminar in Philadelphia. Thanks to Miguel Caballero for suggesting this feature.

#16 Eliminate Pivot Table Annoyances

I am on an eight-year mission to convince the Excel team to offer a setting somewhere in Excel 2018 to allow people to specify whether they prefer Compact Layout, Outline Layout, or Tabular Layout. I began this mission after the team added Repeat All Item Labels to Excel 2010. I had been asking for *that* feature since 2002. Now that's been added, my new passion is to allow everyone who prefers Tabular to Compact to have a checkbox somewhere to make Tabular be the default. If you also prefer Tabular Layout, get ready to wait until Excel 2018. Plus two years for your IT department to decide to up-grade. That puts the feature out to 2020 for most of us.

If you don't want to wait until the Excel team finally gets tired of my lobbying and adds the feature you can invest $30 today to buy an amazing add-in called Pivot Power Premium from Debra Dalgleish at Contextures.com. Here you see the Add-In's Set Preferences dialog, where you can specify the default layout plus dozens of other settings.

This add-in will force all new Values fields to Sum. You will never have to deal with Counts! Plus it offers a way to control the number format.

This add-in takes all the obscure pivot functionality that is buried deep in the Options dialog and exposes it in the Ribbon. Let's stop talking about it. It is worth every penny of the $30 license fee. Just go buy it: http://mrx.cl/pppdebra.

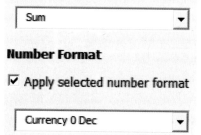

Ctrl+T Table Before Adding New Data

In almost every seminar, someone asks why their pivot tables default to counting a numeric field instead of summing. There are two possible answers: Either there are a few blank cells in the numeric column, or the person is selecting entire columns in the data set (such as A:C instead of A1:C16).

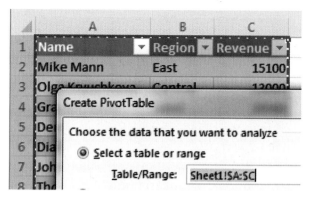

I understand the logic behind the second possibility. If you choose all of columns A:C and you later want to add more records below the data, it takes only a simple Refresh to add the new data instead of having to find the Change Data Source icon. In the past, this made sense. But today, Change Data Source is right next to the Refresh button and not hard to find. Plus, there is a workaround in the Ctrl+T Table.

When you choose your data set and select Format as Table by using Ctrl+T, the pivot table source will grow as the table grows. You can even do this retroactively, after the pivot table exists.

This figure shows a data set and a pivot table. The pivot table source is A1:C16.

	A	B	C	D	E	F
1	Name	Region	Revenue			
2	Mike Mann	East	15100		Region ▾	Revenue
3	Olga Kryuchkova	Central	13000		Central	$282,800
4	Graham Stent	West	20500		East	$176,500
5	Dennis P Jancsy	East	29800		West	$350,900
6	Diana McGunigale	Central	27800		Grand Total	$810,200
7	John Henning	West	39000			
8	Thomas Fries	East	7200			
9	Aiman Sadeq	Central	47700			
10	John Cockerill	West	36200			
11	Greg Heyman	East	39900			
12	Rick Grantham	Central	78600			
13	DeLisa Lee	West	100900			
14	Mark E Luhdorff	East	84500			
15	John T Lutz	Central	115700			
16	Mario Garcia	West	154300			
17						

You want to be able to easily add new data below the pivot table.

Select one cell in the data and press Ctrl+T. Make sure that My Table Has Headers is checked in the Create Table dialog and click OK.

Some nice formatting is applied to the data set. But the formatting is not the important part.

You have some new records to add to the table. Copy the records.

Go to the blank row below the table and paste. The new records pick up the formatting from the table. The angle-bracket-shaped End-of-Table marker moves to C19. But notice that the pivot table has not updated yet.

	A	B	C	D	E	F
1	Name ▼	Region ▼	Revenue ▼			
2	Mike Mann	East	15100		**Region** ▼	**Revenue**
3	Olga Kryuchkova	Central	13000		Central	$282,800
4	Graham Stent	West	20500		East	$176,500
5	Dennis P Jancsy	East	29800		West	$350,900
6	Diana McGunigale	Central	27800		**Grand Total**	**$810,200**
7	John Henning	West	39000			
8	Thomas Fries	East	7200			
9	Aiman Sadeq	Central	47700			
10	John Cockerill	West	36200			
11	Greg Heyman	East	39900			
12	Rick Grantham	Central	78600			
13	DeLisa Lee	West	100900		**Pasted data**	
14	Mark E Luhdorff	East	84500			
15	John T Lutz	Central	115700		**No change yet**	
16	Mario Garcia	West	154300			
17	Erik Svensen	East	42800		**End of Table mark**	
18	Melanie Breden	Central	98300			
19	J Maltais	West	68400			
20					(Ctrl) ▼	

Click the Refresh button in the Pivot Table Tools Analyze tab. Excel adds the new rows to your pivot table.

Developer	Power Pivot	Analyze
Filter	Refresh	Change Data Source
Connections		
	Data	

	E	F	G
	Region ▼	**Revenue**	
	Central	$381,100	
	East	$219,300	
	West	$419,300	
	Grand Total	**$1,019,700**	

1

Bonus Tip: Ctrl+T Helps VLOOKUP and Charts

In this figure, the VLOOKUP table is in E5:F9. Item A106 is missing from the table and the VLOOKUP is returning #N/A. Conventional wisdom says to add A106 to the middle of your VLOOKUP table so you don't have to rewrite the formula.

	A	B	C	D	E	F	G
1	Qty	Item	Price?				
2	7	A104	37.95	=VLOOKUP(B2,$E$5:$F$9,2,0)			
3	8	A101	10.95				
4	2	A101	10.95		Item	Price	
5	9	A106	#N/A		A101	10.95	
6	7	A102	19.95		A102	19.95	
7	2	A103	28.95		A103	28.95	
8					A104	37.95	
9					A105	46.95	
10							

Instead, use Ctrl+T to format the lookup table. Note that the formula is still pointing to E5:F9; nothing changes in the formula.

	A	B	C	D	E	F
1	Qty	Item	Price?			
2	7	A104	37.95	=VLOOKUP(B2,$E$5:$F$9,2,0)		
3	8	A101	10.95		**Ctrl+t**	
4	2	A101	10.95		Item	Price
5	9	A106	#N/A		A101	10.95
6	7	A102	19.95		A102	19.95
7	2	A103	28.95		A103	28.95
8					A104	37.95
9	**No change**				A105	46.95
10	**in formula**					

But when you type a new row below the table, it becomes part of the table and the VLOOKUP formula automatically updates to reflect the new range.

	A	B	C	D	E	F	G
1	Qty	Item	Price?	**Formula changes**			
2	7	A104	37.95	=VLOOKUP(B2,$E$5:$F$10,2,0)			
3	8	A101	10.95				
4	2	A101	10.95		Item	Price	
5	9	A106	24.95		A101	10.95	
6	7	A102	19.95		A102	19.95	
7	2	A103	28.95		A103	28.95	
8					A104	37.95	
9	**Add new row**				A105	46.95	
10					A106	24.95	
11							

The same thing happens with charts. The chart on the left is based on A1:B5 which is not a table. Format A1:B5 as a table by pressing Ctrl+T. Add a new row. The row is automatically added to the chart.

It is fairly cool that you can use Ctrl+T after setting up the pivot table, VLOOKUP, or chart, and Excel still makes the range expand.

Bonus Tip: Readable References with Ctrl+T

Not only do these tables make refreshing the data easier, they also make reading formulas much easier! The only thing you need to do is to press Ctrl+T before writing the formula.

Let's go back to the VLOOKUP formula from above. This time, convert your items table and your purchase table to an Excel table with Ctrl+T right from the start! To make things easier, give each table a friendly name using the Table Tools tab:

Now type in the VLOOKUP again without doing anything differently than you normally do, your formula in C2 now is =VLOOKUP([@Item],Items,2,0) instead of =VLOOKUP(B2,$E$5:$F$10,2,0)!

	A	B	C	D	E	F
1	Qty	Item	Price			
2	7	A104	37.95	=VLOOKUP([@Item],Items,2,0)		
3	8	A101	10.95	=VLOOKUP([@Item],Items,2,0)		
4	2	A101	10.95	=VLOOKUP([@Item],Items,2,0)		
5	9	A106	24.95	=VLOOKUP([@Item],Items,2,0)		
6	7	A102	19.95	=VLOOKUP([@Item],Items,2,0)	Item	Price
7	2	A103	28.95	=VLOOKUP([@Item],Items,2,0)	A101	10.95
8					A102	19.95
9					A103	28.95
10					A104	37.95
11					A105	46.95
12					A106	24.95

Even if the Items table is on a different worksheet, the formula is the same, instead of the less readable =VLOOKUP(B2,Items!$A$2:$B$7,2,0).

The [@Item] in the formula refers to the cell in the Item column of this table (in the same row as the formula) and is therefore the same in the whole column. And Items refers to the whole items table (without the headers). Best of all, you don't need to type any of this. Once this is a table, Excel will place these names in your formula as you select the cells/ranges!

Let's take this one step further. Add another column to the Sales table to calculate the revenue with the formula =[@Price]*[@Qty]. If you now want to calculate the total revenue, the formula is =SUM(Sales[Revenue]); which is really easy to understand, no matter where the data is or how many rows it covers!

	A	B	C	D	E
1	Qty	Item	Price	Revenu	
2	7	A104	37.95	265.65	=[@Price]*[@Qty]
3	8	A101	10.95	87.6	=[@Price]*[@Qty]
4	2	A101	10.95	21.9	=[@Price]*[@Qty]
5	9	A106	24.95	224.55	=[@Price]*[@Qty]
6	7	A102	19.95	139.65	=[@Price]*[@Qty]
7	2	A103	28.95	57.9	=[@Price]*[@Qty]
8					
9	Total revenue			797.25	=SUM(Sales[Revenue])
10					

Bonus Tip: Running Totals in Tables

A running total is, for a list of numeric values, a sum of the values from the first row to the row of the running total. Common uses of a running total are in a checkbook register or an accounting sheet. There are many ways to create a running total—two of which are described below.

The simplest technique is to, on each row, add the running total from the row above to the value in the row. So the first formula in row 2 is:

```
=SUM(D1,C2)
```

The reason we use the SUM function is because, in the first row, we are looking at the header in the row above. If we use the simpler, more intuitive formula of =D1+C2 then an error will be generated because the header value is text versus numeric. The magic is that the SUM function ignores text values, which are added as zero values. When the formula is copied down to all of the rows in which a running total is desired, the cell references are adjusted accordingly:

D2 · : × ✓ fx =SUM(D1,C2)

	A	B	C	D	E
1	Month	Customer	Sales	Running Total	Formula
2	Jan	Data Automation Professionals	13,093	13,093	=SUM(D1,C2)
3	Jan	Lugh Information Services Consulting	33,588	46,681	=SUM(D2,C3)
4	Feb	Lugh Information Services Consulting	41,721	88,402	=SUM(D3,C4)
5	Mar	Lugh Information Services Consulting	17,221	105,623	=SUM(D4,C5)
6	Mar	MrExcel Consulting	39,996	145,619	=SUM(D5,C6)
7	Apr	Lugh Information Services Consulting	26,760	172,379	=SUM(D6,C7)
8	May	Data Automation Professionals	5,242	177,621	=SUM(D7,C8)
9	May	Lugh Information Services Consulting	19,817	197,438	=SUM(D8,C9)
10	Jun	Lugh Information Services Consulting	48,000	245,438	=SUM(D9,C10)
11	Jul	Data Automation Professionals	47,933	293,371	=SUM(D10,C11)
12	Jul	Lugh Information Services Consulting	4,447	297,818	=SUM(D11,C12)
13	Jul	MrExcel Consulting	8,870	306,688	=SUM(D12,C13)
14	Aug	Lugh Information Services Consulting	49,552	356,240	=SUM(D13,C14)

The other technique also uses the SUM function but each formula sums all of the values from the first row to the row displaying the running total. In this case we use a dollar sign ($) to make the first cell in the reference an absolute reference which means it is not adjusted when copied:

| D2 | | | f_x | =SUM(C$1:C2) | |

	A	B	C	D	E
1	Month	Customer	Sales	Running Total	Formula
2	Jan	Data Automation Professionals	13,093	13,093	=SUM(C$2:C2)
3	Jan	Lugh Information Services Consulting	33,588	46,681	=SUM(C$2:C3)
4	Feb	Lugh Information Services Consulting	41,721	88,402	=SUM(C$2:C4)
5	Mar	Lugh Information Services Consulting	17,221	105,623	=SUM(C$2:C5)
6	Mar	MrExcel Consulting	39,996	145,619	=SUM(C$2:C6)
7	Apr	Lugh Information Services Consulting	26,760	172,379	=SUM(C$2:C7)
8	May	Data Automation Professionals	5,242	177,621	=SUM(C$2:C8)
9	May	Lugh Information Services Consulting	19,817	197,438	=SUM(C$2:C9)
10	Jun	Lugh Information Services Consulting	48,000	245,438	=SUM(C$2:C10)
11	Jul	Data Automation Professionals	47,933	293,371	=SUM(C$2:C11)
12	Jul	Lugh Information Services Consulting	4,447	297,818	=SUM(C$2:C12)

Both techniques are unaffected by sorting and deleting rows but, when inserting rows, the formula has to be copied into the new rows.

Excel 2007 introduced the Table which is a re-implementation of the List in Excel 2003. Tables introduced a number of very useful features for data tables such as formatting, sorting, and filtering. With the introduction of Tables we were also provided a new way of referencing the parts of a Table. This new referencing style is called structured referencing.

To convert the above example into a Table, we select the data we want to include in the Table and press CTRL+T. After displaying a prompt asking us to confirm the Table's range and whether or not there are existing headers, Excel converts the data into a formatted Table:

| D2 | | | f_x | =SUM(C$1:C2) | |

	A	B	C	D	E
1	Month	Customer	Sales	Running Total	Formula
2	Jan	Data Automation Professionals	13,093	13,093	=SUM(C$2:C2)
3	Jan	Lugh Information Services Consulting	33,588	46,681	=SUM(C$2:C3)
4	Feb	Lugh Information Services Consulting	41,721	88,402	=SUM(C$2:C4)
5	Mar	Lugh Information Services Consulting	17,221	105,623	=SUM(C$2:C5)
6	Mar	MrExcel Consulting	39,996	145,619	=SUM(C$2:C6)
7	Apr	Lugh Information Services Consulting	26,760	172,379	=SUM(C$2:C7)
8	May	Data Automation Professionals	5,242	177,621	=SUM(C$2:C8)
9	May	Lugh Information Services Consulting	19,817	197,438	=SUM(C$2:C9)
10	Jun	Lugh Information Services Consulting	48,000	245,438	=SUM(C$2:C10)
11	Jul	Data Automation Professionals	47,933	293,371	=SUM(C$2:C11)
12	Jul	Lugh Information Services Consulting	4,447	297,818	=SUM(C$2:C12)
13	Jul	MrExcel Consulting	8,870	306,688	=SUM(C$2:C13)
14	Aug	Lugh Information Services Consulting	49,552	356,240	=SUM(C$2:C14)
15	Sep	Lugh Information Services Consulting	19,685	375,925	=SUM(C$2:C15)
16	Oct	MrExcel Consulting	16,776	392,701	=SUM(C$2:C16)
17	Nov	Lugh Information Services Consulting	5,942	398,643	=SUM(C$2:C17)
18	Dec	Lugh Information Services Consulting	15,408	414,051	=SUM(C$2:C18)

Note that the formulas we entered earlier remain the same.

One of the useful features Tables offers is automatic formatting and formula maintenance as rows are added, removed, sorted, and filtered. It is the formula maintenance in particular that we will focus on and which can be problematic. To keep Tables working while they are manipulated, Excel utilizes calculated columns which are columns with formulas such as column D in the above example. When new rows are inserted are added to the bottom, Excel automatically populates the new rows with the "default" formula for that column. The problem with the above example is that Excel gets confused with standard formulas and does not always handle them correctly. This is made apparent when new rows are added to the bottom of the Table (by selecting the bottom right cell in the Table and pressing TAB):

D18		fx	=SUM(C$1:C21)		

	A	B	C	D	E	F G
1	Month	Customer	Sales	Running Total	Formula	
2	Jan	Data Automation Professionals	13,093	13,093	=SUM(C$2:C2)	Correct
3	Jan	Lugh Information Services Consulting	33,588	46,681	=SUM(C$2:C3)	Correct
4	Feb	Lugh Information Services Consulting	41,721	88,402	=SUM(C$2:C4)	Correct
5	Mar	Lugh Information Services Consulting	17,221	105,623	=SUM(C$2:C5)	Correct
6	Mar	MrExcel Consulting	39,996	145,619	=SUM(C$2:C6)	Correct
7	Apr	Lugh Information Services Consulting	26,760	172,379	=SUM(C$2:C7)	Correct
8	May	Data Automation Professionals	5,242	177,621	=SUM(C$2:C8)	Correct
9	May	Lugh Information Services Consulting	19,817	197,438	=SUM(C$2:C9)	Correct
10	Jun	Lugh Information Services Consulting	48,000	245,438	=SUM(C$2:C10)	Correct
11	Jul	Data Automation Professionals	47,933	293,371	=SUM(C$2:C11)	Correct
12	Jul	Lugh Information Services Consulting	4,447	297,818	=SUM(C$2:C12)	Correct
13	Jul	MrExcel Consulting	8,870	306,688	=SUM(C$2:C13)	Correct
14	Aug	Lugh Information Services Consulting	49,552	356,240	=SUM(C$2:C14)	Correct
15	Sep	Lugh Information Services Consulting	19,685	375,925	=SUM(C$2:C15)	Correct
16	Oct	MrExcel Consulting	16,776	392,701	=SUM(C$2:C16)	Correct
17	Nov	Lugh Information Services Consulting	5,942	398,643	=SUM(C$2:C17)	Correct
18	Dec	Lugh Information Services Consulting	1◇08	471,905	=SUM(C$2:C21)	Incorrect
19	Dec		23,419	471,905	=SUM(C$2:C21)	Incorrect
20	Dec		3,910	471,905	=SUM(C$2:C21)	Incorrect
21	Dec		30,525	471,905	=SUM(C$2:C21)	Correct

This deficiency is resolved by using the newer structured referencing. Structured referencing eliminates the need to reference specific cells using the A1 or R1C1 referencing style and instead uses column names and other keywords to identify and reference the parts of a Table. For example, to create the same running total formula used above but using structured referencing we have:

=SUM(INDEX([Sales],1):[@Sales])

In this example we have a reference to the column name, "Sales", along with the ampersand (@) to reference the row in the column in which the formula is located which is also known as the current row.

D2   fx   =SUM(INDEX([Sales],1):[@Sales])

	Month ▼	Customer ▼	Sales ▼	Running Total ▼
2	Jan	Data Automation Professionals	13,093	13,093
3	Jan	Lugh Information Services Consulting	33,588	46,681
4	Feb	Lugh Information Services Consulting	41,721	88,402
5	Mar	Lugh Information Services Consulting	17,221	105,623
6	Mar	MrExcel Consulting	39,996	145,619
7	Apr	Lugh Information Services Consulting	26,760	172,379
8	May	Data Automation Professionals	5,242	177,621
9	May	Lugh Information Services Consulting	19,817	197,438
10	Jun	Lugh Information Services Consulting	48,000	245,438
11	Jul	Data Automation Professionals	47,933	293,371
12	Jul	Lugh Information Services Consulting	4,447	297,818
13	Jul	MrExcel Consulting	8,870	306,688
14	Aug	Lugh Information Services Consulting	49,552	356,240
15	Sep	Lugh Information Services Consulting	19,685	375,925
16	Oct	MrExcel Consulting	16,776	392,701
17	Nov	Lugh Information Services Consulting	5,942	398,643
18	Dec	Lugh Information Services Consulting	15,408	414,051
19	Dec		23,419	437,470
20	Dec		3,910	441,380
21	Dec		30,525	471,905

To implement the first example above where we added the running total value in the preceding row to the sales amount in the current row, you can use the OFFSET function:

```
=SUM(OFFSET([@[Running Total]],-1,0),[@Sales])
```

If the amounts used to calculate the running total are in two columns, for example one for "Debits" and one for "Credits", then the formula is:

```
=SUM(INDEX( [Credit],1):[@Credit])- SUM(INDEX( [Debit],1):[@Debit])
```

Here we are using the INDEX function to locate the first row's Credit and Debit cells, and summing the entire column up to and including the current row's values. The running total is the sum of all credits up to and including the current row less the sum of all the debits up to and including the current row.

For a more information on structured references in particular and Tables in general, we recommend the book Excel Tables: A Complete Guide for Creating, Using and Automating Lists and Tables by Zack Barresse and Kevin Jones.

When I asked readers to vote for their favorite tips, tables were popular. Thanks to Peter Albert, Snorre Eikeland, Nancy Federice, Colin Michael, James E. Moede, Keyur Patel, and Paul Peton for suggesting this feature. Peter Albert wrote the Readable References bonus Tip. Zack Barresse wrote the Running Totals bonus tip. Four readers suggested using OFFSET to create expanding ranges for dynamic charts: Charley Baak, Don Knowles, Francis Logan, and Cecelia Rieb. Tables now do the same thing in most cases.

#17 Replicate a Pivot Report For Each Rep

Here is a great trick that I learned from my coauthor Szilvia Juhasz.

The pivot table below shows products across the top and customers down the side. The pivot table is sorted so the largest customers are at the top. The Sales Rep field is in the Report Filter.

	A	B	C	D	E
1	Rep	(All)			
2					
3	Sum of Revenue	Product			
4	Customer	Gizmo	Gadget	WhatsIt	Grand Total
5	Harlem Globetrotters	382,878	414,502	402,311	1,199,691
6	MySpreadsheetLab	341,902	444,299	362,269	1,148,470
7	CPASelfStudy.com	335,541	267,607	285,829	888,977
8	Reports Wand	126,769	88,354	101,966	317,089
9	The Lab with Leo Crew	57,281	72,643	164,236	294,160

If you open the Rep filter dropdown, you can filter the data to any one sales rep.

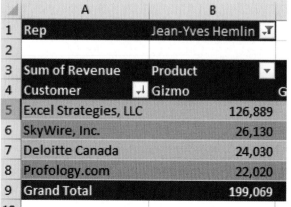

This is a great way to create a report for each sales rep. Each report summarizes the revenue from a particular salesperson's customers, with the biggest customers at the top. And you get to see the split between the various products.

	A	B
1	Rep	Jean-Yves Hemlin
2		
3	Sum of Revenue	Product
4	Customer	Gizmo G
5	Excel Strategies, LLC	126,889
6	SkyWire, Inc.	26,130
7	Deloitte Canada	24,030
8	Profology.com	22,020
9	Grand Total	199,069

The Excel team has hidden a feature called Show Report Filter Pages. Select any pivot table that has a Report Filter. Go to the Analyze tab (or the Options tab in Excel 2007/2010). On the far left side is the large Options button. Next to the large Options button is a tiny dropdown arrow. Click this dropdown and choose Show Report Filter Pages.

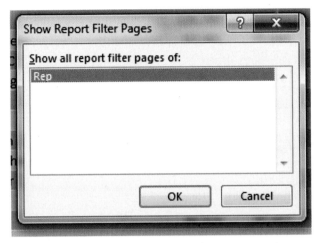

Excel asks which field you want to use. Select the one you want (in this case the only one available) and click OK.

Over the next few seconds, Excel starts inserting new worksheets, one for each sales rep. Each sheet tab is named after the sales rep. Inside each worksheet, Excel replicates the pivot table but changes the name in the Report Filter to this sales rep.

	A	B	C	D
1	Rep	Mark E Luhdorff 🔽		
2				
3	Sum of Revenue	Product 🔽		
4	Customer	Gizmo	Gadget	WhatsIt
5	The Lab with Leo Crew	57,281	72,643	
6	myexcelonline.com	12,838	108,373	
7	XLYOURFINANCES, LLC	33,993	13,723	
8	Hartville Marketplace & Flea Market	0	15,394	
9	Grand Total	104,112	210,133	
10				
11				
12				

◀ ▶ ... | Jean-Yves Hemlin | **Mark E Luhdorff** | Melanie Breden | Peter Albert

You end up with a report for each sales rep.

This would work with any field. If you want a report for each customer, product, vendor, or so on, add it to the Report Filter and use Show Report Filter Pages.

Thanks to Szilvia Juhasz for showing me this feature during a seminar I was teaching at the University of Akron many years ago. For the record, Szilvia was in row 1.

#18 Use a Pivot Table to Compare Lists

When you think of comparing lists, you probably think of VLOOKUP. If you have two lists to compare, you need to add two columns of VLOOKUP. In the figure below, you are trying to compare Tuesday to Monday and Wednesday to Tuesday and maybe even Wednesday to Monday. It is going to take a lot of VLOOKUP columns to figure out who added and dropped from each list.

	Monday			Tuesday			Weds	
	A	B	C	D	E	F	G	H
1	Monday			Tuesday			Weds	
2								
3	**Name**	**RSVP**		Name	RSVP		Name	RS
4	Carl Hjortsjö	2		Andrew Spain	3		Andrew Spain	3
5	Caroline Bonner	2		Caroline Bonner	2		Jean-Yves Hemlin	1
6	Dawn Kosmakos	2		Dawn Kosmakos	1		Jeffrey P. Coulson	2
7	Jeff Long	1		Kathryn Sullivan	2		John Durran	1
8	M.R. Rosenkrantz	1		M.R. Rosenkrantz	1		Kathryn Sullivan	1
9	Martin Lucas	2		Martin Lucas	2		Kevin Lehrbass	1
10	Paul Hannelly	2		Melissa Esquibel	2		M.R. Rosenkrantz	2
11	Roger Fisher	1		Michael Karpfen	2		Martin Lucas	1
12	Sabine Hanschitz	1		Peter Harvest	2		Melissa Esquibel	2
13	Ute Simon	2		Roger Fisher	1		Michael Karpfen	2
14	Yesenia Garcia	2		Sabine Hanschitz	1		Peter Harvest	1
15				Ute Simon	2		Roger Fisher	1
16				Yesenia Garcia	2		Sabine Hanschitz	2
17							Ute Simon	2
18								

You can use pivot tables to make this job far easier. Combine all of your lists into a single list with a new column called Source. In the Source column, identify which list the data came from. Build a pivot table from the combined list, with Name in ROWS, RSVP in VALUES and Source in COLUMNS. Turn off the Grand Total row and you have a neat list showing a superset from day to day.

	A	B	C
1	Combine all Lists		
2			
3	**Name**	**RSVP**	**Source**
13	Ute Simon	2	Monday
14	Yesenia Garcia	2	Monday
15	Andrew Spain	3	Tuesday
16	Caroline Bonner	2	Tuesday
17	Dawn Kosmakos	1	Tuesday
18	Kathryn Sullivan	2	Tuesday
19	M.R. Rosenkrantz	1	Tuesday
20	Martin Lucas	2	Tuesday
21	Melissa Esquibel	2	Tuesday
22	Michael Karpfen	2	Tuesday
23	Peter Harvest	2	Tuesday
24	Roger Fisher	1	Tuesday
25	Sabine Hanschitz	1	Tuesday
26	Ute Simon	2	Tuesday
27	Yesenia Garcia	2	Tuesday
28	Andrew Spain	3	Wednesday
29	Jean-Yves Hemlin	1	Wednesday

Sum of RSVP	Source		
Name	Monday	Tuesday	Wednesday
Andrew Spain		3	3
Carl Hjortsjö	2		
Caroline Bonner	2	2	
Dawn Kosmakos	2	1	
Jean-Yves Hemlin			1
Jeff Long	1		
Jeffrey P. Coulson			2
John Durran			1
Kathryn Sullivan		2	1
Kevin Lehrbass			1
M.R. Rosenkrantz	1	1	2
Martin Lucas	2	2	1
Melissa Esquibel		2	2
Michael Karpfen		2	2
Paul Hannelly	2		
Peter Harvest		2	1
Roger Fisher	1	1	1
Sabine Hanschitz	1	1	2
Ute Simon	2	2	2
Yesenia Garcia	2	2	
Grand Total	**18**	**23**	**22**

Bonus Tip: Showing Up/Down Markers

There is a super-obscure way to add up/down markers to a pivot table to indicate an increase or a decrease.

Somewhere outside the pivot table, add columns to show increases or decreases. In the figure below, the difference between I6 and H6 is 3, but you just want to record this as a positive change. Asking for the SIGN(I6-H6) will provide either +1, 0, or -1.

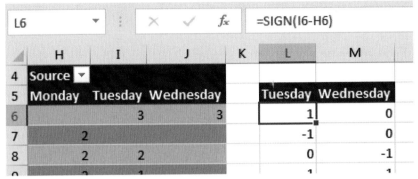

Select the two-column range showing the sign of the change and then select Home, Conditional Formatting, Icon Sets, 3 Triangles. (I have no idea why Microsoft called this option Three Triangles, when it is clearly Two Triangles and a Dash.)

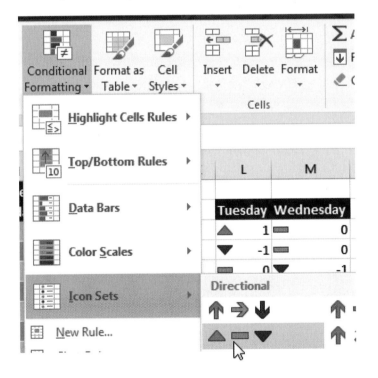

With the same range selected, now select Home, Conditional Formatting, Manage Rules, Edit Rule. Check the Show Icon Only checkbox.

With the same range selected, press Ctrl+C to copy. Select the first Tuesday cell in the pivot table. From the Home tab, open the Paste Dropdown and choose Linked Picture. Excel pastes a live picture of the icons above the table.

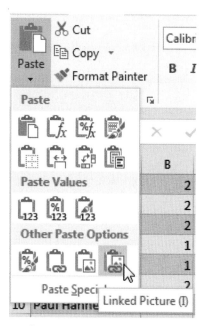

At this point, adjust the column widths of the extra two columns showing the icons so that the icons line up next to the numbers in your pivot table.

Name	Monday	Tuesday	Wednesday
Andrew Spain		△ 3	▭ 3
Carl Hjortsjö	2	▼	▭
Caroline Bonner	2	▭ 2	▼
Dawn Kosmakos	2	▼ 1	▼
Jean-Yves Hemlin		▭	△ 1

After seeing this result, I don't really like the thick yellow dash to indicate "no change". If you don't like it either, select Home, Conditional Formatting, Manage Rules, Edit. Open the dropdown for the thick yellow dash and choose No Cell Icon.

Andrew Spain		△ 3	3
Carl Hjortsjö	2	▼	
Caroline Bonner	2	2	▼
Dawn Kosmakos	2	▼ 1	▼

#19 Custom Chart Labels in Excel 2013

Using Excel custom chart labels is a great way to create a more insightful chart without having to show another whole series. Consider the chart below, which has custom labels showing the year-on-year percentage change:

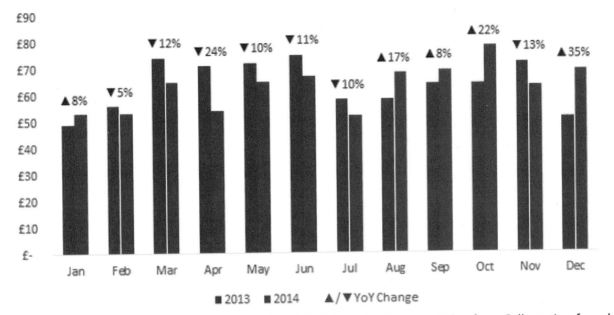

In Excel 2013 you can easily insert custom chart labels by using the new Value from Cells option found in the Label Options menu.

Format Data Labels

LABEL OPTIONS

⊿ **LABEL OPTIONS**

Label Contains

☑ Value From Cells

☐ Series Name

☐ Category Name

☐ Value

To do this, set up your chart source data, like this:

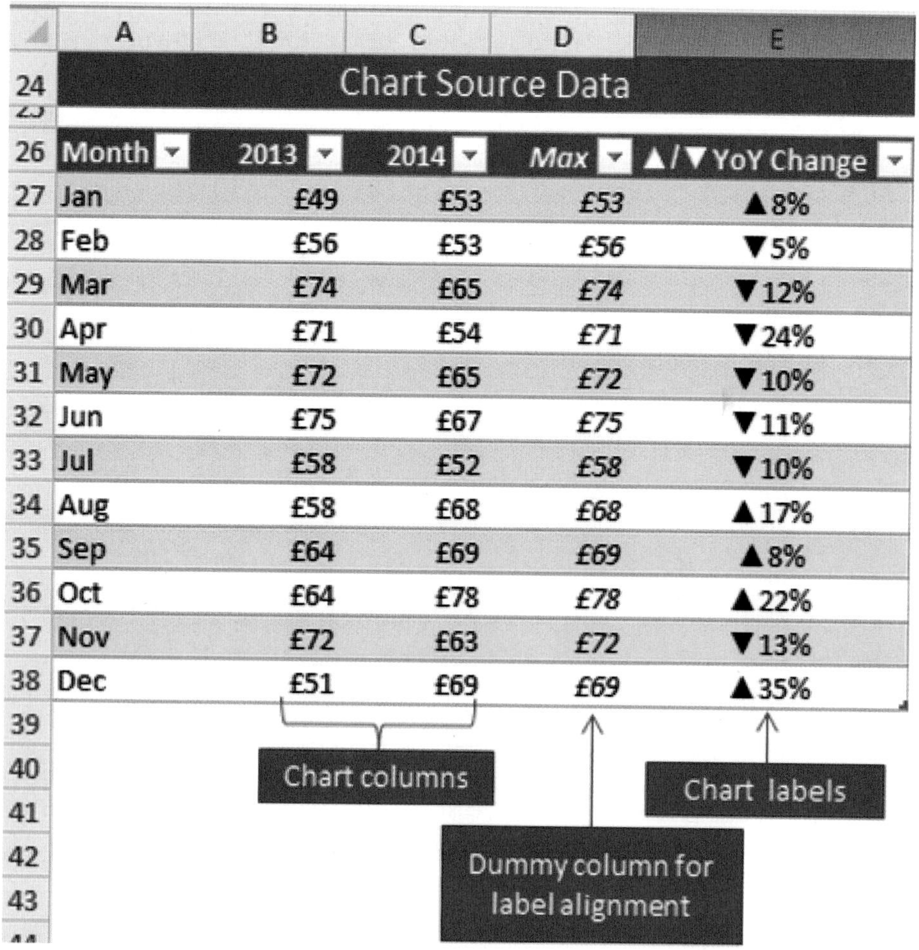

	A	B	C	D	E
24			Chart Source Data		
25					
26	Month ▼	2013 ▼	2014 ▼	Max ▼	▲/▼ YoY Change ▼
27	Jan	£49	£53	£53	▲ 8%
28	Feb	£56	£53	£56	▼ 5%
29	Mar	£74	£65	£74	▼ 12%
30	Apr	£71	£54	£71	▼ 24%
31	May	£72	£65	£72	▼ 10%
32	Jun	£75	£67	£75	▼ 11%
33	Jul	£58	£52	£58	▼ 10%
34	Aug	£58	£68	£68	▲ 17%
35	Sep	£64	£69	£69	▲ 8%
36	Oct	£64	£78	£78	▲ 22%
37	Nov	£72	£63	£72	▼ 13%
38	Dec	£51	£69	£69	▲ 35%

Chart columns (B and C)

Dummy column for label alignment (D)

Chart labels (E)

Take special note of columns D and E as these are required for the labels.

A brief word on the Max column: This column simply returns the MAX from columns B and C for each row. I used Max as a dummy series in this chart to dynamically position the labels just above the columns.

1. Select cells A26:D38 and insert a column chart

2. Select the Max series and plot it on the secondary axis by double-clicking the Max series and then selecting Format Data Series, Secondary Axis:

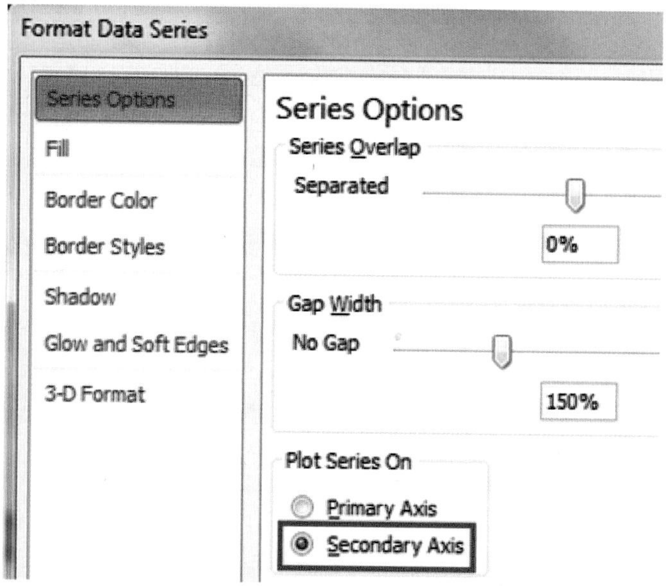

Format Data Series

Series Options	Series Options
Fill	Series Overlap
Border Color	Separated
Border Styles	0%
Shadow	Gap Width
Glow and Soft Edges	No Gap
3-D Format	150%

Plot Series On

○ Primary Axis

◉ Secondary Axis

3. Insert labels on the Max series, by right-clicking the series and selecting Add Data Labels:

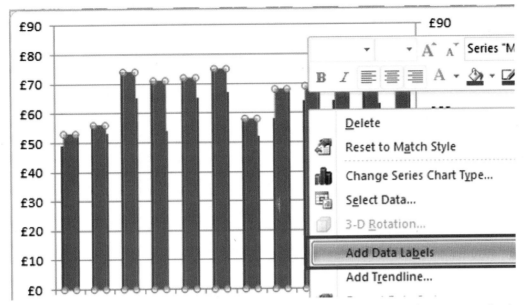

4. Change the horizontal category axis for the Max series, right-click the series and select Data. Then select Max under Legend Entries and Edit under Horizontal Axis Labels:

5. Select the labels in cells E27:E38 and click OK. (Don't worry if the chart doesn't look any different yet.)

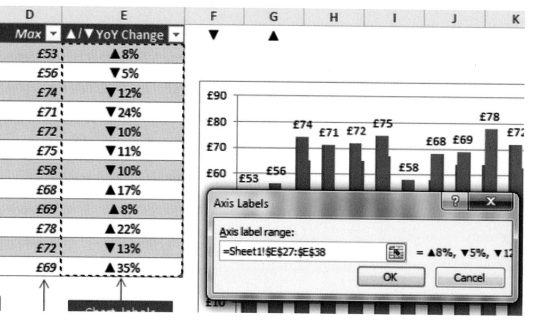

6. Replace the default labels with your custom labels by right-clicking the labels and selecting Format Data Labels:

7. From the Label Contains list choose Category Name.

8. To hide the Max series columns, double-click the Max columns in the chart to open the Format Data Point dialog box. Under Fill select No fill:

9. To tidy up the chart, hide the secondary axis by double-clicking it to open the Format Axis dialog box. Then select Axis Options and make sure Major Tick Mark Type, Minor Tick Marks Type, and Axis Labels are all set all to None:

10. Also in the Format Axis dialog box, select Line Color and then select No Line. Then move the legend to the bottom by double-clicking the legend, choosing Legend Position, Bottom.

11. Get rid of the gridlines by selecting them and pressing the Delete key.

12. To format the legend point for Max to pick up the value in cell E26, right-click the columns and select Data, and then select Max under Legend Entries and click Edit.

In the Edit Series dialog box, with the Series Name textbox selected, click on cell E26 and then click OK.

Thanks to Excel MVP Mynda Treacy for this trip. Twice each year, Mynda offers an amazing online Excel Dashboarding Class. Check it out at http://mrx.cl/dashcourse.

#20 Build Dashboards with Sparklines and Slicers

New tools debuted in Excel 2010 that let you create interactive dashboards that do not look like Excel. This figure shows an Excel workbook with two slicers, Region and Line, used to filter the data. Also in this figure, pivot charts plus a collection of sparkline charts illustrate sales trends.

You can use a setup like this and give your manager's manager a touch screen. All you have to do is teach people how to use the slicers, and they will be able to use this interactive tool for running reports. Touch the East region and the Books line. All of the charts update to reflect sales of books in the East region.

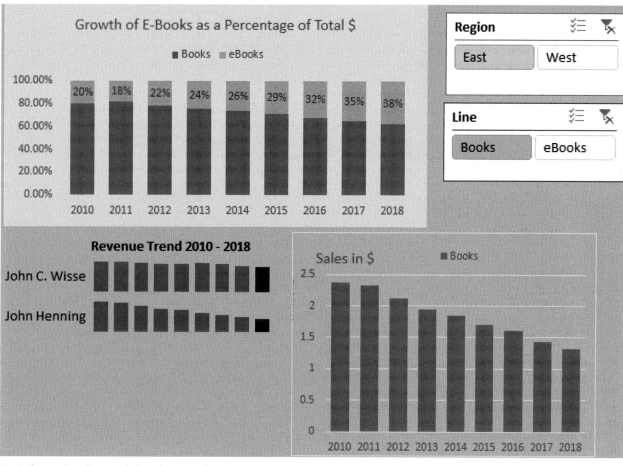

Switch to eBooks, and the data updates.

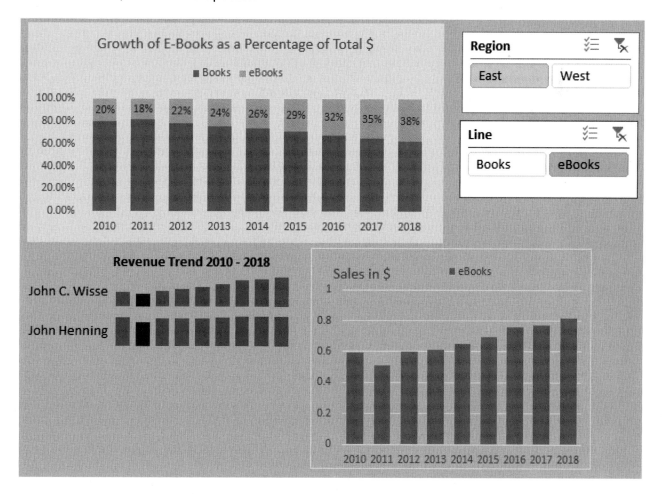

Pivot Tables Galore

Behind all the charts and reports just shown is a series of pivot tables. These pivot tables are scattered below and to the right of the first screen of data. Each pivot table should be based on the same data set and should share a pivot table cache.

Sum of Value	Year								
Name	2010	2011	2012	2013	2014	2015	2016	2017	2018
John C. Wisse	956500	928600	928600	919400	957700	1008100	1050100	1009700	1009700
John Henning	2018800	1904500	1796700	1633400	1540900	1400800	1321500	1201400	1133400
Lynda Maynard	510400	567100	630100	900100	677900	864300	960300	1067000	1185500
Roger Fisher	1639986	1570536	1358259	1512143	1299871	1313699	1098237	1127465	909300
Todd A Lesko	981200	1095500	1203300	1366600	1259100	1199200	1078500	998600	1866600

Sum of Value	Line			Sum of Value	Line	
Year	Books	eBooks		Year	Books	eBooks
2010	84.83%	15.17%		2010	5180706.28	926179.72
2011	86.19%	13.81%		2011	5228740.352	837495.648
2012	82.55%	17.45%		2012	4884163.302	1032795.698
2013	81.16%	18.84%		2013	5138671.568	1192971.432

Slicers Can Filter Multiple Pivot Tables

Slicers provide a visual way to filter. Choose the first pivot table and select Analyze, Slicers. Add slicers for region and line. Use the Slicer Tools tab in the ribbon to change the color and the number of columns in each slicer. Resize the slicers to fit and then arrange them on your dashboard.

Initially, the slicers are tied to only the first pivot table. Select a cell in the second pivot table and choose Filter Connections (aka Slicer Connections in Excel 2010). Indicate which slicers should be tied to this pivot table. In many cases, you will tie each pivot table to all slicers. But not always. For example, in the chart showing how Books and eBooks add up to 100%, you need to keep all lines. The Filter Connections dialog box choices for that pivot table connect to the Region slicer but not the Line slicer.

Sparklines Are Word-Sized Charts

Professor Edward Tufte introduced sparklines in his 2007 book *Beautiful Evidence*. Excel 2010 implemented sparklines as either line, column, or win/loss charts, where each series fills a single cell.

Personally, I like my sparklines to be larger. In this example, I changed the row height to 30 and <gasp> merged B14:D14 into a single cell to make the charts wider. The labels in A14:A18 are formulas that point to the first column of the pivot table.

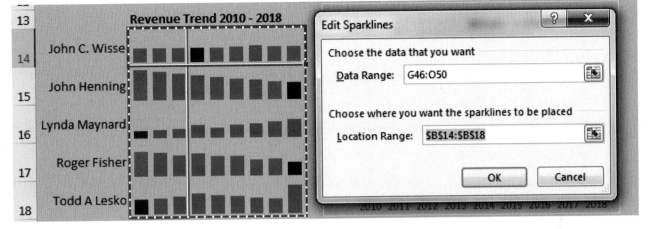

To change the color of the low and high points, choose these boxes in the Sparkline Tools tab:

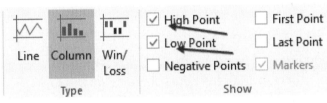

Then change the color for the high and low points:

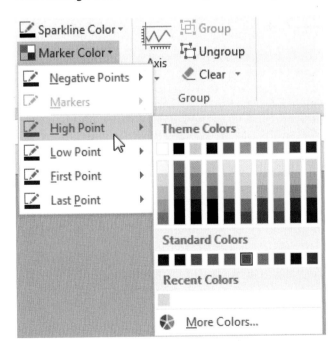

By default, sparklines are scaled independently of each other. I almost always go to the Axis settings and choose Same for All Sparklines for Minimum and Maximum. Below, I set Minimum to 0 for all sparklines.

Making Excel Not Look Like Excel

With several easy settings you can make a dashboard look less like Excel.

- Select all cells and apply a light fill color to get rid of the gridlines.

- On the View tab, uncheck Formula Bar, Headings, and Gridlines.

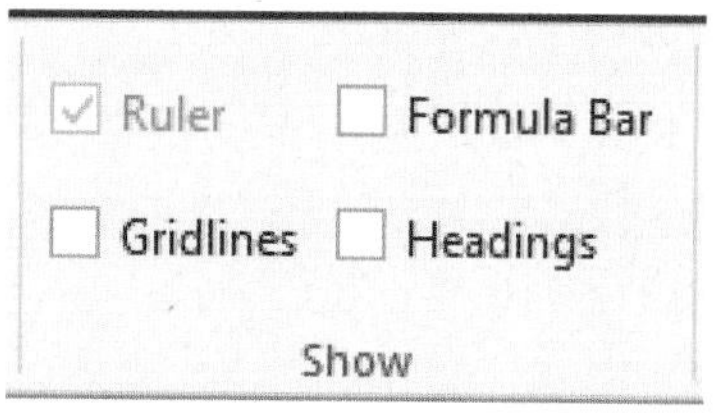

✓ Ruler	☐ Formula Bar
☐ Gridlines	☐ Headings

Show

- At the right edge of the ribbon, use the ^ to collapse the Ribbon.

- Use the arrow keys to move the active cell so it is hidden behind a chart or slicer.

- Hide all sheets except for the dashboard sheet.

- In Excel Options, Advanced, you can hide the scrollbars and sheet tabs.

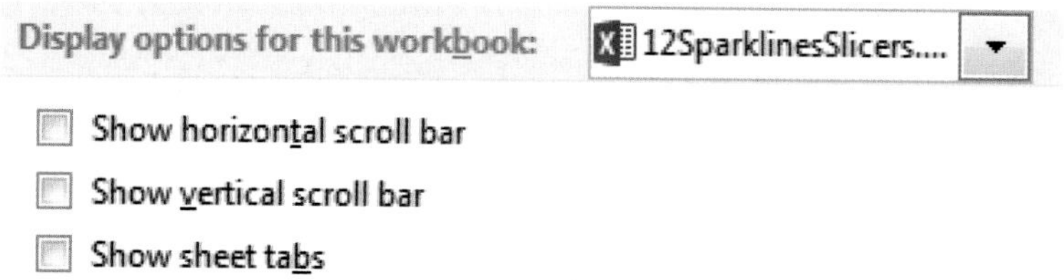

Display options for this workbook: [X] 12SparklinesSlicers.... ▼

- ☐ Show horizontal scroll bar
- ☐ Show vertical scroll bar
- ☐ Show sheet tabs

Bonus Tip: Make Your Workbook into an Web App

Create a named range such as DisplayMe that surrounds your dashboard. To do so, select File, Browser View Options. Choose Items in the Workbook on the Show tab and select the named range DisplayMe.

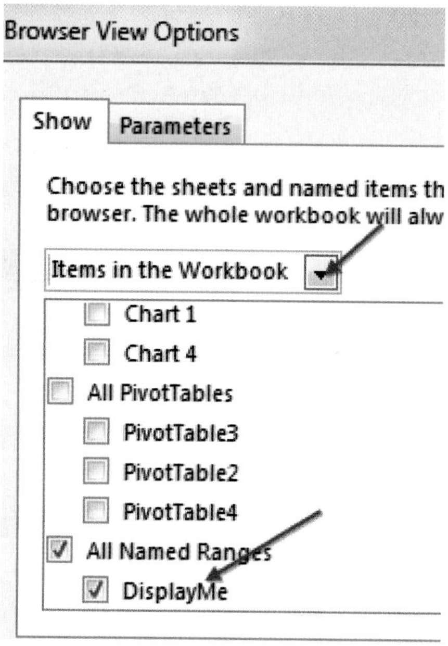

Browser View Options

| Show | Parameters |

Choose the sheets and named items th browser. The whole workbook will alw

Items in the Workbook ▼

- ☐ Chart 1
- ☐ Chart 4
- ☐ All PivotTables
- ☐ PivotTable3
- ☐ PivotTable2
- ☐ PivotTable4
- ✓ All Named Ranges
- ✓ DisplayMe

Save your workbook to a OneDrive location. Use File, Share and ask for a Sharing Link.

Share

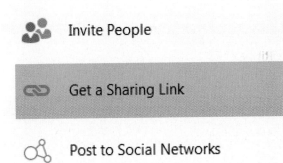

12SparklinesSlicers

Mary Ellen Jelen's OneDrive » Public

Share

👥 Invite People

🔗 Get a Sharing Link

⚤ Post to Social Networks

Get a Sharing Link

Sharing Links are useful for sharing with large group

View Link

https://onedrive.live.com/redir?page=view&resid=

Edit Link

Anyone with an edit link can edit this document

Shared with

Anyone who has the link can open the file in a browser and interact with the slicers. Try it: http://mrx.cl/
xlonedrive77.

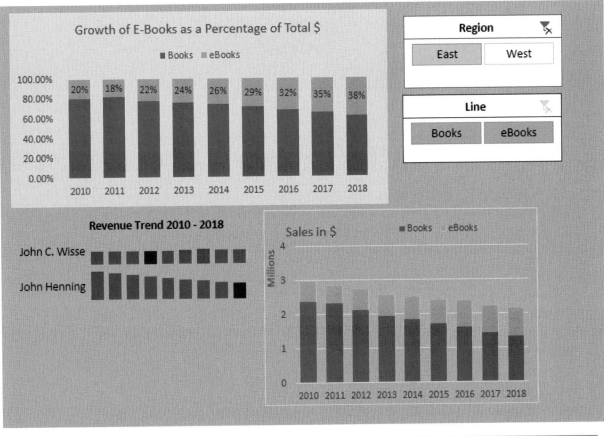

Caution: Anyone who has the link can download the workbook and unhide the data sheets.

Thanks to Ghaleb Bakri for suggesting a similar technique using dropdown boxes. Ryan Wilson suggested making Excel not look
like Excel. Jon Wittwer of Vertex42 suggested sparklines and slicers.

#21 GETPIVOTDATA Might Not Be Entirely Evil

Most people first encounter GETPIVOTDATA when they try to build a formula outside a pivot table that uses numbers in the pivot table. For example, this variance percentage won't copy down to the other months due to Excel inserting GETPIVOTDATA functions.

✕ ✓ fx		=GETPIVOTDATA("Sales",$B$3,"Date",1, "Years",2019)/GETPIVOTDATA("Sales",$B$3, "Date",1,"Years",2018)-1				

B	C	D	E	F	G
Sales	**Years** ▾				
Date ▾	**2018**	**2019**	% Change		
Jan	80772	77864	-3.6%		
Feb	81151	84640	-3.6%		
Mar	80773	77381	-3.6%		
Apr	81695	84963	-3.6%		
May	80774	77705	-3.6%		
Jun	81827	85673	-3.6%		

Excel inserts GETPIVOTDATA any time you use the mouse or arrow keys to point to a cell inside the pivot table while building a formula outside the pivot table.

By the way, if you don't want the GETPIVOTDATA function to appear, simply type a formula such as =D5/C5-1 without using the mouse or arrow keys to point to cells. That formula copies without any problems.

✕ ✓ fx	=D5/C5-1				

B	C	D	E	F
Sales	**Years** ▾			
Date ▾	**2018**	**2019**	% Change	
Jan	80772	77864	-3.6%	
Feb	81151	84640	4.3%	
Mar	80773	77381	-4.2%	

Here is a data set that contains one plan number per month per store. There are also actual sales per month per store for the months that are complete. Your goal is to build a report that shows actuals for the completed months and plan for the future months.

	A	B	C	D
1	**Store**	**Month**	**Type**	**Sales**
1727	Fair Oaks Mall	Dec	Plan	123700
1728	Bellevue Square	Dec	Plan	140500
1729	U Village	Dec	Plan	126600
1730	Park Place	Jan	Actual	13475
1731	Kierland Commons	Jan	Actual	11708
1732	Scottsdale Fashion Square	Jan	Actual	12415
1733	Chandler Fashion Center	Jan	Actual	12848

Build a pivot table with Store in ROWS. Put Month and Type in the COLUMNS. You get the report shown below, with January Actual, January Plan, and the completely nonsensical January Actual+Plan.

▲	A	B	C	D	E
1					
2					
3	Sum of Sales	Month ▾	Type ▾		
4		⊟Jan		Jan Total	⊟Feb
5	Store ▾	Actual	Plan		Actual
6	Ala Moana	11739	11100	22839	16105
7	Altamonte Mall	11421	11400	22821	14854
8	Annapolis Mall	11689	10800	22489	14675
9	Aventura Mall	13646	12900	26546	17473
10	Baybrook	12366	12100	24466	16625

If you select a month cell and go to Field Settings, you can change subtotals to None.

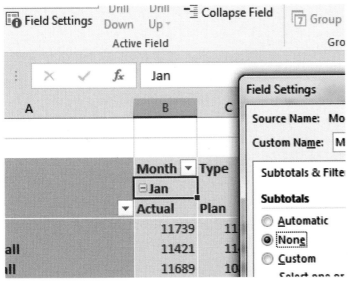

This removes the useless Actual+Plan. But you still have to get rid of the plan columns for January through April. There is no good way to do this inside of the pivot table.

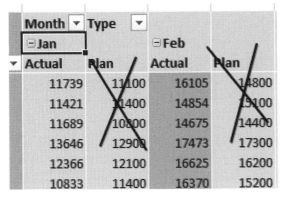

So, your monthly workflow becomes:

1. Add the actuals for the new month to the data set.

2. Build a new pivot table from scratch.

3. Copy the pivot table and paste as values so it is not a pivot table anymore.

4. Delete the columns that you don't need.

There is a better way to go. The following very small figure shows a new Excel worksheet added to the workbook. This is all just straight Excel, no pivot tables. The only bit of magic is an IF function in row 4 that toggles from Actual to Plan based on the date in cell P1.

| E4 | | × ✓ *fx* | =IF((1+MONTH($P1))>COLUMN(A1),"Actual","Plan") |

	A	B	C	D	E	F	G	H	I	J	K	L	M	N	O	P	Q	R
1	**XYZ Company Super Report**														Actuals Through:	4/30		
2																		
3					Jan	Feb	Mar	Apr	May	Jun	Jul	Aug	Sep	Oct	Nov	Dec		
4					Actual	Actual	Actual	Actual	Plan	Plan	Plan	Plan	Plan	Plan	Plan	Plan	Total	
5			Houston Area															
6				Baybrook													$0K	
7				Highland Village													0K	
8				Willowbrook													0K	
9				The Woodlands Mall													0K	
10			Houston Total		$0K	$0K	$0K	$0K	$0K	$0K	$0K	$0K	$0K	$0K	$0K	$0K	$0K	
11																		
12			Dallas/Forth Worth Area															
13				Firewheel													$0K	
14				Galleria													0K	
15				Hulen Mall													0K	
16				Northeast Mall													0K	
17				Northpark Center													0K	
18				The Parks													0K	
19				Southlake Town Square													0K	
20				Stonebriar Mall													0K	
21				Willowbend													0K	
22			Dallas Total		$0K	$0K	$0K	$0K	$0K	$0K	$0K	$0K	$0K	$0K	$0K	$0K	$0K	
23																		
24			Other															
25				Huebner Oaks													$0K	
26				La Cantera													0K	
27				Northstar Mall													0K	
28				Cielo Vista Mall													0K	
29				The Domain													0K	
30				Lakeline													0K	
31			Other Total		$0K	$0K	$0K	$0K	$0K	$0K	$0K	$0K	$0K	$0K	$0K	$0K	$0K	
32																		
33			Grand Total		$0K	$0K	$0K	$0K	$0K	$0K	$0K	$0K	$0K	$0K	$0K	$0K	$0K	
34																		

The very first cell that needs to be filled in is January, Actuals for Baybrook. Click in that cell and type an

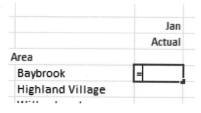

equal sign. Using the mouse, navigate back to the pivot table. Find the cell for January Actuals for Baybrook. Click on that cell and press Enter. As usual, Excel builds one of those annoying GETPIVOTDATA functions that cannot be copied.

But today, let's study the syntax of GETPIVOTDATA.

The first argument below is the numeric field "Sales". The second argument is the cell where the pivot table resides. The remaining pairs of arguments are field name and value. Do you see what the auto-generated formula did? It hard-coded "Baybrook" as the name of the store. That is why you cannot copy these auto-generated GETPIVOTDATA formulas. They actually hard-code names into formulas. Even though you can't copy these formulas, you can edit them. In this case, it would be better if you edited the formula to point to cell $D6.

	D	E	F	G	H	I	J	K	L	M	N
1	**uper Report**										Ac
2											
3		Jan	Feb	Mar	Apr	May	Jun	Jul	Aug	Sep	
4		Actual	Actual	Actual	Actual	Plan	Plan	Plan	Plan	Plan	
5	Area										
6	Baybrook	=GETPIVOTDATA("Sales",Sheet3!$A$3,"Store","Baybrook","Month","Jan","Type","Actual")									
7	Highland Village										
8	Willowbrook										

Here is the formula after you edit it. Gone are "Baybrook", "Jan", and "Actual". Instead, you are pointing to $D6, E$3, E$4.

ny Super Report

		Jan	Feb	Mar	Apr	May	Jun	Jul	Aug
		Actual	Actual	Actual	Actual	Plan	Plan	Plan	Plan
Area									
Baybrook		=GETPIVOTDATA("Sales",Sheet3!$A$3,"Store",$D6,"Month",E$3,"Type",E$4)							
Highland Village									
W	GETPIVOTDATA(data_field, pivot_table, [field1, item1], [field2, item2], [field3, **item3**], [field4, item4],
The Woodlands Mall									

Copy this formula and then choose Paste Special, Formulas in all of the other numeric cells.

Jan
Actual

Paste Special

Paste
○ All
◉ Formulas

$12K

Now here's your annual workflow:

1. Build an ugly pivot table that no one will ever see.

2. Set up the report worksheet.

Each month, you have to:

1. Paste new actuals below the data.

2. Refresh the ugly pivot table.

3. Change cell P1 on the report sheet to reflect the new month. All the numbers update.

		Jan	Feb	Mar	Apr	May	Jun	Jul	Aug	Sep	Oct	Nov	Dec	
ompany Super Report											Actuals Through:		5/31	
		Actual	Actual	Actual	Actual	Actual	Plan	Plan	Plan	Plan	Plan	Plan	Plan	Total
Houston Area														
	Baybrook	$12K	$17K	$22K	$25K	$24K	$32K	$28K	$24K	$20K	$32K	$49K	$121K	$406K
	Highland Village	13K	17K	20K	24K	23K	33K	29K	24K	20K	33K	49K	122K	406K
	Willowbrook	15K	19K	24K	30K	30K	37K	32K	28K	23K	37K	55K	138K	467K
	The Woodlands Mall	14K	19K	24K	28K	27K	36K	32K	27K	23K	36K	54K	135K	453K
Houston Total		$54K	$71K	$90K	$106K	$103K	$138K	$120K	$103K	$86K	$138K	$207K	$516K	$1,732K
Dallas/Forth Worth Area														
	Firewheel	$11K	$15K	$18K	$23K	$22K	$29K	$25K	$22K	$18K	$29K	$43K	$108K	$364K
	Galleria	11K	15K	19K	25K	24K	30K	27K	23K	19K	30K	46K	114K	383K
	Hulen Mall	13K	17K	23K	26K	27K	34K	30K	26K	21K	34K	51K	128K	430K
	Northeast Mall	11K	15K	19K	23K	24K	31K	27K	23K	20K	31K	47K	117K	390K
	Northpark Center	12K	18K	22K	27K	28K	35K	30K	26K	22K	35K	52K	130K	437K
	The Parks	13K	17K	20K	26K	26K	33K	28K	24K	20K	33K	49K	122K	410K
	Southlake Town Squar	14K	17K	22K	25K	26K	34K	29K	25K	21K	34K	50K	126K	422K
	Stonebriar Mall	11K	14K	19K	22K	23K	28K	25K	21K	18K	28K	42K	106K	357K
	Willowbend	13K	17K	23K	28K	28K	34K	30K	26K	22K	34K	52K	129K	436K
Dallas Total		$109K	$144K	$186K	$225K	$227K	$288K	$252K	$216K	$180K	$288K	$432K	$1,081K	$3,629K
Other														
	Huebner Oaks	$11K	$15K	$18K	$23K	$21K	$29K	$25K	$22K	$18K	$29K	$43K	$107K	$361K
	La Cantera	13K	18K	22K	26K	26K	34K	30K	25K	21K	34K	51K	127K	426K
	Northstar Mall	13K	16K	21K	24K	25K	32K	28K	24K	20K	32K	48K	119K	400K
	Cielo Vista Mall	12K	18K	22K	26K	24K	34K	29K	25K	21K	34K	50K	126K	421K
	The Domain	15K	19K	25K	29K	29K	37K	32K	28K	23K	37K	55K	139K	468K
	Lakeline	13K	17K	23K	27K	28K	34K	30K	26K	21K	34K	51K	127K	430K
Other Total		$76K	$102K	$132K	$155K	$153K	$199K	$174K	$149K	$124K	$199K	$298K	$745K	$2,506K
Grand Total		$239K	$318K	$408K	$486K	$484K	$625K	$546K	$468K	$390K	$625K	$937K	$2,342K	$7,867K

You have to admit that using a plain report that pulls numbers from a pivot table gives you the best of both worlds. You are free to format the report in ways that you cannot format a pivot table. Blank rows are fine. You can have currency symbols on the first and last rows but not in between. You get double-under-lines under the grand totals, too.

Thanks to @iTrainerMX for suggesting this feature.

#22 Eliminate VLOOKUP with the Data Model

Say that you have a data set with product, customer, and sales information.

	A	B	C	D
1	Product	Date	Customer	Quantity
545	Gizmo	12/8/2019	Calleia Company	100
546	Gizmo	12/9/2019	Budget Wand	900
547	Widget	12/10/2019	excelisfun	1000
548	Gadget	12/10/2019	JEVS Human Services	200
549	Gadget	12/11/2019	Calleia Company	200

The IT department forgot to put sector in there. Here is a lookup table that maps customer to sector. Time for a VLOOKUP, right?

Table Name:	Summarize with PivotTable		
Sectors	Remove Duplicates	Insert Slicer	Export
Resize Table	Convert to Range		
Properties	Tools		

H4		× ✓ fx	Access Analytic

	H	I
3	Customer	Sector
4	Access Analytic	Consulting
5	adaept information management	Consulting
6	All Systems Go Consulting	Consulting
7	Analytic Minds	Consulting
8	Areef Ali & Associates	Consulting
9	Association for Computers & Taxation	Associations
10	Berghaus Corporation	Consulting
11	Bits of Confetti	Retail

There is no need to do VLOOKUPs to join these data sets if you have Excel 2013 or Excel 2016. Both of these versions of Excel have incorporated the Power Pivot engine into the core Excel. (You could also do this using the Power Pivot add-in for Excel 2010, but there are a few extra steps.)

In both the original data set and the lookup table, use Home, Format as Table. On the Table Tools tab, rename the table from Table1 to something meaningful. I've used Data and Sectors.

Select one cell in the data table. Choose Insert, Pivot Table. Starting in Excel 2013, there is an extra box Add This Data to the Data Model that you should select before clicking OK.

Choose where you want the PivotTable report to be placed

◉ New Worksheet

◯ Existing Worksheet

Location: [   ]

Choose whether you want to analyze multiple tables

☑ Add this data to the Data Model

[OK]   [Cancel]

The Pivot Table Fields list appears with the fields from the Data table. Choose Revenue. Because you are using the Data Model, a new line appears at the top of the list, offering Active or All. Click All.

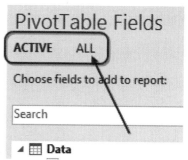

Surprisingly, the PivotTable Fields list offers all the other tables in the workbook. This is groundbreaking. You haven't done a VLOOKUP yet. Expand the Sectors table and choose Sector. Two things happen to warn you that there is a problem.

First, the pivot table appears with the same number in all the cells.

Row Labels	Sum of Revenue
Applications	6707812
Associations	6707812
Consulting	6707812
Retail	6707812
Services	6707812
Training	6707812
Utilities	6707812
Grand Total	6707812

Perhaps the more subtle warning is a yellow box appears at the top of the PivotTable Fields list indicating that you need to create a relationship. Choose Create. (If you are in Excel 2010 or 2016, take your luck with Auto-Detect.)

PivotTable Fields

ACTIVE   ALL

Choose fields to add to report:

Relationships between tables may be needed.

AUTO-DETECT...   CREATE...

In the Create Relationship dialog, you have four dropdown menus. Choose Data under Table, Customer under Column (Foreign), and Sectors under Related Table. Power Pivot will automatically fill in the matching column under the Related Column (Primary). Click OK.

Create Relationship

Pick the tables and columns you want to use for this relationship

Table:
Data

Column (Foreign):
Customer

Related Table:
Sectors

Related Column (Primary):
Customer

The resulting pivot table is a mashup of the original data and the lookup table. No VLOOKUPs required.

Sector	Sum of Revenue
Applications	482,074
Associations	418,988
Consulting	2,904,312
Retail	570,426
Services	877,055
Training	935,397
Utilities	519,560
Grand Total	6,707,812

Bonus Tip: Count Distinct

Here is an annoyance with pivot tables. Drag the Customer column from the Data table to the VALUES area. The field says Count of Customer, but it is really a count of how many invoices belong to each sector. What if you really want to see how many unique customers belong to each sector?

Sector	Sum of Revenue	Count of Customer
Applications	482,074	44
Associations	418,988	32
Consulting	2,904,312	238
Retail	570,426	49
Services	877,055	79
Training	935,397	75
Utilities	519,560	46
Grand Total	6,707,812	563

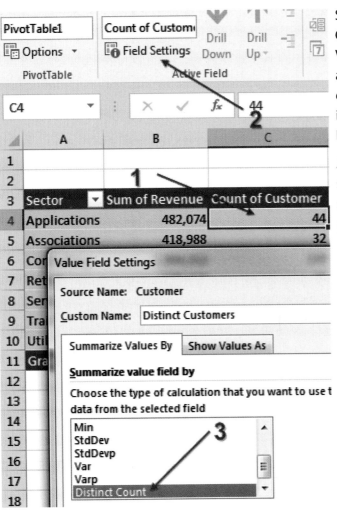

Select a cell in the Count of Customer column. Click Field Settings. At first, the Summarize Values By looks like the same Sum, Average, and Count that you've always had. But scroll down to the bottom. Because the pivot table is based on the Data Model, you now have Distinct Count.

After you select Distinct Count, the pivot table shows a distinct count of customers for each sector. This was very hard to do in regular pivot tables.

Sector	Revenue	Distinct Customers
Applications	482,074	6
Associations	418,988	5
Consulting	2,904,312	30
Retail	570,426	5
Services	877,055	10
Training	935,397	11
Utilities	519,560	6
Grand Total	6,707,812	73

Count Distinct in Excel 2010

To join two tables in Excel 2010, you have to download the free Power Pivot add-in from Microsoft. Once you have that installed, here are the extra steps to get your data into Power Pivot:

1. Select a cell in the Data table. On the PowerPivot tab, choose Create Linked Table. If Excel leaves you in the PowerPivot grid, use Alt+Tab to get back to Excel.

2. Select a cell in the Sectors table. Choose Create Linked Table.

3. From either the PowerPivot tab in the Excel ribbon or the Home tab in the PowerPivot ribbon, choose to create a pivot table.

When it comes time to create relationships, you have only one button called Create. Excel 2010 will attempt to AutoDetect relationships first. In this simple example, it will get the relationship correct.

Thanks to Colin Michael and Alejandro Quiceno for suggesting Power Pivot in general.

#23 Budget Versus Actual via Power Pivot

Budgets are done at the top level – revenue by product line by region by month. Actuals accumulate slowly over time – invoice by invoice, line item by line item. Comparing the small Budget file to the voluminous Actuals data has been a pain forever. I love this trick from Rob Collie, aka PowerPivotPro.com.

To set up the example, you have a 54-row budget table: one row per month per region per product.

	A	B	C	D
1	Budget - Top Level			
2				
3	Product	Region	Date	Budget
52	Whatsit	West	1/31/2018	10,300
53	Whatsit	West	2/28/2018	10,600
54	Whatsit	West	3/31/2018	10,900
55	Whatsit	West	4/30/2018	11,200
56	Whatsit	West	5/31/2018	11,500
57	Whatsit	West	6/30/2018	11,800

The invoice file is at the detail level: 422 rows so far this year.

	M	N	O	P	Q
1	Invoice Detail				
2					
3	Invoice	Date	Region	Product	Revenue
417	1414	6/26/2015	Central	Widget	1728
418	1415	6/29/2015	West	Gadget	1719
419	1416	6/29/2015	East	Widget	2199
420	1417	6/29/2015	Central	Widget	2087
421	1418	6/29/2015	East	WhatsIt	2309
422	1419	6/29/2015	Central	Widget	1652
423	1420	6/30/2015	Central	Gadget	1994
424	1421	6/30/2015	Central	WhatsIt	2055
425	1422	6/30/2015	East	Gadget	1931

There is no VLOOKUP in the world that will ever let you match these two data sets. But, thanks to Power Pivot (aka the Data Model in Excel 2013+), this becomes easy.

You need to create tiny little tables that I call "joiners" to link the two larger data sets. In my case, Product, Region, and Date are in common between the two tables. The Product table is a tiny four-cell table. Ditto for Region. Create each of those by copying data from one table and using Remove Duplicates.

"Joiners"

Product	Region	Date	Month
Gadget	Central	1/2/2018	2018-01
WhatsIt	East	1/5/2018	2018-01
Widget	West	1/6/2018	2018-01
		1/7/2018	2018-01
		1/8/2018	2018-01
		1/9/2018	2018-01

George Berlin

The calendar table on the right was actually tougher to create. The budget data has one row per month, always falling on the end of the month. The invoice data shows daily dates, usually weekdays. So, I had to copy the Date field from both data sets into a single column and then remove duplicates to make sure that all dates are represented. I then used =TEXT(J4,"YYYY-MM") to create a Month column from the daily dates.

If you don't have the full Power Pivot add-in, you need to create a pivot table from the Budget table and check the box for Add This Data to the Data Model.

Choose whether you want to analyze multiple tables
☑ Add this data to the Data Model

As discussed in the previous tip, as you add fields to the pivot table, you will have to define six relationships. While you could do this with six visits to the Create Relationship dialog, I fired up my Power Pivot add-in and used the diagram view to define the six relationships.

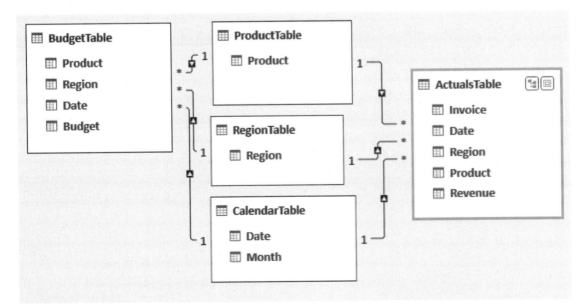

Here is the key to making all of this work: You are free to use the numeric fields from Budget and from Actual. But if you want to show Region, Product, or Month in the pivot table, they must come from the joiner tables!

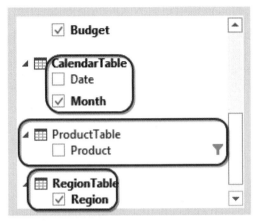

Here is a pivot table with data coming from five tables. Column A is coming from the Region joiner. Row 2 is coming from the Calendar joiner. The Product slicer is from the Product joiner. The Budget numbers come from the Budget table, and the Actual numbers come from the Invoice table.

	A	B	C	D	E	F	G	H	I
1			Month ▼						
2	Regio ▼	Values	2018-01	2018-02	2018-03	2018-04	2018-05	2018-06	Grand Total
3	Central	Budget	15450	15900	16350	16800	17250	17700	99450
4	Central	Actuals	24203	24703	19815	28208	27555	26961	151445
5	East	Budget	10300	10600	10900	11200	11500	11800	66300
6	East	Actuals	17949	23174	17538	25180	29175	17967	130983
7	West	Budget	20600	21200	21800	22400	23000	23600	132600
8	West	Actuals	24378	11971	14170	11162	11229	10501	83411
9	Total Budget		46350	47700	49050	50400	51750	53100	298350
10	Total Actuals		66530	59848	51523	64550	67959	55429	365839
11									
12		Product							
13									
14		Gadget		WhatsIt		Widget			

This works because the joiner tables apply filters to the Budget and Actual table. It is a beautiful technique and shows that Power Pivot is not just for big data.

Bonus Tip: Portable Formulas

If you have the full version of Power Pivot, you can use the DAX formula language to create new calculated fields. From the Power Pivot tab in the ribbon, choose Insert Calculated Field.

Give the field a name, such as Variance. When you go to type the formula, type =[. As soon as you type the square bracket, Excel gives you a list of fields to choose from.

Note that you can also assign a numeric format to these calculated fields. Wouldn't it be great if regular pivot tables brought the numeric formatting from the underlying data?

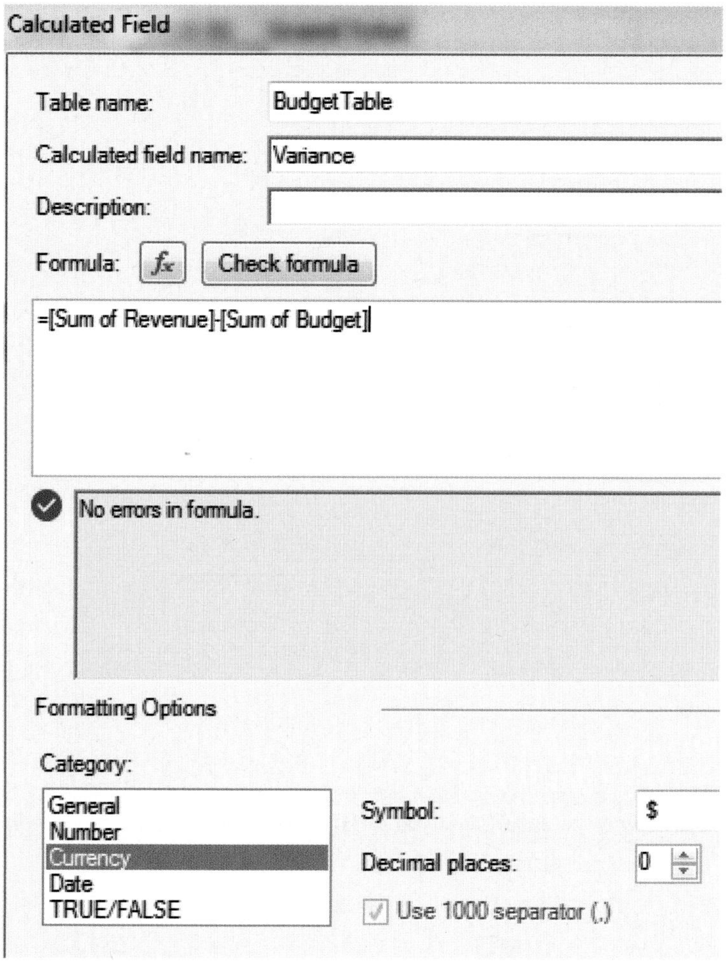

Calculated Field

Table name:	Budget Table
Calculated field name:	Variance
Description:	

Formula: *fx* [Check formula]

=[Sum of Revenue]-[Sum of Budget]

✓ No errors in formula.

Formatting Options

Category:

General	
Number	
Currency	Symbol: $
Date	Decimal places: 0
TRUE/FALSE	✓ Use 1000 separator (,)

In the next calculation, the VariancePercent is reusing the Variance field that you just defined.

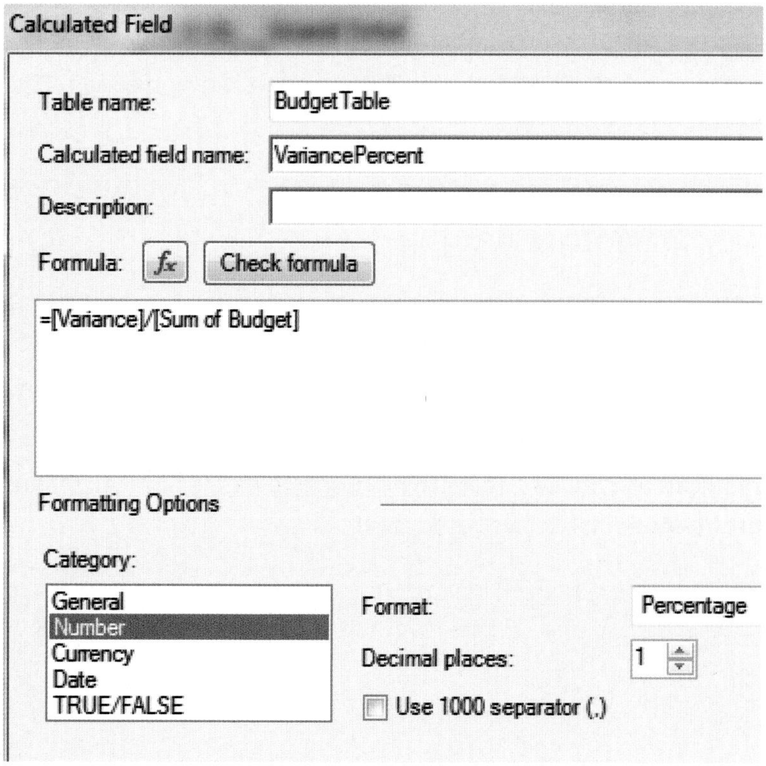

Calculated Field

Table name:	Budget Table
Calculated field name:	VariancePercent
Description:	

Formula: *fx* [Check formula]

=[Variance]/[Sum of Budget]

Formatting Options

Category:

General	
Number	Format: Percentage
Currency	Decimal places: 1
Date	
TRUE/FALSE	☐ Use 1000 separator (,)

This is great – all of those fields in the pivot table:

Region ▼	Values	Month ▼ 2018-01	2018-02
Central	Sum of Budget	7730	7950
Central	Sum of Revenue	10539	13909
Central	Variance	$2,809	$5,959
Central	VariancePercent	36.3 %	75.0 %

But you don't have to leave any of those fields in the pivot table. If your manager only cares about the variance percentage, you can remove all of the other numeric fields.

VariancePercent Month ▼	Region ▼ Central	East	West	Grand Total
2018-01	▲ 36.3 %	▲ 27.8 %	▼ -76.8 %	▼ -15.8 %
2018-02	▲ 75.0 %	▲ 9.8 %	▼ -83.0 %	▼ -9.7 %
2018-03	▼ -22.6 %	▲ 120.9 %	▼ -56.4 %	▼ -5.7 %
2018-04	▲ 187.3 %	▲ 2.7 %	▼ -66.9 %	▲ 33.3 %
2018-05	▲ 158.9 %	▲ 191.4 %	▼ -33.4 %	▲ 80.7 %
2018-06	▲ 7.1 %	▲ 108.9 %	▼ -48.5 %	▲ 5.0 %
Grand Total	▲ 74.4 %	▲ 78.8 %	▼ -60.2 %	▲ 15.6 %

Product ⧮ ⧩

Gadget	WhatsIt	Widget

Note that the DAX in this bonus tip is barely scratching the surface of what is possible. If you want to explore Power Pivot, you need to get a copy of *DAX Formulas for Power Pivot* by Rob Collie and Avi Singh

Thanks to Rob Collie for teaching me this feature. Find Rob at www.PowerPivotPro.com

#24 F4 for Absolute and Repeat Last Command

The mighty F4 key should be in your Excel arsenal for two completely different reasons:

- Use F4 to add dollar signs in formula references to make them absolute, mixed, or relative.

- When you are not editing a formula, use F4 to repeat the last command.

Illustration: Bob D'Amico

Making a Reference Absolute

In the following figure, the tax in C2 is B2 times F1.

C2		f_x	=B2*F1			
	A	B	C	D	E	F
1	Customer	Merchandise $	Tax $		Rate	6.25%
2	Robert Jelen	24.95	1.56			
3	Sam Radakovitz	114.95				
4	Judy A Glaser	69.95				
5	Diana McGunigale	34.95				
6	Edwin Deo	9.95				
7	Mario Garcia	169.95				
8	Anne Troy	129.95				
9	Robert S. McClellan	154.95				
10	David Gainer	199.95				
11	David Haggarty	109.95				

But when you copy this formula down, none of the sales tax calculations are working. As you copy the formula down the column, the B2 reference automatically changes to B3, B4, and so on. That is what you want. But unfortunately, the reference to the sales tax in F1 is changing as well. That is not what you want.

SUM	▼ ⋮	✕ ✓ f_x	=B5*F4				

◢	A	B	C	D	E	F	G
1	Customer	Merchandise $	Tax $		Rate	6.25%	
2	Robert Jelen	24.95	1.56				
3	Sam Radakovitz	114.95	0.00				
4	Judy A Glaser	69.95	0.00				
5	Diana McGunigale	34.95	=B5*F4				
6	Edwin Deo	9.95	0.00				
7	Mario Garcia	169.95	0.00				
8	Anne Troy	129.95	0.00				

The solution? Edit the original formula and press F4. Two dollar signs are added to the final element of the formula. The $F$1 says that no matter where you copy this formula, that part of the formula always needs to point to F1. This is called an absolute reference. Pressing F4 while the insertion point is touching the F1 reference is a fast way to add both dollar signs.

SUM	▼ ⋮	✕ ✓ f_x	=B2*$F$1			

◢	A	B	C	D	E	F
1	Customer	Merchandise $	Tax $		Rate	6.25%
2	Robert Jelen	24.95	=B2*$F$1	**F4**		
3	Sam Radakovitz	114.95	7.18			
4	Judy A Glaser	69.95	4.37			
5	Diana McGunigale	34.95	2.18			

There are other times when you need only part of the reference to be locked. In the following example, you need to multiply H2 by A3 by C1. The H1 will always point to H1, so you need both dollar signs in $H$1. The A3 will always point back to column A, so you need $A3. The C1 will always point to row 1, so you need C$1.

◢	A	B	C	D	E	F	G	H
1			105%	107%	103%	115%		Base
2		Name	Q1	Q2	Q3	Q4		10000
3	113%	Micheal Reynolds	=$H$2*$A3*C$1					
4	112%	John Cockerill						
5	115%	Adam Weaver						
6	112%	Michael Dietterick						
7	113%	Ryan Wilson						
8	113%	James Williams						
9	112%	Mike Dolan Fliss						
10	112%	Paul Hannelly						
11	115%	Dawn Kosmakos						
12	112%	Jeff Long						

To enter the above formula, you would press F4 once after clicking on H1, three times after clicking on A3, and twice after clicking on C1. What if you screw up and press F4 too many times? Keep pressing F4: It will toggle back to relative then absolute, then row absolute, then column absolute.

The result? A single formula that can be copied to C3:F12.

F12		▼	⋮	×	✓	f_x	=$H$2*$A12*F$1	

◢	A	B	C	D	E	F	G	H
1			105%	109%	103%	115%		Base
2		Name	Q1	Q2	Q3	Q4		12000
3	113%	Micheal Reynolds	14238	14780	13967	15594		
4	112%	John Cockerill	14112	14650	13843	15456		
5	115%	Adam Weaver	14490	15042	14214	15870		
6	110%	Michael Dietterick	13860	14388	13596	15180		
7	113%	Ryan Wilson	14238	14780	13967	15594		
8	113%	James Williams	14238	14780	13967	15594		
9	114%	Mike Dolan Fliss	14364	14911	14090	15732		
10	112%	Paul Hannelly	14112	14650	13843	15456		
11	115%	Dawn Kosmakos	14490	15042	14214	15870		
12	112%	Jeff Long	14112	14650	13843	15456		
13								

Repeating the Last Command

Keyboard shortcuts are great. Alt+E, D, C Enter will delete a column. But even if you are really fast at doing Alt+E, D, C Enter, it can be a pain to do a lot of these in a row.

◢	A	B	C	D	E	F	G	H	I
1	Name		Q1		Q2		Q3		Q4
2	Jeffrey P. Coulson		161		153		136		163
3									
4	Robert Phillips		150		143		198		161
5									
6	Peter Harvest		132		185		167		150
7			Alt+EDC						
8	Trace Cordell		149		140		167		176
9									
10	Eddie Stephen		195		158		162		108
11									
12	Patrick Wirz		119		161		141		188
13									
14	M.R. Rosenkrantz		105		169		200		166
15									
16	Dawn Gilbert		186		158		108		141
17									
18	Rick Grantham		182		198		197		183
19									
20	DeLisa Lee		128		135		146		122

After deleting column B, press the Right arrow key to move to the next column that needs to be deleted. Instead of doing Alt+E, D, C Enter again, simply press F4. This beautiful command repeats the last command that you invoked.

	A	B	C	D	E
1	Name	Q1		Q2	
2	Jeffrey P. Coulson	161		153	
3					
4	Robert Phillips	150		143	
5					
6	Peter Harvest	132		185	
7					

Rt Arrow
F4

To delete the remaining columns, keep pressing Right arrow then F4.

	A	B	C	D	E	F	G
1	Name	Q1	Q2		Q3		Q4
2	Jeffrey P. Coulson	161	153		136		163
3							
4	Robert Phillips	150	143		198		161
5							
6	Peter Harvest	132	185		167		150
7							

Rt Arrow
F4

Next you need to delete a row. Alt+E, D, R Enter will delete the row.

	A	B	C	D	E
1	Name	Q1	Q2	Q3	Q4
2	Jeffrey P. Coulson	161	153	136	163
3					
4	Robert Phillips	150	143	198	161
5					
6	Peter Harvest	132	185	167	150

Alt+EDR Enter

To keep deleting rows, press the Down arrow followed by F4 until all the blank rows are gone.

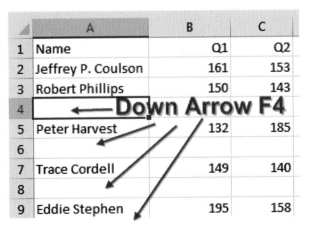

	A	B	C
1	Name	Q1	Q2
2	Jeffrey P. Coulson	161	153
3	Robert Phillips	150	143
4			
5	Peter Harvest	132	185
6			
7	Trace Cordell	149	140
8			
9	Eddie Stephen	195	158

Down Arrow F4

The F4 command works for a surprising number of commands. Perhaps you just built a custom format to display numbers in thousands: #,##0,K. If you see a few more cells that need the same format, select the cells and press F4.

There are a few annoying commands that do not work with F4. For example, going into Field Settings in a Pivot Table and changing the number format and calculation is one that would be nice to repeat. But it does not work.

Thanks to Myles Arnott, Glen Feechan, Shelley Fishel, Colin Legg, and Nathan Zelany for suggesting this feature.

#25 The Fastest Way to Convert Formulas to Values

I always say there are five ways to do anything in Excel. Converting live formulas to values is a task that has far more than five ways. But I will bet that I can teach you two ways that are faster than what you are using now.

The goal is to convert the formulas in column D to values.

You are probably using one of the ways shown here:

	A	B	C	D
1	Customer	Revenue	Profit	GP%
2	Analytic Minds	369,567	164,599	44.5%
3	Areef Ali & Associates	1,248,598	515,469	41.3%
4	Berghaus Corporation	606,128	273,935	45.2%
5	data2impact	490,827	218,470	44.5%
6	Excel Learning Zone	329,597	145,571	44.2%
7	Excel-Translator.de	505,279	221,591	43.9%
8	How To Excel At Excel.Com	460,086	206,861	45.0%
9	MyOnlineTrainingHub.com	922,134	407,530	44.2%
10	NetCom Computer	430,540	190,598	44.3%
11	Steve Comer	448,241	196,403	43.8%
12	XLYOURFINANCES, LLC	486,697	235,678	48.4%
13	Yesenita	410,118	181,689	44.3%
14	Grand Total	6,707,812	2,978,394	44.4%

D2 = =C2/B2

Some Ways to Paste Values

Ctrl+C, Paste Dropdown, Values

Ctrl+C, Alt+E, S, V Enter

Ctrl+C, Ctrl+Alt+V, V, Enter

Ctrl+C, Ctrl+V, Ctrl, V

Ctrl+C, Alt, H, V, V

Rt-Click, Copy, Rt-Click, Paste Options Values

Paste Options:

You Prefer using the Mouse

If you prefer to use the mouse, nothing is faster than this trick that I learned from Dave in Columbus, Indiana. You don't even have to copy the cells using this technique:

1. Select the data.

2. Go to the right edge of the selection box.

3. Hold down the right mouse button while you drag the box to the right.

C	D	E	F	G
Profit	GP%			
164,599	44.5%			
515,469	41.3%			
273,935	45.2%			
218,470	44.5%			
145,571	44.2%			
221,591	43.9%			
206,861	45.0%			F2:F14

4. Keep holding down the right mouse button while you drag the box back to the original location.

5. When you release the right mouse button, in the menu that pops up select Copy Here As Values Only.

How does anyone ever randomly discover right-click, drag right, drag left, let go? It is not something that you would ever accidentally do.

GP%
44.5%
41.3%
45.2%
44.5%
44.2%
43.9%
45.0%
44.2%
44.3%
43.8%

Move Here
Copy Here
Copy Here as Values Only
Copy Here as Formats Only
Link Here
Create Hyperlink Here
Shift Down and Copy

It turns out the menu is called the Alternate Drag and Drop Menu. You get this menu any time you right-drag a selection somewhere.

In this case, you want the values to cover the original formulas, so you have to drag right and then back to the left.

You Prefer Keyboard Shortcuts

I love keyboard shortcuts. I can Ctrl+C, Alt+E, S, V, Enter faster than you can blink. But starting in Excel 2010, there is a faster way. Look at the bottom row of your keyboard. To the left of the spacebar, you usually have Ctrl, Windows, Alt. To the right of the spacebar is Alt, *Something*, and Ctrl.

What is that key between the right Alt and the right Ctrl? It has a picture of a mouse pointer and a pop-up menu. I've heard it called the Program key. I've heard it called the Application key. I've heard it called the Right-Click key. I don't care what you call it, but here is a picture of it:

Here is the fastest keyboard shortcut for copying and pasting values. Press Ctrl+C. Press and release the Program/Application/Right-Click key. Press V.

Again, this only works in Excel 2010 or newer.

And, if you have a Lenovo laptop, it is likely that you don't even have this key. On a keyboard without this key, you can press Shift+F10 instead.

Thanks to Ed Bott, Ken McLean, Melih Met, and Bryony Stewart-Seume for suggesting this feature.

#26 See All Formulas at Once

You inherit a spreadsheet from a former co-worker. You need to figure out how the calculations work. You could visit each cell one at a time and look at the formula in the formula bar. Or, you could quickly toggle between pressing F2 and Esc to see the formula right in the cell.

	A	B	C	D
1	Vendor	Last Year	Growth	Next Year
2	adaept information management	190,716	7%	204,100
3	Orange County Health Department	188,874	8%	204,000
4	MrExcel.com	188,173	5%	197,600
5	Access Analytic	177,972	7%	190,400
6	Excelerator BI	185,529	4%	193,000
7	MyOnlineTrainingHub.com	181,901	6%	192,800
8	Cambia Factor	153,609	6%	162,800
9	data2impact	154,605	8%	117,000
10	Blockhead Data Consultants	121,751	8%	131,500
11	Bits of Confetti	100,308	8%	108,300
12	Total	1,643,438		1,701,500

But there is a faster way. On most U.S. keyboards, just below the Esc key is a key with two accent characters: the tilde from Spanish and the grave accent from French. It is an odd key. I don't know how I would ever use this key to actually type Piñata or Café.

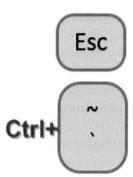

If you hold down Ctrl and this key, you toggle into something called Show Formulas mode. Each column gets wider, and you see all of the formulas.

B	C	D
Last Year	Growth	Next Year
190716	=RANDBETWEEN(4,8)/100	=ROUND(B2*(1+C2),-2)
188874	=RANDBETWEEN(4,8)/100	=ROUND(B3*(1+C3),-2)
188173	=RANDBETWEEN(4,8)/100	=ROUND(B4*(1+C4),-2)
177972	=RANDBETWEEN(4,8)/100	=ROUND(B5*(1+C5),-2)
185529	=RANDBETWEEN(4,8)/100	=ROUND(B6*(1+C6),-2)
181901	=RANDBETWEEN(4,8)/100	=ROUND(B7*(1+C7),-2)
153609	=RANDBETWEEN(4,8)/100	=ROUND(B8*(1+C8),-2)
154605	=RANDBETWEEN(4,8)/100	=ROUND(B9*(1+C9),-2)-50000
121751	=RANDBETWEEN(4,8)/100	=ROUND(B10*(1+C10),-2)
100308	=RANDBETWEEN(4,8)/100	=ROUND(B11*(1+C11),-2)
1643438		=SUM(D2:D11)

This gives you a view of all the formulas at once. It is great for spotting "plug" numbers or when someone added the totals with a calculator and typed the number instead of using =SUM(). This is great you can see that the co-worker left RANDBETWEEN functions in this model.

Bonus Tip: Highlight All Formula Cells

If you are going to be auditing the worksheet, it would help to mark all of the formula cells. Here are the steps:

1. Select all cells using the box just above and to the left of cell A1.

2. Press Ctrl+G for Go To and then Alt+S for Special. In the Go To Special dialog, choose Formulas and click OK. Alternatively, you can choose Home, Find & Select, Formulas.

3. All of the formula cells will be selected. Mark them in a different font color, or, heck, use Home, Cell Styles, Calculation.

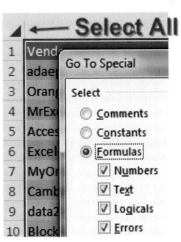

To mark all of the input cells, follow the same steps, but choose Constants in the Go To Special dialog. I prefer to then uncheck Text, Logical, and Errors, leaving only the numeric constants.

Why Is the F1 Key Missing from Your Keyboard?

I served as a judge for the ModelOff Financial Modeling Championships in NYC twice. On my first visit, I was watching contestant Martijn Reekers work in Excel. He was constantly pressing F2 and Esc with his left hand. His right hand was on the arrow keys, swiftly moving from cell to cell.

F2 puts the cell in Edit mode so you can see the formula in the cell. Esc exits Edit mode and shows you the number.

Martijn would press F2 and Esc at least three times every second.

But here is the funny part: What dangerous key is between F2 and Esc? F1. If you accidentally press F1, you will have a 10-second delay while Excel loads online Help. If you are analyzing three cells a second, a 10-second delay would be a disaster. You might as well go to lunch. So, Martijn had pried the F1 key from his keyboard so he would never accidentally press it.

Photo Credit: MrsExcel

Martijn was competing for a $10,000 first prize, but I still thought this was a little over-the-top. However, as I talked to the other 15 finalists, most admitted to having removed F1 from their keyboards, along with Caps Lock and Insert.

Thanks to Ron Armstrong, Olga Kryuchkova, and Sven Simon for suggesting this feature.

#27 Discover New Functions Using fx

There are 400+ functions in Excel. I only have room for 40 tips this book, so there is no way I can cover them all. But instead of taking 450 pages to describe every function, I am going to teach you how to find the function that you need.

The Excel 2007 formulas tab introduced a huge *fx* Insert Function icon. But you don't need to use the one on the Formulas tab; the same icon has been to the left of the formula bar ever since I can remember.

If you are trying to figure out how to calculate a loan payment, the Insert Function dialog will help. Click the icon next to the formula bar. In the Search for a Function box, type what you are trying to do. Click Go. The Select a Function box will show functions related to your search term. Click on a function in that box to see the description at the bottom of the dialog.

When you find the correct function and click OK, Excel takes you into the Function Arguments dialog. This is an amazing tool when you are new to a function. As you click into each argument box, help appears at the bottom of the window, with specifics on that argument.

Function Arguments   ?   X

PMT

Rate		= number
Nper		= number
Pv		= number
Fv		= number
Type		= number

=

Calculates the payment for a loan based on constant payments and a constant interest rate.

> **Rate** is the interest rate per period for the loan. For example, use 6%/4 for quarterly payments at 6% APR.

Personally, I could never get the PMT function to work correctly because I always forgot that the Rate had to be the interest rate per period. Instead of pointing to the 5.25% in B3, you have to point to B3/12. Below, the help for Nper explains that it is the total number of payments for the loan, also known as the Term, from B2.

Rate	B3/12	= 0.004375
Nper	B2	= 60
Pv		= number
Fv		= number
Type		= number

=

it for a loan based on constant payments and a constant interest rate.

> **Nper** is the total number of payments for the loan.

PV is the loan amount. Since I never write a check for negative $493, I want the answer from PMT to be positive instead of negative. That is why I always use –B1 for the PV argument. If you use B1 instead, you will get the correct $493.45065 answer, but it will appear as negative in your worksheet. Think of the original $25,995 as money leaving the bank; that is why the PV is negative.

Rate	B3/12	= 0.004375
Nper	B2	= 60
Pv	-B1|	= -25995
Fv		= number
Type		= number

= 493.54065

Calculates the payment for a loan based on constant payments and a constant interest rate.

> **Pv** is the present value: the total amount that a series of future payments is worth now.

Formula result = 493.54065

Help on this function   OK   Cancel

Notice in the above figure that three argument names are bold. These are the required arguments. Once you finish the required arguments, the Function Arguments dialog shows you the answer in two places. I always use this as a sanity check. Does this answer sound like a typical car payment?

This one topic really covered three things: how to calculate a loan payment, how to use the *fx* icon to discover new functions, and how to use Function Arguments to get help on any function. If you are in a situation where you remember the function name but still want to use the Function Arguments dialog, type =PMT(with the opening parenthesis then press Ctrl+A.

Note: Thanks to Tony DeJonker and Cat Parkinson for suggesting the function arguments.

#28 Calculate Nonstandard Work Weeks

In my live Power Excel seminar, it is pretty early in the day when I show how to right-click the Fill Handle, drag a date, and then choose Fill Weekdays. This fills Monday through Friday dates. I ask the audience, "How many of you work Monday through Friday?" A lot of hands go up. I say, "That's great. For everyone else, Microsoft clearly doesn't care about you." Laughter.

It certainly seems that if you work anything other than Monday through Friday or have a year ending any day other than December 31, a lot of things in Excel don't work very well.

However, two functions in Excel show that the Excel team does care about people who work odd work weeks: NETWORKDAYS.INTL and WORKDAY.INTL.

But let's start with their original Monday-Friday antecedents. The following figure shows a start date in B and an end date in C. If you subtract =C5-B5, you will get the number of days elapsed between the two dates. To figure out the number of weekdays, you would use =NETWORKDAYS(B2,C2).

	A	B	C	D	E
E2			fx	=NETWORKDAYS(B2,C2)	
1	Name	Start	End	Days	Work Days
2	Aaron Culbertson	5/1/2018	5/9/2018	8	7
3	Celine Loos	5/1/2018	5/16/2018	15	12
4	Rob Collie	5/1/2018	6/1/2018	31	24
5	Mike Dolan Fliss	5/1/2018	6/12/2018	42	31
6	Cecelia Rieb	5/1/2018	7/17/2018	77	56
7	Todd A Lesko	5/1/2018	7/28/2018	88	64
8	Micheal Reynolds	5/1/2018	8/14/2018	105	76
9	Robert Jelen	5/1/2018	10/3/2018	155	112
10	Michael Seeley	5/1/2018	11/2/2018	185	134
11	Judy A Glaser	5/1/2018	11/9/2018	192	139
12	Will Riley	5/1/2018	11/23/2018	206	149
13	Brian Canes	5/1/2018	4/16/2019	350	251

It gets even better. The old NETWORKDAYS allows for an optional third argument where you specify work holidays. In the next figure, the list of holidays in H3:H15 allows the Work Days Less Holidays calculation in column F.

`=NETWORKDAYS(B4,C4,$H$3:$H$15)`

	D	E	F	G	H
	Days	Work Days	Work Days less Holidays		Holidays
'2018	8	7	7		5/28/2018
'2018	15	12	12		7/4/2018
'2018	31	24	23		9/3/2018
'2018	42	31	30		10/8/2018
'2018	77	56	54		11/12/2018
'2018	88	64	62		11/22/2018
'2018	105	76	74		11/23/2018
'2018	155	112	109		12/24/2018
'2018	185	134	130		12/25/2018
'2018	192	139	135		1/1/2019
'2018	206	149	142		1/21/2019
'2019	350	251	239		2/18/2019
					5/27/2019

Prior to Excel 2007, the NETWORKDAYS and WORKDAY function were available if you enabled the Analysis ToolPak add-in that shipped with every copy of Excel. For Excel 2007, those add-ins were made a part of the core Excel. Microsoft added INTL versions of both functions with a new Weekend argument. This argument allowed for any two consecutive days as the weekend and also allowed for a one-day weekend.

D	E	F	G	H

Working Saturdays

s	Work Days less Holidays
8	`=NETWORKDAYS.INTL(B4,C4,`
15	NETWORKDAYS.INTL(start_date, end_date, [weekend], [holidays])
31	23
42	30
77	54
88	62
105	74
155	109
185	130
192	135
206	142
350	239

- 1 - Saturday, Sunday
- 2 - Sunday, Monday
- 3 - Monday, Tuesday
- 4 - Tuesday, Wednesday
- 5 - Wednesday, Thursday
- 6 - Thursday, Friday
- 7 - Friday, Saturday
- 11 - Sunday only
- 12 - Monday only
- 13 - Tuesday only
- 14 - Wednesday only
- 15 - Thursday only

I've seen a manufacturing plant switch to six day weeks in order to meet excess demand.

| E4 | ▼ | : | ✕ | ✓ | *fx* | =NETWORKDAYS.INTL(B4,C4,11,$G$5:$G$17) |

Manufacturing Plant Starts Working Saturdays

	A	B	C	D	E
3	Name	Start	End	Days	Work Days less Holidays
4	Aaron Culbertson	5/1/2018	5/9/2018	8	8
5	Celine Loos	5/1/2018	5/16/2018	15	14
6	Rob Collie	5/1/2018	6/1/2018	31	27
7	Mike Dolan Fliss	5/1/2018	6/12/2018	42	36
8	Cecelia Rieb	5/1/2018	7/17/2018	77	65
9	Todd A Lesko	5/1/2018	7/28/2018	88	75
10	Micheal Reynolds	5/1/2018	8/14/2018	105	89
11	Robert Jelen	5/1/2018	10/3/2018	155	131
12	Michael Seeley	5/1/2018	11/2/2018	185	156
13	Judy A Glaser	5/1/2018	11/9/2018	192	162
14	Will Riley	5/1/2018	11/23/2018	206	171
15	Brian Canes	5/1/2018	4/16/2019	350	289

Plus, there are several countries with weekends that don't fall on Saturday and Sunday. All of the countries shown below except Bruneei Darussalem gained functionality with NETWORKDAYS.INTL and WORKDAY.INTL.

Weekend Countries	
Fri-Sat	Algeria, Bahrain, Bangladesh, Egypt, Iraq, Israel, Jordan, Kuwait, Libya, Maldives, Mauritania, Malaysia, Oman, Palestine, Qatar, Saudi Arabia, Sudan, Syria, UAE, Yemen
Sat	Nepal
Thu-Fri	Afghanistan
Fri	Djibouti, Iran
Fri, Sun	Brunei Darussalam
Sat-Sun	Rest of World

However, there are still cases where the weekend does not meet any of the 14 weekend definitions added in Excel 2007.

I happen to live in the same county as the Pro Football Hall of Fame in Canton, Ohio. But the top tourism destination in our county is not the hall of fame. The top tourism destination is the Hartville Marketplace and Flea Market. Started in 1939, this place is a hot spot for people looking for fresh produce and bargains. The original lunch stand became the Hartville Kitchen restaurant. And the nearby Hartville Hardware is so big, they built an entire house inside the hardware store. But the Marketplace is the beneficiary of the new, secret weekend argument for NETWORKDAYS and WORKDAY. The Marketplace is open Monday, Thursday, Friday, and Saturday. That means their weekend is Tuesday, Wednesday and Sunday.

Starting in Excel 2010, instead of using 1-7 or 11-17 as the weekend argument, you can pass a 7-digit binary text to indicate if a company is open or closed on a particular day. It seems a bit unusual, but you use a 1 to indicate that the store is closed for the weekend and a 0 to indicate that the store is open. After all, 1 normally means On and 0 normally means Off. But the name of the argument is Weekend, so 1 means it is a day off, and 0 means you don't have the day off.

Thus, for the Monday, Thursday, Friday, Saturday schedule at the Hartville Marketplace, you would use "0110001". Every time I type one of these text strings, I have to silently say in my head, "Monday, Tuesday, Wednesday…" as I type each digit.

Marion Coblentz at the Hartville Marketplace could use the following formula to figure out how many Marketplace days there are between two dates.

| C8 | | | f_x | =NETWORKDAYS.INTL(A8,B8,"0110001") |

	A	B	C	D	E	F	G
1	Hartville Marketplace and Flea Market						
2	Open Monday, Thursday, Friday, Saturday						
3	Closed Tuesday, Wednesday, Sunday						
4	7 Binary Digits, starting with Monday						
5	1=Weekend, 0=Open						
6							
7	Start	End	Work Days				
8	5/1/2018	5/9/2018	4	=NETWORKDAYS.INTL(A8,B8,"0110001")			
9	5/1/2018	5/16/2018	8				
10	5/1/2018	6/1/2018	18				
11	5/1/2018	6/12/2018	24				
12	5/1/2018	7/17/2018	44				
13	5/1/2018	7/28/2018	51				

By the way I did not use the optional Holidays argument above because Memorial Day, July 4, and Labor Day are the biggest customer days in Hartville.

If you are ever in northeastern Ohio, you need to stop by Hartville to see the 100% American-Made house inside of the Hartville Hardware and to try the great food at the Hartville Kitchen. Give me a call; I will meet you there.

Bonus Tip: Use WORKDAY.INTL for a Work Calendar

While NETWORKDAYS calculates the work days between two dates, the WORKDAY function takes a starting date and a number of days, and it calculates the date that is a certain number of work days away.

Say that a new hire is on probation for 30 work days. But no one really uses work days for that calculation. By far the most common use is to calculate the next work day. In the following figure, the start date is the date on the previous row. The number of days is always 1. Specify the weekend and/or holiday. Drag the formula down, and you will generate an employee calendar of work days.

	A	B	C	D
1	Using WORKDAY.INTL to Create Work Calendar			
2	Hartville Marketplace and Flea Market			
3	Open Monday, Thursday, Friday, Saturday			
4	Closed Tuesday, Wednesday, Sunday			
5				
6	Start			
7	Monday, April 30, 2018			
8	Thursday, May 03, 2018	=WORKDAY.INTL(A7,1,"0110001")		
9	Friday, May 04, 2018	=WORKDAY.INTL(A8,1,"0110001")		
10	Saturday, May 05, 2018	=WORKDAY.INTL(A9,1,"0110001")		
11	Monday, May 07, 2018	=WORKDAY.INTL(A10,1,"0110001")		
12	Thursday, May 10, 2018	=WORKDAY.INTL(A11,1,"0110001")		
13	Friday, May 11, 2018	=WORKDAY.INTL(A12,1,"0110001")		
14	Saturday, May 12, 2018	=WORKDAY.INTL(A13,1,"0110001")		
15	Monday, May 14, 2018	=WORKDAY.INTL(A14,1,"0110001")		

#29 Handle Multiple Conditions in IF

When you need to do a conditional calculation, the IF function is the answer. If <something is true> then <this formula> otherwise <that formula>. In the following figure, a simple IF calculates a bonus if your sales were $20,000 or more.

| D4 | | ✓ | ✓ | fx | =IF(B4>=20000,0.02*B4,0) |

⊿	A	B	C	D	E
1	Pay a 2% bonus for sales > 20000				
2					
3	Sales Rep	Revenue	GP%	Bonus	
4	Richard B Lanza	22810	45.9%	456.2	
5	David Haggarty	2257	54.0%	0	
6	Anthony J. LoBello Jr.	18552	46.3%	0	
7	Jon Higbed	9152	50.5%	0	
8	David Colman	8456	46.1%	0	
9	Eddie Stephen	21730	54.4%	434.6	
10	Mike excelisfun Girvin	16416	48.2%	0	
11	Leonard LaFrenier	21438	52.0%	428.76	
12	Victor E. Scelba II	6267	53.7%	0	

But what happens when two conditions need to be met? Most people will nest one IF statement inside another, like this:

1	Bonus for sales > 20000 + GP%>50%			
2	=IF(B4>20000,IF(C4>0.5,0.02*B4,0),0)			
3	Sales Rep	Revenue	GP%	Bonus
4	Richard B Lanza	22810	45.9%	0
5	David Haggarty	2257	54.0%	0
6	Anthony J. LoBello Jr.	18552	46.3%	0
7	Jon Higbed	9152	50.5%	0
8	David Colman	8456	46.1%	0
9	Eddie Stephen	21730	54.4%	434.6
10	Mike excelisfun Girvir	16416	48.2%	0
11	Leonard LaFrenier	21438	52.0%	428.76
12	Victor E. Scelba II	6267	53.7%	0

But this gets out of hand if you have many conditions that have to be met. The AND function will shorten and simplify the formula. =AND(Test,Test,Test,Test) will only be True if all of the logical tests are True. The following example shows a shorter formula with the same results.

▲	A	B	C	D	
1	Bonus for sales > 20000 + GP%>50%				
2	=IF(AND(B4>20000,C4>0.5),0.02*B4,0)				
3	Sales Rep	Revenue	GP%	Bonus	
4	Richard B Lanza	22810	45.9%	0	
5	David Haggarty	2257	54.0%	0	
6	Anthony J. LoBello Jr.	18552	46.3%	0	
7	Jon Higbed	9152	50.5%	0	
8	David Colman	8456	46.1%	0	
9	Eddie Stephen	21730	54.4%	434.6	
10	Mike excelisfun Girvi	16416	48.2%	0	
11	Leonard LaFrenier	21438	52.0%	428.76	
12	Victor E. Scelba II	6267	53.7%	0	

If you like AND, you might find a use for OR and NOT. =OR(Test,Test,Test,Test) will be True if any one of the logical tests are True. NOT will reverse an answer. =NOT(True) is False. =NOT(False) is True. If you ever have to do something fancy like a NAND, you can do NOT(AND(Test,Test,Test,Test)).

> **Caution**: Although Excel 2013 introduced XOR as an Exclusive Or, it does not work the way that accountants would expect. =XOR(True,False,True,True) is True for reasons that are too complicated to explain here. XOR really counts whether you have an odd number of True values. Odd. Really odd.

Bonus Tip: Using Boolean Logic

I always cover IF in my seminars. And I always ask how people would solve the two-conditions problem. The results are often the same; 70-80% of people use nested IF and 20-30% use AND. Just one time, in Virginia, a woman from Price Waterhouse offered this formula:

▲	A	B	C	D	
1	Bonus for sales > 20000 + GP%>50%				
2	=B4*0.02*(B4>20000)*(C4>0.5)				
3	Sales Rep	Revenue	GP%	Bonus	
4	Richard B Lanza	22810	45.9%	0	
5	David Haggarty	2257	54.0%	0	
6	Anthony J. LoBello Jr.	18552	46.3%	0	
7	Jon Higbed	9152	50.5%	0	
8	David Colman	8456	46.1%	0	
9	Eddie Stephen	21730	54.4%	434.6	
10	Mike excelisfun Girvi	16416	48.2%	0	
11	Leonard LaFrenier	21438	52.0%	428.76	
12	Victor E. Scelba II	6267	53.7%	0	

It works. It gives the same answer as the other formulas. Calculate the bonus .02*B4. But then multiply that bonus by logical tests in parentheses. When you force Excel to multiply a number by True or False, the True becomes 1, and the False becomes 0. Any number times 1 is itself. Any number times 0 is 0. Multiplying the bonus by the conditions ensures that only rows that meet both conditions are paid.

It is cool. It works. But it seems confusing when you first see it. My joke in the seminar always is, "If you are leaving your job next month and you hate your co-workers, start using this formula."

#30 Cure Triskaidekaphobia with a Killer Formula

Triskaidekaphobia is the fear of Friday the 13th. This topic won't cure anything, but it will show you an absolutely amazing formula that replaces 110,268 formulas. In real life, I never have to count how many Friday the 13ths have occurred in my lifetime, but the power and the beauty of this formula illustrates the power of Excel.

Say that you have a friend who is superstitious about Friday the 13th. You want to illustrate how many Friday the 13ths your friend has lived through.

why be afraid?

you've been alive for 86 of them.

Illustration Credit: Chelsea Besse

Set up the simple worksheet below, with birthdate in B1 and =TODAY() in B2. Then a wild formula in B6 evaluates every day that your friend has been alive to figure out how many of those days were Friday and fell on the 13th of the month. For me, the number is 86. Nothing to be afraid of.

	A	B	C	D	E	F
1	Birth Date	2/17/1965				
2	Today	6/12/2015				
3						
4	Number of Friday the 13th's					
5	that you've survived:					
6		86				
7						
8	=SUMPRODUCT(					
9	--(DAY(ROW(INDIRECT(B1&":"&B2)))=13),					
10	--(WEEKDAY(ROW(INDIRECT(B1&":"&B2)),2)=5))					
11						
12						

By the way, 2/17/1965 really is my birthday. But I don't want you to send me a birthday card. Instead, for my birthday, I want you to let me explain how that amazing formula works, one small step at a time.

Have you ever used the INDIRECT function? When you ask for =INDIRECT("C3"), Excel will go to C3 and return whatever is in that cell. But INDIRECT is more powerful when you calculate the cell reference on-the-fly. You could set up a prize wheel where someone picks a letter between A and C and then picks a number between 1 and 3. When you concatenate the two answers, you will have a cell address, and whatever is at that cell address is the prize. Looks like I won a photo book instead of the resort stay.

| fx | =INDIRECT(C5&C6) |

	A	B	C	D	E	F
1	Movie Rental	Big Mac	Photo Book			
2	$50	Gift Card	Camera			
3	Screen Cleaner	Plane Ticket	Resort Stay			
4						
5		Choose A,B,C:	C			
6		Choose 1,2,3:	1			
7						
8	Your Prize:		Photo Book			
9	=INDIRECT(C5&C6)					
10	=INDIRECT("C1")					

Do you know how Excel stores dates? When Excel shows you 2/17/1965, it is storing 23790 in the cell, because 2/17/1965, was the 23790th day of the 20th century. At the heart of the formula is a concatenation that joins the start date and a colon and the end date. Excel doesn't use the formatted date. Instead, it uses the serial number behind the scenes. So B3&":"&B4 becomes 23790:42167. Believe it or not, that is a valid cell reference. If you wanted to add up everything in rows 3 through 5, you could use =SUM(3:5). So, when you pass 23790:42167 to the INDIRECT function, it points at all of the rows.

| B6 | fx | =B3&":"&B4 |

	A	B	C	D
1	How does Excel Store Dates?			
2				
3	Birth Date	2/17/1965		
4	Today	6/12/2015		
5				
6		23790:42167		
7		=B3&":"&B4		
8				
9		18378		
10		{=COUNT(ROW(INDIRECT(B6)))}		
11				

The next thing the killer formula does is to ask for the ROW(23790:42167). Normally, you pass a single cell: =ROW(D17) is 17. But in this case, you are passing thousands of cells. When you ask for ROW(23790:42167) and finish the formula with Ctrl+Shift+Enter, Excel actually returns every number from 23790, 23791, 23792, and so on up to 42167.

This step is the amazing step. In this step, we go from two numbers and "pop out" an array of 18378 numbers. Now, we have to do something with that array of answers. Cell B9 of the previous figure just counts how many answers we get, which is boring, but it proves that ROW(23790:42167) is returning 18378 answers.

Let's dramatically simplify the original question so you can see what is happening. In this case we'll find the number of Fridays in July 2015. The formula shown below in B7 provides the correct answer in B6.

	A	B	C	D	E	F	G
1	How many Fridays this July						
2							
3	Start	7/1/2015					
4	End	7/31/2015					
5							
6		5					
7		=SUMPRODUCT(--(WEEKDAY(ROW(INDIRECT(B3&":"&B4)),2)=5))					
8							
9			Wed 7/1	3 =WEEKDAY(C9,2)			
10			Thu 7/2	4 =WEEKDAY(C10,2)			
11			Fri 7/3	5 =WEEKDAY(C11,2)			
12			Sat 7/4	6 =WEEKDAY(C12,2)			
13			Sun 7/5	7 =WEEKDAY(C13,2)			
14			Mon 7/6	1 =WEEKDAY(C14,2)			
15			Tue 7/7	2 =WEEKDAY(C15,2)			

At the heart of the formula is ROW(INDIRECT(B3&":"&B4)). This is going to return the 31 dates in July 2015. But the formula then passes those 31 dates to the WEEKDAY(<date>,2) function. This function will return a 1 for Monday, 5 for Friday, and so on. So the big question is how many of those 31 dates return a 5 when passed to the WEEKDAY(,2) function.

You can watch the formula calculate in slow motion by using the Evaluate Formula command on the Formula tab of the ribbon.

This is after INDIRECT converts the dates to a row reference.

Evaluation:

SUMPRODUCT(--(WEEKDAY(ROW($42186:$42216),2)=5))

In the next step, Excel is about to pass 31 numbers to the WEEKDAY function. Now, in the killer formula, it would pass 18,378 numbers instead of 31.

Evaluation:

```
SUMPRODUCT(--(WEEKDAY((42186;42187;42188;42189;42190;
42191;42192;42193;42194;42195;42196;42197;42198;42199;
42200;42201;42202;42203;42204;42205;42206;42207;42208;
42209;42210;42211;42212;42213;42214;42215;42216),2)=5))
```

Here are the results of the 31 WEEKDAY functions. Remember, we want to count how many are 5.

Evaluation:

```
SUMPRODUCT(--((3;4;5;6;7;1;2;3;4;5;6;7;1;2;3;4;5;6;7;1;2;3;4;5;6;7;1;
2;3;4;5)=5))
```

Checking to see if the previous array is 5 returns a whole bunch of True/False values. There are 5 True values, one for each Friday.

Evaluation:

```
SUMPRODUCT(--((FALSE;FALSE;TRUE;FALSE;FALSE;FALSE;FALSE;
FALSE;FALSE;TRUE;FALSE;FALSE;FALSE;FALSE;FALSE;FALSE;TRUE;
FALSE;FALSE;FALSE;FALSE;FALSE;FALSE;TRUE;FALSE;FALSE;FALSE;
FALSE;FALSE;FALSE;TRUE)))
```

I cannot show you what happens next, but I can explain it. Excel cannot SUM a bunch of True and False values. It is against the rules. But if you multiply those True and False values by 1 or if you use the double-negative or the N() function, you convert the True values to 1 and the False values to 0. Send those to SUM or SUMPRODUCT, and you will get the count of the True values.

Here is a similar example to count how many months have a day 13 in them. This is trivial to think about: Every month has a 13th, so the answer for a whole year better be 12. Excel is doing the math, generating 365 dates, sending them all to the DAY() function, and figuring out how many end up on the 13th of the month. The answer, as expected, is 12.

	A	B	C	D	E	F	G
17	How many 13ths of the months this year?						
18							
19	Start	1/1/2015					
20	End	12/31/2015					
21							
22		12					
23		=SUMPRODUCT(--(DAY(ROW(INDIRECT(B19&":"&B20)))=13))					

The next figure is a worksheet that does all of the logic the one killer formula shown at the start of this topic. I've created a row for every day that I've been alive. In column B, I get the DAY() of that date. In column C, I get the WEEKDAY() of the date. In column D, is B equal to 13? In Column E, is C=5? I then multiply D*E to convert the True/False to 1/0.

I've hidden a lot of the rows, but I show you three random days in the middle which happen to be both a Friday and the 13th.

The total in F18381 is the same 86 that my original formula returned. A great sign. But this worksheet has 110,268 formulas. My original killer formula does all of the logic of these 110,268 formulas in a single formula.

	A	B	C	D	E	F
1	Date	Day	Weekday(,2)	Day=13?	Weekday=5?	Both?
2	Wednesday, February 17, 1965	17	3	FALSE	FALSE	0
3	Thursday, February 18, 1965	18	4	FALSE	FALSE	0
4	Friday, February 19, 1965	19	5	FALSE	TRUE	0
5	Saturday, February 20, 1965	20	6	FALSE	FALSE	0
179	Friday, August 13, 1965	13	5	TRUE	TRUE	1
7515	Friday, September 13, 1985	13	5	TRUE	TRUE	1
13724	Friday, September 13, 2002	13	5	TRUE	TRUE	1
18376	Tuesday, June 09, 2015	9	2	FALSE	FALSE	0
18377	Wednesday, June 10, 2015	10	3	FALSE	FALSE	0
18378	Thursday, June 11, 2015	11	4	FALSE	FALSE	0
18379	Friday, June 12, 2015	12	5	FALSE	TRUE	0
18381				Total		86
18382		# of Formula Cells:		110268		
18384	Formula in B2:	=DAY(A2)				
18385	Formula in C2:	=WEEKDAY(A2,2)				
18386	Formula in D2:	=B2=13				
18387	Formula in E2:	=C2=5				
18388	Formula in F2:	=D2*E2				

Wait. I want to clarify. There is nothing magical in the original formula that gets smart and shortens the logic. That original formula *really is doing 110,268 steps,* probably even more, because the original formula has to calculate the ROW() array twice.

Find a way to use this ROW(INDIRECT(Date:Date)) in real life and send it to me in an e-mail (pub at mrexcel dot com). I'll send a prize to the first 100 people to answer. Probably not a resort stay. More likely a Big Mac. But that's the way it goes with prizes. Lots of Big Macs and not many resort stays.

I first saw this formula posted at the MrExcel.com message board in 2003 by Ekim. Credit was given to Harlan Grove. The formula also appeared in Bob Umlas's book *This Isn't Excel, It's Magic.* Mike Delaney, Meni Porat, and Tim Sheets all suggested the minus/minus trick. SUMPRODUCT was suggested by Audrey Lynn and Steven White. Thank you all.

#31 Troubleshooting VLOOKUP

VLOOKUP is my favorite function in Excel. If you can do VLOOKUP, you are able to solve many problems in Excel. But there are things that can trip up a VLOOKUP. This topic talks about a few of them.

But first, the basics of VLOOKUP in plain English.

The data in A:C came from the IT department. You asked for sales by item and date. They gave you Item number. You need Item Description. Rather than wait for the IT department to re-run the data, you find the table shown in column F:G.

	A	B	C	D	E	F	G	H
1	Item	Date	Qty	Description				
2	W25-6	8/1/2018	878			SKU	Description	
3	CR 50-4	8/1/2018	213			BG33-3	14K Gold Bangle Bracelet with Vin	
4	CR 50-4	8/2/2018	744			CR50-3	14K Gold Cross with Onyx	
5	BR26-3	8/3/2018	169			RG75-3	14K Gold RAY OF LIGHT Onyx Me	
6	CR50-6	8/3/2018	822			RG78-25	14K Gold Ballerina Ring w/ Blue &	
7	ER46-14	8/3/2018	740			W25-6	18K Italian Gold Women's Watch	
8	RG78-25	8/3/2018	638			BR26-3	18K Italian Gold Men's Bracelet	
9	BR15-3	8/4/2018	817			BR15-3	14K Gold Onyx Men's Bracelet	

You want VLOOKUP to find the item in A2 while it searches through the first column of the table in $F$3:$G$30. When VLOOKUP finds the match in F7, you want VLOOKUP to return the description found in the second column of the table. Every VLOOKUP that is looking for an exact match has to end in False (or zero, which is equivalent to False). The formula below is set up properly.

D2	▼	:	×	✓	f_x	=VLOOKUP(A2,$F$3:$G$30,2,FALSE)

	A	B	C	D	E	F
1	Item	Date	Qty	Description		
2	W25-6	8/1/2018	878	18K Italian Gold Women's Watch	SKU	Descri
3	CR 50-4	8/1/2018	213	14K Gold Onyx Cross	BG33-3	14K G
4	CR 50-4	8/2/2018	744	14K Gold Onyx Cross	CR50-3	14K G
5	BR26-3	8/3/2018	169	18K Italian Gold Men's Bracelet	RG75-3	14K G
6	CR50-6	8/3/2018	822	14K Gold Onyx Cross with White	RG78-25	14K G
7	ER46-14	8/3/2018	740	14K Gold Fish Hoop Earrings	W25-6	18K Ita

Notice that you use F4 to add four dollar signs to the address for the lookup table. As you copy the formula down column D, you need the address for the lookup table to remain constant. There are two common alternatives: You could specify the entire columns F:G as the lookup table. Or, you could name F3:G30 with a name such as ItemTable. If you use =VLOOKUP(A2,ItemTable,2,False), the named range acts like an absolute reference.

Any time that you do a bunch of VLOOKUPs, you need to sort the column of VLOOKUPs. Sort ZA, and any #N/A errors will come to the top. In this case, there is one. Item BG33-9 is missing from the lookup table. Maybe it is a typo. Maybe it is a brand-new item. If it is new, insert a new row anywhere in the middle of your lookup table and add the new item.

	A	B	C	D Sort ZA	E	F
1	Item	Date	Qty	Description		
2	BG33-9	8/19/2018	37	#N/A		SKU
3	W25-6	8/1/2018	878	18K Italian Gold Women's Watch		BG33-3
4	W25-6	8/21/2018	254	18K Italian Gold Women's Watch		CR50-3
5	W25-6	8/22/2018	832	18K Italian Gold Women's Watch		RG75-3
6	W25-6	8/29/2018	581	18K Italian Gold Women's Watch		RG78-25
7	BR26-3	8/3/2018	169	18K Italian Gold Men's Bracelet		W25-6
8	BR26-3	8/5/2018	541	18K Italian Gold Men's Bracelet		BR26-3
9	BR26-3	8/6/2018	849	18K Italian Gold Men's Bracelet		BR15-3
10	BR26-3	8/10/2018	881	18K Italian Gold Men's Bracelet		BG33-8
11	BR26-3	8/12/2018	737	18K Italian Gold Men's Bracelet		BG33-17

It is fairly normal to have a few #N/A errors. But in the figure below, exactly the same formula is returning nothing but #N/A. When this happens, I see if I can solve the first VLOOKUP. You are looking up the BG33-8 found in A2. Start cruising down through the first column of the lookup table. As you can see, the matching value clearly is in F10. Why can you see this, but Excel cannot see it?

D2			f_x	=VLOOKUP(A2,$F$3:$G$30,2,FALSE)	

	A	B	C	D	E	F	G
1	Item	Date	Qty	Description			
2	BG33-8	8/1/2018	580	#N/A		SKU	Description
3	Cross50-5	8/1/2018	422	#N/A		BG33-3	14K Gold Bar
4	RG78-25	8/2/2018	638	#N/A		CR50-3	14K Gold Cro
5	BG33-8	8/3/2018	775	#N/A		RG75-3	14K Gold RA\`
6	BG33-8	8/3/2018	331	#N/A		RG78-25	14K Gold Ball
7	ER46-7	8/3/2018	140	#N/A		W25-6	18K Italian Gc
8	RG75-3	8/3/2018	231	#N/A		BR26-3	18K Italian Gc
9	W25-6	8/4/2018	878	#N/A		BR15-3	14K Gold Ony
10	CR50-6	8/4/2018	571	#N/A		BG33-8	14K Gold Bar
11	ER41-4	8/4/2018	208	#N/A		BG33-17	14K Gold Bar

Go to each cell and press the F2 key. Here is F10. Note that the insertion cursor appears right after the 8.

W25-6	1ur
BR26-3	18ŀ
BR15-3	14ŀ
BG33-8	14ŀ
BG33-17	14ŀ
CR 50-4	14ŀ
CR50-2	14ŀ

Here is cell A2 in Edit mode. The insertion cursor is a couple of spaces away from the 8. This is a sign that at some point, this data was stored in an old COBOL data set. Back in COBOL, if the Item field was defined as 10 characters and you only typed 6 characters, COBOL would pad it with 4 extra spaces.

	A	D
1	Item	
2	BG33-8	
3	Cross50-5	
4	RG78-25	
5	BG33-8	
6	BG33-8	

The solution? Instead of looking up A2, look up the TRIM(A2).

D2			f_x	=VLOOKUP(TRIM(A2),$F$3:$G$30,2,FALSE)	

	A	B	C	D	E	F	G
1	Item	Date	Qty	Description			
2	BG33-8	8/1/2018	580	14K Gold Bangle		SKU	Description
3	Cross50-5	8/1/2018	422	14K Gold Onyx C		BG33-3	14K Gold Bangle Br
4	RG78-25	8/2/2018	638	14K Gold Ballerin		CR50-3	14K Gold Cross with
5	BG33-8	8/3/2018	775	14K Gold Bangle		RG75-3	14K Gold RAY OF L
6	BG33-8	8/3/2018	331	14K Gold Bangle		RG78-25	14K Gold Ballerina F

The TRIM() function removes leading and trailing spaces. If you have multiple spaces between words, TRIM will convert them to a single space. In the figure below there are spaces before and after both names in A1. =TRIM(A1) removes all but one space in A3.

| A3 | | ▼ | ⋮ | × | ✓ | f_x | =TRIM(A1) |

	A	B	C
1	John Durran		
2	* John Durran *	="*"&A1&"*"	
3	John Durran	=TRIM(A1)	
4	*John Durran*	="*"&A3&"*"	
5			

By the way, what if the problem had been trailing spaces in column F instead of column A? Add a column of TRIM() functions to E, pointing to column F. Copy those and paste as values in F to make the lookups start working again.

The other very common reason that VLOOKUP won't work is shown here. Column F has real numbers. Column A has text that looks like numbers.

| D2 | | ▼ | ⋮ | × | ✓ | f_x | =VLOOKUP(A2,$F$3:$G$30,2,FALSE) |

Numbers

	A	B	C	D	E	F	G
1	Item	Date	Qty	Description			
2	4399	8/1/2018	30	#N/A		SKU	Description
3	4250	8/1/2018	422	#N/A		6041	14K Gold Ban
4	3712	8/2/2018	638	#N/A		2304	14K Gold Cros
5	4399	8/3/2018	775	#N/A		1242	14K Gold RAY
6	4399	8/3/2018	?? 331	#N/A		3712	14K Gold Ball
7	3363	8/3/2018	140	#N/A		5805	18K Italian Go
8	1242	8/3/2018	231	#N/A		1995	18K Italian Go
9	5805	8/4/2018	878	#N/A		2619	14K Gold Ony
10	2925	8/4/2018	571	#N/A		4399	14K Gold Ban
11	3270 Text	4/2018	208	#N/A		4101	14K Gold Ban
12	3270	8/5/2018	429	#N/A		5403	14K Gold Ony
	4499	9/5/2018	922	#N/A		2710	14K Gold Ony

Select all of column A. Press Alt+D, E, F. This does a default Text to Columns and will convert all text numbers to real numbers. The lookup starts working again.

Alt+D, E, F

	A	B	C	D	E
1	Item	Date	Qty	Description	
2	4399	8/1/2018	580	14K Gold Bangle Bra	
3	4250	8/1/2018	422	14K Gold Onyx Cross	
4	3712	8/2/2018	638	14K Gold Ballerina Ri	
5	4399	8/3/2018	775	14K Gold Bangle Bra	
6	4399	8/3/2018	331	14K Gold Bangle Bra	
7	3363	8/3/2018	140	14K Gold Hollow Earr	
8	1242	8/3/2018	231	14K Gold RAY OF LI	
9	5805	8/4/2018	878	18K Italian Gold Won	
10	2925	8/4/2018	571	14K Gold Onyx Cross	

Bonus Tip: Replacing Columns of VLOOKUP with a Single MATCH

In the following figure, you are going to have to do 12 VLOOKUP functions for each account number. VLOOKUP is powerful, but it takes a lot of time to do calculations.

| B4 | | | × | ✓ | f_x | =VLOOKUP($A4,$O$4:$AA$227,2,FALSE) |

	A	B	C	D	E	F	G	H	I	J	K	L	M	N		O	P	Q	R	S	T	U	V	W	X	Y	Z	AA
1																												
2																												
3	Acct	Jan	Feb	Mar	Apr	May	Jun	Jul	Aug	Sep	Oct	Nov	Dec			Acct	J	F	M	A	M	J	J	A	S	O	N	D
4	A308	6														A101	5	2	0	8	3	1	1	0	6	1	4	7
5	A219															A102	3	0	7	0	4	9	4	3	5	3	7	1
6	A249															A103	1	4	9	0	3	4	3	3	8	0	5	6

Plus, the formula has to be edited in each cell as you copy across. The third argument has to change from 2 to 3 for February, then 4 for March, and so on.

| C4 | | | × | ✓ | f_x | =VLOOKUP($A4,$O$4:$AA$227,3,FALSE) |

	A	B	C	D	E	F	G	H	I	J	K	L	M	N	O
1															
2															
3	Acct	Jan	Feb	Mar	Apr	May	Jun	Jul	Aug	Sep	Oct	Nov	Dec		Acct
4	A308	6	1												A101
5	A219														A102
6	A249														A103
7	A154														A104

One workaround is to add a row with the column numbers. Then, the 3rd argument of VLOOKUP can point to this row. At least you can copy the same formula from B4 and paste to C4:M4 before copying the whole set down.

| G4 | | | × | ✓ | f_x | =VLOOKUP($A4,$O$4:$AA$227,G$1,FALSE) |

	A	B	C	D	E	F	G	H	I	J	K	L	M	N	O	P
1		2	3	4	5	6	7	8	9	10	11	12	13			
2																
3	Acct	Jan	Feb	Mar	Apr	May	Jun	Jul	Aug	Sep	Oct	Nov	Dec		Acct	J
4	A308	6	1	9	2	9	1	5	4	4	4	7	3		A101	5
5	A219	0	0	5	0	2	8	8	7	8	3	0	0		A102	3
6	A249	1	7	1	3	2	9	6	7	1	2	9	5		A103	1
7	A154	2	5	8	0	3	3	5	5	2	8	9	3		A104	0

But here is a much faster approach. Add a new column B with Where? as the heading. Column B contains a MATCH function. This function is very similar to VLOOKUP: You are looking for the value in A4 in the column P4:P227. The 0 at the end is like the False at the end of VLOOKUP. It specifies that you want an exact match. Here is the big difference: MATCH returns where the value is found. The answer of 208 says that A308 is the 208th cell in the range P4:P227. From a recalc time perspective, MATCH and VLOOKUP are about equal.

B4 f_x =MATCH(A4,$P$4:$P$227,0)

	A	B	C	D	E	F	G	H	I	J	K	L	M
1													
2													
3	Acct	Where?	Jan	Feb	Mar	Apr	May	Jun	Jul	Aug	Sep	Oct	No
4	A308	208											
5	A219	119											
6	A249	149											
7	A154	54											

I can hear what you are thinking. "What good is it to know where something is located? I've never had a manager call up and ask, 'What row is that receivable in?'"

While humans rarely ask what row something is in, the INDEX function can use that position. The following formula tells Excel to return the 208th item from Q4:Q227.

SUM f_x =INDEX(Q$4:Q$227,$B4)

	A	B	C	D	E	F	G	H	I	J	K	L	M	N	O	P	Q	R	S	T
1																				
2																				
3	Acct	Where?	Jan	Feb	Mar	Apr	May	Jun	Jul	Aug	Sep	Oct	Nov	Dec		Acct	J	F	M	A
4	A308	208	=INDEX(Q$4:Q$227,$B4)													A101	5	2	0	8
5	A219	119														A102	3	0	7	0
6	A249	149														A103	1	4	9	0
7	A154	54														A104	0	4	2	5
8	A128	28														A105	9	4	8	1
9	A229	129														A106	6	3	6	2

As you copy this formula across, the array of values moves across the lookup table. For each row, you are doing one MATCH and 12 INDEX functions. The INDEX function is incredibly fast compared to VLOOKUP. The entire set of formulas will calculate 85% faster than 12 columns of VLOOKUP.

SUM f_x =INDEX(Y$4:Y$227,$B4)

	A	B	C	D	E	F	G	H	I	J	K	L	M	N	O	P	Q	R	S	T	U	V	W	X	Y	Z	AA	AB
1																												
2																												
3	Acct	Where?	Jan	Feb	Mar	Apr	May	Jun	Jul	Aug	Sep	Oct	Nov	Dec		Acct	J	F	M	A	M	J	J	A	S	O	N	D
4	A308	208	6	1	9	2	9	1	5	4	=INDEX(Y$4:Y$227,$B4)						5	2	0	8	3	1	1	0	6	1	4	7
5	A219	119	0	0	5	0	2	8	8	7	8	3	0	0		A102	3	0	7	0	4	9	4	3	5	3	7	1
6	A249	149	1	7	1	3	2	9	6	7	1	2	9	5		A103	1	4	9	0	3	4	3	3	8	0	5	6
7	A154	54	2	5	8	0	3	3	5	5	2	8	9	3		A104	0	4	2	5	0	0	9	7	6	8	8	5
8	A128	28	4	1	8	6	2	5	7	8	4	0	9	5		A105	9	4	8	1	3	4	5	7	7	7	9	7

Bonus Tip: VLOOKUP Left with INDEX/MATCH

What if your lookup value is to the right of the information that you want VLOOKUP to return? The conventional wisdom says VLOOKUP cannot handle a negative column number in order to go left of the key.

	A	B	C	D	E
1	Name	Department			
2	Alex Pilar	=VLOOKUP(A2,$D$4:$E$11,-1,FALSE)			
3	Gary Kane			Department	Name
4	Leonard LaFrenier			Accounting	Allan Matz
5	Allan Matz			Finance	Gary Kane
6	Alex Pilar	**Won't**		Accounting	Alex Pilar
7	Alex Pilar	**Work!**		Finance	Larry Vance
8	Larry Vance			Tax	Leonard LaFrenier
9	Larry Vance			Finance	Lorna Banuilos
10	Alex Pilar			Accounting	Erik Svensen
11	Larry Vance			Finance	Victor E. Scelba II
12	Lorna Banuilos				

> Note: In the second section of this book, Szilvia Juhasz reveals how VLOOKUP can look left. See "#19 VLOOKUP – to the Left!" on page 194.

The solution is to use a MATCH to find where the name is located, and then use INDEX to return the correct value.

fx =INDEX($D$4:$D$11,MATCH(A2,$E$4:$E$11,0))

	A	B	C	D	E	F	G
1	Name	Department					
2	Alex Pilar	=INDEX($D$4:$D$11,MATCH(A2,$E$4:$E$11,0))					
3	Gary Kane	Finance		Department	Name		
4	Leonard LaFrenier	Tax		Accounting	Allan Matz		
5	Allan Matz	Accounting		Finance	Gary Kane		
6	Alex Pilar	Accounting		Accounting	Alex Pilar		
7	Alex Pilar	Accounting		Finance	Larry Vance		
8	Larry Vance	Finance		Tax	Leonard LaFrenier		
9	Larry Vance	Finance		Finance	Lorna Banuilos		
10	Alex Pilar	Accounting		Accounting	Erik Svensen		
11	Larry Vance	Finance		Finance	Victor E. Scelba II		
12	Lorna Banuilos	Finance					
13	Alex Pilar	Accounting					

VLOOKUP was suggested by Rod Apfelbeck, Patty Hahn, John Henning, @ExcelKOS, and @tomatecaolho. INDEX/MATCH came from Mark Domeyer, Jon Dow, Justin Fishman, Donna Gilliland, Alex Havermans, Jay Killeen, Martin Lucas, Patrick Matthews, Mike Petry, Michael Tarzia, and @beatexcel. Thanks to all of you.

1

A VALUE TO THE LEFT.....

VLOOKUP'S KRYPTONITE

This message brought to you by:

INDEX & MATCH

= INDEX (X2:X99,MATCH(A2,Z2:Z99,0))

YOUR **1** STOP FOR EXCEL SOLUTIONS

MrEXCeL.com

Poster Credit: Bobby Rosenstock
justAjar Design Press, http://www.justajar.com/

#32 Replace Nested IFs with a Lookup Table

A long time ago, I worked for the vice president of sales at work. I was always modeling some new bonus program or commission plan. I became pretty used to commission plans with all sorts of conditions. The one below is pretty tame.

The normal approach is to start building a nested IF formula. You always start at either the high end or the low end of the range. "If sales are over $500K, then the discount is 20%; otherwise…." The third argument of the IF function is a whole new IF function that tests for the second level: If sales are over $250K, then the discount is 15%; otherwise,…."

These formulas get longer and longer as there are more levels. The toughest part of such a formula is remembering how many closing parentheses to put at the end of the formula.

Mini Bonus Tip: Matching the Parentheses

Excel cycles through a variety of colors for each new level of parentheses. While Excel reuses the colors, it uses black only for the opening parenthesis and for the matching closing parenthesis. As you are finishing the formula below, just keep typing closing parentheses until you type a black parenthesis.

	A	B	C	D
1	**Next Year Discount Level Rules**			
2	*Based on last year's revenue:*			
3	*Anyone over $500K: 20% discount*		=IF(B10>500000,20%,	
4	*Anyone over $250K: 15% discount*		IF(B10>250000,15%,	
5	*Anyone over $100K: 10% discount*		IF(B10>100000,10%,	
6	*Anyone over $50K: 5% discount*		IF(B10>50000,5%,	
7	*Anyone over $10K: 1% Discount*		IF(B10>10000,1%,0)))))	
9	Customer	Revenue	Future Discount	
10	SpringBoard	550000	20%	
11	LaFrenier Sons Septic	503500	20%	

Back to the Nested Formula Tip

If you're using Excel 2003, your formula is already nearing the limit. Back then, you could not nest more than 7 IF functions. It was an ugly day when the powers that be changed the commission plan and you needed a way to add an eighth IF function. Today, you can nest 64 IF functions. You should never do this, but it is nice to know there is no problem nesting 8 or 9.

Rather than use the nested IF function, try using the unusual use for the VLOOKUP function. When the fourth argument of VLOOKUP changes from False to True, the function is no longer looking for an exact match.

Well, first VLOOKUP tries to find an exact match. But if an exact match is not found, then Excel settles into the row just less than what you are searching for.

Consider the table below. In cell C13, Excel will be looking for a match for $28,355 in the table. When it can't find 28355, Excel will return the discount associated with the value that is just less. In this case, the 1% discount for the $10K level.

When you convert the rules to the table in E13:F18, you need to start from the smallest level and proceed to the highest level. Although it was unstated in the rules, if someone is below $10,000 in sales, the discount will be 0%. You need to add this as the first row in the table.

=VLOOKUP(B10,$E$13:$F$18,2,TRUE

	Customer	Revenue	Future Discount			
10	SpringBoard	550000	20%			
11	LaFrenier Sons Septic	503500	20%			
12	myexcelonline.com	18699	1%			
13	California Blazing Chile Farms	28355	1%			
14	Cambia Factor	4860	0%			
15	All Systems Go Consulting	123750	10%			
16	Vertex42	201250	10%			
17	Mary Maids	255750	15%			
18	leanexcelbooks.com	328250	15%			
19	MN Excel Consulting	444050	15%			

Lookup Table

Sales	Discount
0	0%
10000	1%
50000	5%
100000	10%
250000	15%
500000	20%

Caution: When you are using the "True" version of VLOOKUP, your table has to be sorted ascending. Many people believe that all lookup tables have to be sorted. But a table needs to be sorted only in the case of doing an approximate match.

What if your manager wants a completely self-contained formula and does not want to see the bonus table off to the right? After building the formula, you can embed the table right into the formula.

Put the formula in Edit mode by double-clicking the cell or by selecting the cell and pressing F2.

Using the cursor, select the entire second argument: $E$13:$F$18.

Discount

=VLOOKUP(B10,$E$13:$F$18,2,TRUE)

VLOOKUP(lookup_value, **table_array**, col_index_num, [rar

Press the F9 key. Excel will embed the lookup table as an array constant. In the array constant, a semicolon indicates a new row, and a comma indicates a new column.

P(B10,{0,0;10000,0.01;50000,0.05;100000,0.1;250000,0.15;500000,0.2},:

Press Enter. Copy the formula down to the other cells.

You can now delete the table. The final formula is shown below.

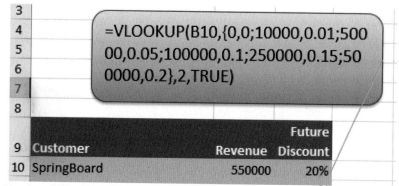

=VLOOKUP(B10,{0,0;10000,0.01;500 00,0.05;100000,0.1;250000,0.15;50 0000,0.2},2,TRUE)

	Customer	Revenue	Future Discount
10	SpringBoard	550000	20%

Thanks to Mike Girvin for teaching me about the matching parentheses. The VLOOKUP technique was suggested by Danny Mac, Boriana Petrova, Andreas Thehos, and @mvmcos.

#33 Speed Up VLOOKUP

VLOOKUP is a relatively expensive function. When you are looking for an exact match, Excel has to look through the lookup table one row at a time.

The workbook that I am using today is doing 7000 VLOOKUPs into a table of 116,000 items. On a really fast 64-bit machine with 8 cores, the recalc time is 3.01 seconds.

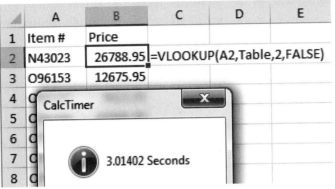

One way to improve VLOOKUP is to move the best-selling items to the top of the lookup table. Get a report of the top 100 best-selling items and move those items to the top of the list. Sorting by popularity improves the recalc time to 0.369 seconds. This is eight times faster than the first result.

But there is a way to speed things up even more. As you are building your VLOOKUP, when you get to the fourth argument to choose False, there is another option that is hardly ever used. Excel says "True" does an "approximate match." This is not at all correct. If the Excel team were being honest, they would explain that True "provides a correct answer a lot of the time, but other times, without any warning, we are going to slip the wrong answer in there. I hope you don't mind restating your numbers to the Securities and Exchange Commission."

Sure, there is a proper time to use True. See "#32 Replace Nested IFs with a Lookup Table" on page 114. But it would be really bad to use True when you are trying to do an exact match.

If you try to use True for an exact match, you will get the right answer a lot of the time. But when the item you are looking for is not in the table, Excel will give you the value from a different row. This is the part that makes "True" a non-starter for everyone in Accounting. Close is never correct in Accounting.

Note: I learned the following trick from Charles Williams. He is the world's foremost expert on worksheet speed. If you have a slow workbook, hire Charles Williams for a half day of consulting. He can find the bottlenecks and make your worksheet faster. Find Charles at http://www.decisionmodels.com.

While I and all accountants reject the "True" argument of VLOOKUP because of the unpredictability, Charles Williams argues for True. He points out the True is much faster than False. Hundreds of times faster. He concedes that sometimes you get the wrong answer. But he has a way to deal with the wrong answers.

Charles actually wants you to do two VLOOKUPs. First, do a VLOOKUP and return column 1 from the table. See if the result is what you were looking up in the first place. If that result matches, then you know it is safe to do the *real* VLOOKUP in order to return some other column from the table:

=IF(VLOOKUP(A2,Table,1,True)=A2,"All is good","The Answer will be wrong")

On the face of it, this seems insane. To use Charles' method, you have to do twice as many VLOOKUPs. But, when you time the calculation time for this method, it is 35 times faster than the normal VLOOKUP.

1

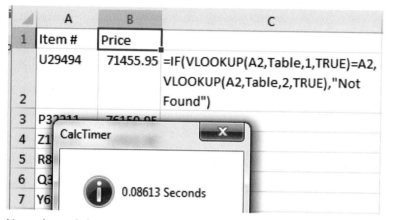

Note that while most lookup tables do not have to be sorted, when you are using True as the fourth argument, the table does have to be sorted. For a 7-minute discussion of how the True version of VLOOKUP hops through the lookup table, see http://mrx.cl/TrueVLOOKUP.

Thanks to Charles Williams for teaching me this feature and to Scott St. Amant for nominating it for a top 40 tip.

Chad Thomas

#34 Protect All Formula Cells

Worksheet protection in Excel is a little strange to use. Using the steps below, you can quickly protect just the formula cells in your worksheet.

It seems unusual, but all 16 billion cells on the worksheet start out with their Locked property set to True. You need to unlock all of the cells first.

1. Select all cells by using the icon above and to the left of cell A1.

2. Press Ctrl+1 (that is the number 1) to open the Format Cells dialog.

3. In the Format Cells dialog, go to the Protection tab. Uncheck the Locked status. Click OK.

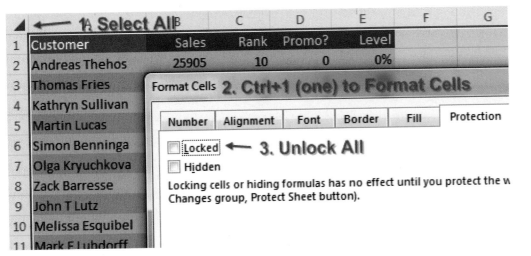

While all cells are still selected, select Home, Find & Select, Formulas.

At this point, only the formula cells are selected. Press Ctrl+1 again to display Format Cells. On the Protection tab, choose Locked to lock all of the formula cells.

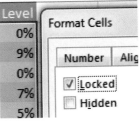

But locking cells does nothing until you protect the worksheet. On the Review tab, choose Protect Sheet. In the Protect Sheet dialog, choose if you want people to be able to select your formula cells or not. Don't bother putting in a password. Passwords are easily broken and easily lost. You will find yourself paying $39 to the Estonians who sell the Office password-cracking software.

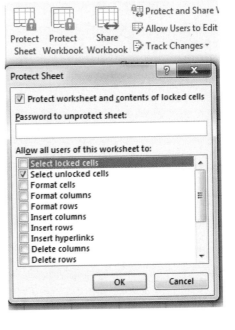

#35 Back into an Answer Using Goal Seek

Do you remember in "#27 Discover New Functions Using fx" on page 94, when I showed you how to calculate a loan payment using the Insert Function dialog? Back in that example, the monthly loan payment was going to be $493.54. I did not mention it at the time, but my monthly budget for car payments is $425.

If you are about the same age as me, and spent your summers watching TV, you might remember a crazy game show called *The Price Is Right*. Long before Drew Carey, the venerable Bob Barker would give away prizes using a variety of games. One that I recall is the Higher/Lower game. Bob would give you the car if you could state the price of the car. You would guess. Bob would shout Higher or Lower. I think you had 20 seconds to narrow your guesses to the exact price.

A lot of times, I feel like those summers watching Bob Barker trained me to find answers in Excel. Have you ever found yourself plugging in successively higher and lower values into an input cell, hoping to arrive at a certain answer?

1

	A	B	C	D	E
1	Goal Seek on the Price is Right TV Show				
3	Principal	Term	Rate	Payment	Bob Barker
4	25995	60	5.25%	$493.54	Lower!
5	20000	60	5.25%	$379.72	Higher!
6	23000	60	5.25%	$436.68	Lower!
7	21500	60	5.25%	$408.20	Higher!
8	22300	60	5.25%	$423.39	Higher!
9	22700	60	5.25%	$430.98	Lower!
10	22500	60	5.25%	$427.18	Lower!
11	22400	60	5.25%	$425.29	Lower!
12	22390	60	5.25%	$425.10	Lower!
13	22380	60	5.25%	$424.91	Higher!
14	22385	60	5.25%	$425.00	Winner!

Illustration: Chad Thomas

A tool that is built in to Excel that does exactly this set of steps. On the Data tab, in the Data Tools group, look for the What-If Analysis dropdown and choose Goal Seek.

Below, you are trying to set the payment in B5 to $425 by changing cell B1

	A	B	C
1	Principal	25995	
2	Term	60	
3	Rate	5.25%	
4			
5	Payment	**$493.54**	
6			
7			
8			
9			
10			
11			

Goal Seek

Set cell: B5
To value: 425
By changing cell: $B$1

OK   Cancel

Goal Seek finds the correct answer within a second.

	A	B	C
1	Principal	22384.9	
2	Term	60	
3	Rate	5.25%	
4			
5	Payment	$425.00	
6			
7			
8			
9			
10			
11			

Goal Seek Status

Goal Seeking with Cell B5 found a solution.

Target value: 425
Current value: $425.00

Step

Pause

OK   Cancel

Note that the formula in B5 stays intact. The only thing that changes is the input value typed in to B1.

Also, with Goal Seek, you are free to experiment with changing other input cells. You can still get the $425 loan payment and the $25,995 car if your banker will offer you a 71.3379-month loan!

	A	B
1	Principal	25995
2	Term	71.3379
3	Rate	5.25%
4		
5	Payment	$425.00

Thanks to Jon Wittwer of Vertex42.com and to @BizNetSoftware for suggesting Goal Seek.

#36 Do 60 What-If Analyses with a Data Table

Goal Seek lets you find the set of inputs that lead to a particular result. Sometimes, you want to see many different results from various combinations of inputs. Provided that you have only two input cells to change, the data table provides a fast way to compare alternatives.

Using the loan payment example, say that you want to calculate the price for a variety of principal balances and for a variety of terms.

▲	A	B	C	D	E	F
1	Principal	25995	Test from $20,995 to $29,995			
2	Term	60	Test from 36 to 72			
3	Rate	5.25%				
4						
5	Payment	$494				

Make sure that the formula you want to model is in the top-left corner of a range. Put various values for one variable down the left column and various values for another variable across the top.

B5	▼	⋮	✕	✓	*fx*	=PMT(B3/12,B2,-B1)		

▲	A	B	C	D	E	F	G	H
5	Payment	$494	36	48	54	60	66	72
6		20,995						
7		21,995						
8		22,995						

From the Data tab, select What-If Analysis, data table.

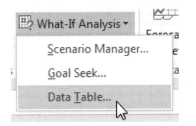

You have values along the top row of the input table. You want Excel to plug those values into a certain input cell. Specify that input cell as the Row Input Cell.

You have values along the left column. You want those plugged into another input cell. Specify that cell as the Column Input Cell.

▲	A	B	C	D	E	F	G
1	Principal	25995	Test from $20,995 to $29,995				
2	Term	60	Test from 36 to 72				
3	Rate	5.25%					
4							
5	Payment	$494	36	48	54	60	
6		20995					
7		21995					
8		22995					
9		23995					
10		24995					
11		25995					

Data Table

Row input cell: $B$2

Column input cell: $B$1

[OK]   [Cancel]

When you click OK, Excel will repeat the formula in the top-left column for all combinations of the top row and left column. In the image below, you see 60 different loan payments based on various results.

$494	36	48	54	60	66	72
20,995	632	486	437	399	367	341
21,995	662	509	458	418	384	357
22,995	692	532	479	437	402	373
23,995	722	555	500	456	419	389
24,995	752	578	521	475	437	405
25,995	782	602	542	494	454	422
26,995	812	625	562	513	472	438
27,995	842	648	583	532	489	454
28,995	872	671	604	550	507	470
29,995	902	694	625	569	524	487

Note that I formatted the table results to have no decimals and used Home, Conditional Formatting, Color Scale to add the red/yellow/green shading.

Here is the great part: This table is "live." If you change the input cells along the left column or top row, the values in the table will recalculate. Below, the values along the left are focused on the $23K to $24K range.

$494	48	51	54	57	60	63
22,995	532	504	479	457	437	418
23,095	534	506	481	459	438	420
23,195	537	508	483	461	440	422
23,295	539	511	485	463	442	424
23,395	541	513	487	465	444	426

Thanks to Owen W. Green for suggesting tables.

Bonus Tip: data table from a Blank Cell

Note: If you took a class on financial modeling in college, you likely used a textbook written by Professor Simon Benninga. I met Simon twice, when we were judges for the ModelOff World Financial Modeling Championships. He truly enjoyed what he was doing and showed me this cool Excel trick.

Simon Benninga tells a story of two illegal pastimes when he was attending private school in New York. The first was smoking in the bathroom. The second was a game called Penny Pitching. You and another student would each flip a penny. If you get one head and one tail, you win the penny. If the coins match (heads/heads or tails/tails), the other student gets the penny.

It is simple to model this game in Excel. If RAND()>.5, you win a penny. Otherwise, you lose a penny. Do that for 25 rows and chart the result. Press F9 to play 25 more rounds.

This is known as a Random Walk Down Wall Street. Simon would always point out a result like this one, where a hot young stock analyst is on fire with a series of wins, but then a series of losses wipe out the gain. This is why most investment prospectuses point out that past results are not a guarantee of future returns.

| B4 | | | × | ✓ | f_x | =IF(RAND()>0.5,1,-1)+B3 |

	A	B	C	D	E	F	G
1	Round						
2	1	1					
3	2	2		25 ROUNDS OF PENNY PITCHING			
4	3	3					
5	4	2					
6	5	3					
7	6	2					
8	7	1					
9	8	0					
10	9	-1					

Instead of 25 trials, extend your table in A and B to run 250 trials. This would be like playing one round of penny pitching every work day for a year. Build a row of statistics about that year:

| | ✓ | f_x | =MAX(B2:B251) |

	G	H	I	J	K	L
	Max	Min	Average	Win Streak	Lose Streak	Final
	3	-30	-14.7	6	8	-30

Create an odd data table where the blank cell in column F is the corner cell. Leave the Row Input Cell blank. Specify any blank cell as the Column Input Cell.

	E	F	G	H	I	J
13			Max	Min	Average	Win St
14			3	-30	-14.7	
15						
16			Data Table		? X	
17						
18			Row input cell:			
19			Column input cell: $E$13			
20						
21			OK	Cancel		

When you create the table, Excel will run the 250 coin flips once per row. This 30-row table models the entire career of a stock analyst. Every time you press F9, Excel runs the 250-row model for each of 30 years. You can watch an entire 30-year career be modeled with the simple press of F9.

	G	H	I	J	K	L
13	Max	Min	Average	Win Streak	Lose Streak	Final
14	2	-16	-5.412	6	9 ▼	-12
15	3	-26	-14.028	5	6 ▼	-22
16	21	-5	6.772	12	7 ▲	+14
44	19	-3	9.78	12	7 ▬	0

Thanks to Professor Simon Benninga for showing me this technique. He had a chance to review this book just before he lost a battle to cancer in 2015. I trust he is in a better place - one where Pivot Tables don't default to Compact Form!

#37 Find Optimal Solutions with Solver

Excel was not the first spreadsheet program. Lotus 1-2-3 was not the first spreadsheet program. The first spreadsheet program was VisiCalc in 1979. Developed by Dan Bricklin and Bob Frankston, VisiCalc was published by Dan Fylstra. Today, Dan runs Frontline Systems. His company wrote the Solver used in Excel. It has also developed a whole suite of analytics software that works with Excel.

If you have Excel, you have Solver. It may not be enabled, but you have it. To enable Solver in Excel, press Alt+T followed by I. Add a checkmark next to Solver.

To successfully use Solver you have to build a worksheet model that has three elements:

- There has to be a single Goal cell. This is a cell that you either want to minimize, maximize, or set to a particular value.

- There can be many input cells. This is one fundamental improvement over Goal Seek, which can only deal with one input cell.

- There can be constraints.

Your goal is to build the scheduling requirements for an amusement park. Each employee will work five straight days and then have two days off. There are seven different possible ways to schedule someone for five straight days and two off days. These are shown as text in A4:A10. The blue cells in B4:B10 are the input cells. This is where you specify how many people you have working each schedule.

The Goal cell is total Payroll per Week, shown in B17. This is straight math: Total People from B11 times $68 salary per person per day. You will ask Solver to find a way to minimize the weekly payroll.

The red box shows values that will not change. This is how many people you need working the park on each day of the week. You need at least 30 people on the busy weekend days – but as few as 12 on Monday and Tuesday. The orange cells use SUMPRODUCT to calculate how many people will be scheduled each day based on the inputs in the blue cells.

The icons in row 15 indicate whether you need more people, or fewer people or whether you have exactly the right number of people.

First, I tried to solve this without Solver. I went with 4 employees each day. That was great, but I did not have enough people on Sunday. So, I started increasing schedules that would give me more Sunday employees. I ended up with something that works: 38 employees and $2,584 of weekly payroll.

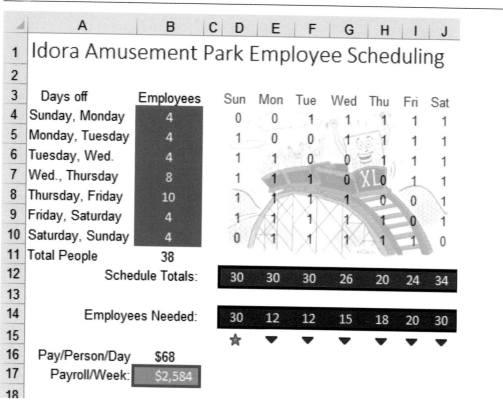

Idora Amusement Park Employee Scheduling

Days off	Employees	Sun	Mon	Tue	Wed	Thu	Fri	Sat
Sunday, Monday	4	0	0	1	1	1	1	1
Monday, Tuesday	4	1	0	0	1	1	1	1
Tuesday, Wed.	4	1	1	0	0	1	1	1
Wed., Thursday	8	1	1	1	0	0	1	1
Thursday, Friday	10	1	1	1	1	0	0	1
Friday, Saturday	4	1	1	1	1	1	0	1
Saturday, Sunday	4	0	1	1	1	1	1	0
Total People	38							
Schedule Totals:		30	30	30	26	20	24	34
Employees Needed:		30	12	12	15	18	20	30
Pay/Person/Day	$68							
Payroll/Week:	$2,584							

Click the Solver icon on the Data tab. Tell Solver that you are trying to set the payroll in B17 to the minimum. The input cells are B4:B10.

Constraints fall into obvious and not-so-obvious categories.

The first obvious constraint is that D12:J12 has to be >= D14:J14.

But, if you tried to run Solver now, you would get bizarre results where you have fractional numbers of people and possibly a negative number of people working certain schedules.

While it seems obvious to you that you can't hire 0.39 people, you need to add constraints to tell Solver that B4:B10 are >= 0 and that B4:B10 are integers.

Solver Parameters

Set Objective: $B$17

To: ○ Max ◉ Min ○ Value Of:

By Changing Variable Cells:

$B$4:$B$10

Subject to the Constraints:

$D$12:$J$12 >= $D$14:$J$14
$B$4:$B$10 = integer
$B$4:$B$10 >= 0

Choose Simplex LP as the solving method and choose Solve. In a few moments, Solver presents one optimal solution.

Solver found a way to cover the amusement park staffing using 30 employees instead of 38. The savings per week is $544 – or more than $7,000 over the course of the summer.

Idora Amusement Park Employee Scheduling

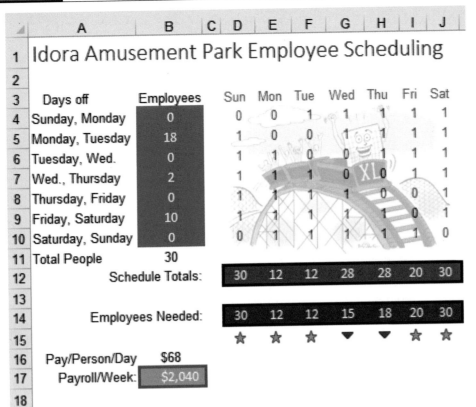

Days off	Employees		Sun	Mon	Tue	Wed	Thu	Fri	Sat
Sunday, Monday	0		0	0	1	1	1	1	1
Monday, Tuesday	18		1	0	0	1	1	1	1
Tuesday, Wed.	0		1	1	0	0	1	1	1
Wed., Thursday	2		1	1	1	0	0	1	1
Thursday, Friday	0		1	1	1	1	0	0	1
Friday, Saturday	10		1	1	1	1	1	0	1
Saturday, Sunday	0		0	1	1	1	1	1	0
Total People	30								
Schedule Totals:			30	12	12	28	28	20	30
Employees Needed:			30	12	12	15	18	20	30
			★	★	★	▼	▼	★	★
Pay/Person/Day	$68								
Payroll/Week:	$2,040								

Notice the five stars below Employees Needed. The schedule that Solver proposed meets your exact needs for five of the seven days. The byproduct is that you will have more employees on Wednesday and Thursday than you really need.

I can understand how Solver came up with this solution. You need a lot of people on Saturday, Sunday, and Friday. One way to get people there on those day is to give them Monday and Tuesday off. That is why Solver put 18 people with Monday and Tuesday off.

But just because Solver came up with an optimal solution does not mean that there are not other equally optimal solutions.

When I was just guessing at the staffing, I didn't really have a good strategy.

Now that Solver has given me one of the optimal solutions, I can put on my logic hat. Having 28 college-age employees on Wednesday and Thursday when you only need 15 or 18 employees is going to lead to trouble. There won't be enough to do. Plus, with exactly the right headcount on five days, you will have to call in someone for overtime if someone else calls in sick.

I trust Solver that I need to have 30 people to make this work. But I bet that I can rearrange those people to even out the schedule and provide a small buffer on other days.

For example, giving someone Wednesday and Thursday off also ensures that the person is at work Friday, Saturday, and Sunday. So, I manually moved some workers from the Monday, Tuesday row to the Wednesday Thursday row. I kept manually plugging in different combinations and came up with this solution which has the same payroll expense as Solver but better intangibles. The overstaff situation now exists on four days instead of two. That means you can handle call-offs on Monday through Thursday without having to call in someone from their weekend.

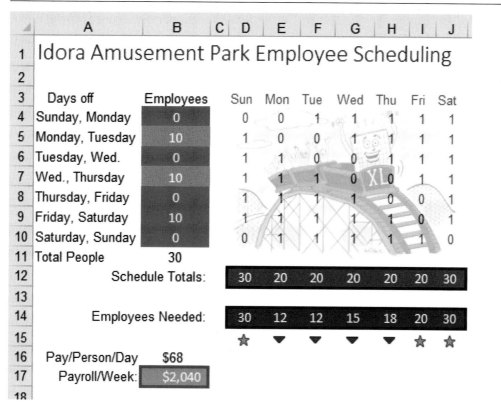

Is it bad that I was able to come up with a better solution than Solver? No. The fact is that I would not have been able to get to this solution without using Solver. Once Solver gave me a model that minimized costs, I was able to use logic about intangibles to keep the same payroll.

If you need to solve problems more complex than Solver can handle, check out the premium Excel solvers available from Frontline Systems: http://mrx.cl/solver77.

Thanks to Dan Fylstra and Frontline Systems for this example. Walter Moore illustrated the XL roller coaster.

#38 Load a File List into Excel with Power Query

Power Query is built in to Excel 2016 and is available as a free download in certain versions of Excel 2010

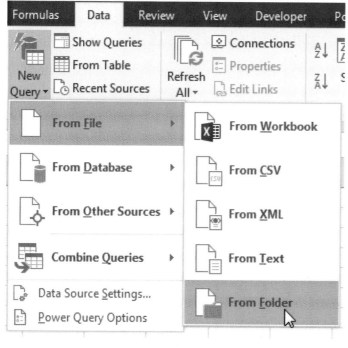

and Excel 2013. The tool is designed to extract, transform and load data into Excel from a variety of sources. The best part: Power Query remembers your steps and will play them back when you want to refresh the data. As this book goes to press, the Power Query features in Excel 2016 are on the Data tab, in the Get & Transform group, under New Query. It is hard to predict whether Microsoft will retroactively rename Power Query to Get & Transform in Excel 2010 and Excel 2013.

This free add-in is so amazing, there could be a whole book about it. But as one of my top 40 tips, I want to cover something very simple: bringing a list of files into Excel, along with the file creation date and maybe size. This is useful for creating a list of budget workbooks or a list of photos.

In Excel 2016, you select Data, New Query, From File, From Folder. In earlier Excel versions, use Power Query, From File, From Folder. Specify the folder:

Folder

Choose a folder.

Folder Path

| ents\All Holy Macros\All Holy Macros\MrExcelXL\Images | Browse... |

While editing the query, right-click any columns that you don't want and choose Remove.

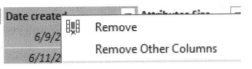

To get File Size, click this icon in the Attributes column:

A large list of Transform options are available.

When you are done editing the query, click Close & Load.

A list of extra attributes appears. Choose Size.

- ☐ ReadOnly
- ☐ ReparsePoin
- ☑ Size
- ☐ SparseFile
- ☐ System

The data loads to Excel as a table.

	A	B	C
1	Name	Date created	Copy of Date created
2	XLFig223.png	0	6:54:53 AM
3	XLFig224.png	0	6:56:38 AM
4	XLFig225.png	0	6:57:18 AM
5	XLFig226.png	0	6:57:51 AM

Later, to update the table, select Data, Refresh All. Excel remembers all the steps and updates the table with a current list of files in the folder.

For a complete description of the feature formerly known as Power Query, check out *M is for (Data) Monkey* by Ken Puls and Miguel Escobar.

Thanks to Miguel Escobar, Rob Garcia, Mike Girvin, Ray Hauser and Colin Michael for nominating Power Query.

#39 Pivot Table on a Map Using 3D Maps

3D Maps (née Power Map) is available in the Office 365 versions of Excel 2013 and all versions of Excel 2016. Using 3D Maps, you can build a pivot table on a map. You can fly through your data and animate the data over time.

3D Maps lets you see five dimensions: latitude, longitude, color, height, and time. Using it is a fascinating way to visualize large data sets.

3D Maps can work with simple one-sheet data sets or with multiple tables added to the Data Model. Select the data. Choose Insert, 3D Maps.

3D Map ▾
Tours

Next, you need to choose which fields are your geography fields. This could be Country, State, County, Zip Code, or even individual street addresses.

GEOGRAPHY
Map by Address (Street)

You are given a list of fields in your data the drop zones HEIGHT, CATEGORY, and TIME.

HEIGHT
Amt (No Aggregation)

CATEGORY
Allotment

TIME
Date (None)

Here is a map of Merritt Island, Florida. The various colors are different housing allotments. Each colored dot on the map is a house with a dock, either on a river or one of many canals dredged out in the 1960s and 1970s.

Using the time slider, you can go back in time to any point. Here is when NASA landed the first man on the Moon. The NASA engineers had just started building waterfront homes a few miles south of Kennedy Space Center.

Use the wheel mouse to scroll in. You can actually see individual streets, canals, and driveways.

Hold down the Alt key and drag sideways to rotate the map. Hold down the Alt key and drag up to tip the map so your view is closer to the ground.

Hover over any point on the map to get details such as last sale date and amount.

In the default state of Power Map, each data point occupies about one city block. To be able to plot many houses on a street, use the Gear Wheel, Layer Options and change the thickness of the point to 10%.

To get the satellite imagery, open the Themes dropdown and use the second theme.

The 3D Maps feature provides a completely new way to look at your data. It is hard to believe that this is Excel.

By the way, my thanks to Tony Giannotti at Serving Brevard Realty for showing me many of the houses in this area. If you need a house near Merritt Island, give Tony a call.

Thanks to Igor Peev and Scott Ruble at Microsoft for this cool new feature.

1

Illustration: Libby Norcross

#40 Avoid Whiplash with Speak Cells

I hate having to hand-key data into Excel. Between the Internet and Power Query, there almost always is a way to find the data somewhere. I hate when people send a PDF where they scanned some numbers and are sending the numbers as a picture. But even then, a free trial of Able2Extract Pro (http://mrx.cl/ ExtractPDF) will get the actual number into Excel. Even so, sometimes, you end up keying data into Excel.

One of the painful parts about keying in data is that you have to proofread the numbers. So, you are looking at the sheet of paper, then the screen, then the paper, then the screen. You will end up with a sore neck. Wouldn't it be nice if you had someone to read you the screen so you can keep your eye on the paper? It's built in to Excel.

Right-click on the Quick Access Toolbar and choose Customize Quick Access Toolbar.

Change the top-left dropdown to Commands Not in the Ribbon. Scroll down to the S entries until you find Speak Cells. Add all five of these commands to the Quick Access Toolbar

Customize the Quick Access Toolbar.

Choose commands from: ⓘ   **1**

All Commands

🔊	Speak Cells
🔊⊗	Speak Cells - Stop Speaking Cells
⬍	Speak Cells by Columns
⬌	Speak Cells by Rows
🔊	Speak Cells on Enter
ABC	Spelling...

Select your range of numbers and click Speak Cells. Excel will read you the numbers.

	A	B	C
1	Name	Amount	
2	David Gainer	$7,936,245.18	
3	Derek Brown	$2,349,561.78	
4	Roger Govier	$6,185,972.34	
5	James N Johnson	$4,789,156.32	
6	Edwin Deo	$5,943,286.71	
7	Emily Mathews	$6,852,479.31	
8	Jonathan Hepplewhite	$6,581,372.94	
9	Lynda Maynard	$4,253,861.97	
10	Arly Hansen	$6,327,851.49	

Tip: You can customize the voice in the Windows Control Panel. Search for Tex to Speech. There is a setting for Voice Speed. Drag that slider to half way between Normal and Fast to have the voice read your cells faster.

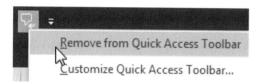

Bonus Tip: A Great April Fool's Day Trick

Do you want a harmless prank to pull on a co-worker? When he leaves his leave their desk to grab a cup of coffee, add the fifth icon to his Quick Access Toolbar: Speak Cells on Enter. Click the icon once and the computer will say, "Cells will now be spoken on Enter."

Once you've turned on Speak Cells on Enter, right-click the icon in the Quick Access Toolbar and choose Remove from Quick Access Toolbar. This will hide any sign that you were there.

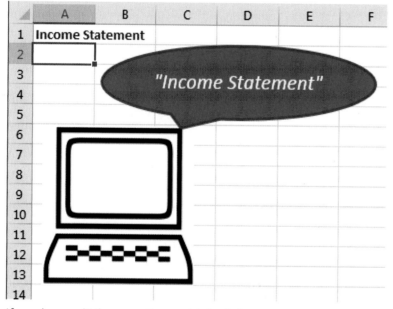

Your co-worker comes back, sits down, and starts to build a worksheet. The computer will repeat back everything the co-worker types.

If you have a little more time, add the following macro to the code pane for the current worksheet. Speak Cells on Enter with attitude:

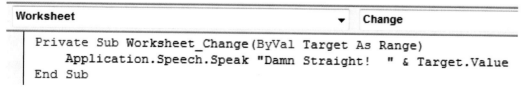

```
Private Sub Worksheet_Change(ByVal Target As Range)
    Application.Speech.Speak "Damn Straight!  " & Target.Value
End Sub
```

If only you could get the voice to be Nichelle Nichols, it would be perfect.

Part 2 - 40 Keyboard Shortcuts

As I started polling readers about their favorite Excel tips, a large number of those were keyboard short-cuts. Some readers, such as Matt Kellett, Olga Kryuchkova, Mike Dolan Fliss, and @model_citizen suggested that one of the 40 best tips has to be keyboard short cuts.

These are presented in order of popularity. If a lot of readers suggested a tip, it is at the top. After the first eight or so, they are then sorted by my subjective sequence.

1. Ctrl+1 to Format the Selection

Ctrl+1 (the number one) works to format whatever is selected. Whether it is a cell, Smart Art, a picture, a

shape, or the March data point in a column chart, press Ctrl+1.

Thanks to Mitja Bezenšek, Alexa Gardner, Andrej Lapajne, Schmuel Oluwa, Jon Peltier, @ExcelNewss, @JulianExcelTips

2. Ctrl[+Shift]+Arrow to Navigate or Select

Your cell pointer is sitting at the top of 50K rows of data and you need to get to the bottom. If you have a

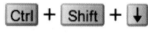

column with no blanks, press Ctrl+Down Arrow to jump to the end of the data set.

In the following figure, Ctrl+Down Arrow will jump to K545. Ctrl+Left Arrow will jump to A1. Ctrl+Right Arrow will jump the gap of empty cells and land on N1.

	A	B	J	K	L	M	N
1	data	data	data	data			other
2	data	data	data	data			other
3	data	data	data	data			other
4	data	data	data	data			other
544	data	data	data	data			other
545	data	data	data	data			other
546							

Add the Shift key in order to select from the active cell to the landing cell. Starting from A1 in the above figure, press Ctrl+Shift+Down Arrow to select A1:A545. While still holding down Ctrl+Shift, press the right arrow to select A1:K545. If it seems awkward at first, try it for a few days until you get the hang of it.

Thanks to Captain Excel, @Cintellis, José de Diego, Mike Girvin, Elchin Khalilov, Crystal Long, Paul Sasur, @XLStudioWorks.

3. Ctrl+. to Jump to Next Corner

Once you have a large range selected, press Ctrl+Period to move to the next corner of the selection. If the selection is rectangular, you move in a clockwise fashion. From the bottom right corner, press Ctrl+. twice to move to the top left.

Thanks to Crystal Long, Steve McCready

4. Ctrl+5 for Strikethrough

This is great for crossing things off your to-do list.

5. Ctrl+* to Select Current Region

This one is easier if you have a number keypad so you don't have to press shift to get to an asterisk. If I could slow down enough to stop pressing Ctrl+Shift+Down Arrow followed by Ctrl+Shift+Right arrow, I would realize that Ctrl+* is much shorter and does not get tripped up by blank cells. It is really superior in every way to keyboard tip #2. But my muscle memory still prefers tip #2. Thanks to @Excelforo

6. Ctrl+Enter to Copy Formula into Entire Selection

Ken Puls, who is the king of Power Query, says, "You would think my favorite Excel tip would be Unpivot with Power Query, but my favorite all-time is Ctrl+Enter." Say that you want to enter a formula into 400 cells. Select the 400 cells. Type the formula in the first cell. Press Ctrl+Enter and Excel enters a similar formula in all cells of the selection.

Gavin White points out another use. You enter a formula in G2. You need to copy the formula down but not the formatting. Select G2:G20. Press the F2 key to put the cell in Edit mode. When you press Ctrl+Enter, the formula is copied but not any formatting. Thanks to Crystal Long, Schmuel Oluwa, Ken Puls, Peter Raiff, Sven Simon, Gavin Whyte.

7. Date or Time Stamp

Press Ctrl+Shift+: to enter the current time. Press Ctrl+; for the current date. Note the shortcut enters the *current* time, not a formula. Thanks to Olga Kryuchkova, Tim O'Mara

8. Ctrl+Backspace to Bring the Active Cell into View

This is a great trick that I never knew. Say that C1 is the active cell. You've used the scroll bars and now you are looking at ZZ999. To bring the window back to encompass the active cell, press Ctrl+Backspace. Thanks to Olga Kryuchkova, Schmuel Oluwa.

9. Alt+= is AutoSum

Press Alt+= to invoke the AutoSum function. Thanks to Dawn Bjork Buzbee, Olga Kryuchkova

10. Ctrl+PageDown and Ctrl+PageUp to Jump to Next Worksheet

If you need to move from Sheet1 to Sheet5, press Ctrl+PageDown four times. If you are at Sheet9 and need to move to Sheet3, press Ctrl+PageUp six times. Thanks to Jeneta Hot.

11. Use Ctrl+Click to Select Noncontiguous Cells

If you have to select two regions, select the first one, then hold down Ctrl while clicking on other cells or regions. – Thomas Fries

12. Tab to AutoComplete

This one is maddening. You type =VL to start VLOOKUP. The AutoComplete shows there is only one function that starts with VL. But if you press Enter, you will get a #NAME? error.

`=vl`

VLOOKUP

The correct way to choose VLOOKUP is to press Tab! Thanks to Ashish Agarwal.

13. Press Shift+F8 for Add to Selection

Select the first range. Press Shift+F8 and you are in Add to Selection mode. Scroll anywhere. Select the next range. Then another range. And so on, without ever touching Ctrl. To return to normal, press Esc. - Neil Charles. A bonus tip from Bill Hazlett: if you select A1, press F8, then click in S20 you will select from A1:S20.

14. Select Entire Column or Row

Ctrl+Spacebar selects the whole column. Shift+Spacebar selects the whole row. How can you remember which is which? The "C" in Ctrl stands for the "C" in column. Also, the "S" in Shift is adjacent in the alphabet to the "R" in Row. Another way to remember which is which: the Shift key is much longer (like a row!) than Ctrl.

Thanks to Michael Byrne, Jeneta Hot, and Bob Umlas.

15. See All Formulas with Ctrl+`

Many folks in the United States think this is Ctrl+~, but it is actually the grave accent to toggle into and out of Show Formulas mode.

16. F3 to Paste a Name into a Formula

I am not a huge fan of this, since you can start typing the name and then choose from AutoComplete. But I know the trick has its fans, include Mike Girvin and Johan van den Brink.

17. Apply Number Format using Ctrl+Shift+1 through 6

I had never memorized these, but I am going to start using some of them. Ctrl+Shift+1 (also known as Ctrl+!), will apply a number format, 2 decimals, thousands separator, and negatives shown with a minus sign. The other five make some reasonable sense, with Ctrl+% doing percentages, Ctrl+@ doing time, Ctrl+$ doing currency, Ctrl+^ doing exponential.

Thanks to Matthew Bernath.

Key	AKA	Formats as	Example
Ctrl+Shift+1	!	Number	-1,234.56
Ctrl+Shift+2	@	Time	2:50 PM
Ctrl+Shift+3	#	Date	29-Jun-15
Ctrl+Shift+4	$	Currency	($1,234.56)
Ctrl+Shift+5	%	Percent	100%
Ctrl+Shift+6	^	Exponential	1.23E+08

18. Control Word Wrap with Alt+Enter

To move to a new row in the current cell, press Alt+Enter. Isn't this the same as turning on Word Wrap? Sort of, but Alt+Enter lets you control where the words wrap. - Olga Kryuchkova

19. Ctrl+[to jump to Linked Cell

You are in a cell that points to Sheet99!Z1000. Press Ctrl+[to jump to that cell. This even works if you have links between workbooks, even if the other workbook is closed! - @Heffa100 with Bob Umlas

20. Alt+F1 Charts the Selected Data

Select some data. Press Alt+F1. You get a chart of the data. You might remember F11 doing the same thing. But F11 creates the chart as a chart sheet. Alt+F1 embeds the chart in the current sheet.

21. Shift+F11 inserts a Worksheet

I never knew this one, but it makes sense as a corollary to F11. If F11 inserted a chart sheet, then Shift+F11 inserted a new worksheet. You can also use Alt+I, W to insert a worksheet, Alt+I, R to insert a row or Alt+I, C to insert a column. - Olga Kryuchkova.

22. Alt+E, S, V to Paste Special Values

I can do Alt+E, S, V Enter with my eyes closed. Alt+E opened the Excel 2003 Edit menu. S chose Paste Special. V chose Values. Enter selected OK. There are a whole series of these to learn: Alt+E, S, T pastes formats. Alt+E, S, F pastes formulas. Alt+E, S, W pastes column widths. Alt+E, S, D, V does a Paste Special Add, but does not screw up the formatting. Alt+E, S, E does a Transpose. To see all the possibilities, press Alt+E, S and then look for the underlined letters. - Matthew Bernath & Laura Lewis.

23. Change Macro Security with Alt+T, M, S. Activate Add-Ins with Alt+T, I

These are really useful now that the settings are buried deep in Excel options. – Ron de Bruin

24. Enable the Filter Dropdowns with Ctrl+Shift+L

Toggle the filters on or off with Ctrl+Shift+L. Or, press and release Alt, A, T. –David Hager, Andew Walker

25. Hold down Alt to Snap to Grid

If you are drawing any shape, Alt will cause that shape to exactly line up with the borders of cells. - Rickard Wärnelid

26. Ctrl+W Closes a Workbook but Leaves Excel Open

If you have one workbook open and you click the "X" in the top right corner, you will close Excel. Ctrl+W will close that workbook but leave Excel open. - Dave Marriott

27. Use F5 to Sneak Into a Hidden Cell

You've hidden column D, but you need to see what is in D2. Press Ctrl+G or F5 to open the Go To dialog. Type D2 and press Enter. The cell pointer moves to the hidden cell D2 and you can see the value in the formula bar. You can now use the down arrow to move within the hidden column D, always seeing the value in the formula bar.

28. Alt+D, E, F to Convert Numbers Stored as Text to Numbers

Select the whole column. Alt+D, E, F. The text numbers are converted to numbers. You are actually doing a default Text to Columns with this shortcut.

29. Alt+O, C, A to AutoFit the Column

Select some cells. Alt+OCA and the column is wide enough for the longest value in the selection.

30. Ctrl+' to Copy the Exact Formula Down (aka Ditto)

You have to sum in D10 and average in D11. Create the AutoSum in D10. When you press Enter, you are in D11. Press Ctrl+' to bring the exact formula down without changing the cell reference. If D10 is =SUM(D2:D9), the formula in D11 will also be =SUM(D2:D9).

From there, you can press F2, Home, Right, AVERAGE, Delete, Delete, Delete, Enter. It sounds crazy, but the engineers at General Electric in Cleveland swear by it.

If you use Ctrl+Shift+" it will bring the value from above into the current cell, eliminating any formula.

31. Alt+W, F, F to Freeze Panes

There are hundreds more shortcuts like this which you can easily learn. Press and release Alt in Excel to see key tips for each tab in the Ribbon (plus numbered key tips for the Quick Access Toolbar. Press the letter corresponding to a Ribbon tab to see the key tips for all of the commands on that tab. In this particular case, clicking Alt+W+F reveals a third level of key tips, so Alt+W, F, F completes the command. - Bradford Myers

32. Ctrl+C to Copy

33. Ctrl+V to Paste

34. Ctrl+X to Cut

35. Ctrl+B for Bold

36. Ctrl+I for Italics

37. Ctrl+U for Underline

38. Ctrl+N for New Workbook

39. Ctrl+T (or Ctrl+L) to Format as Table

40. Never Forget to Right-click

So many timesavers that are linked to the right mouse button that people forget about. – Colin Foster

Hey! This is not a keyboard shortcut! But wait…it is. You can open that right-click menu using the Program key on the bottom right side of your keyboard. Release the Program key then press any underlined letter to invoke the command. Program key, L will invoke the new Excel 2016 Smart Lookup.

Part 3 - Excel 30 Anniversary Tips

#1 Wingdings and Other Unsung Font Heroes

So you want some cool visuals to go on that dashboard. Conditional formatting icon sets are fun but limited.

That's pretty much it. Not much more customization possible.

Unfortunately, you can't really change color schemes, icon size, or the icons themselves. So what if you're bored with all of them?

Enter Excel's unsung font heroes. I'm looking at you, Wingdings, Wingdings 2, and Webdings. These fonts provide a great workaround for conditional formatting's limited icon set options, essentially allowing you to create your own icon sets.

There are Hundreds of Choices

First, let's explore the amazing selection of characters generated by these fonts. One quick way to do this is to create a *character map* you can use for reference. The CHAR() function is what you'll need. CHAR() takes a single argument – a number – and returns a character from your computer's internal character set that corresponds to that number. For instance, character number 65, when formatted as Arial, returns a capital letter A.

| B34 | ▾ | ⋮ | ✕ ✓ ƒx | =CHAR(A34) |

	A	B	C	D	E	F
1	*Code Num*	*Arial*	*Webdings*	*Wingdings*	*Wingdings 2*	*Wingdings 3*
31	62	>	AA	⊛	☜	↓
32	63	?	📦	✍	☞	↴
33	64	@	⚒	✎	➡	↵
34	65	A	🧰	✌	☛	↳
35	66	B	🏚	✌	☜	⤵
36	67	C	🏭	☝	☞	⤶

Supplying CHAR() with a code number, 65, and comparing results using Arial, and then four of your special unsung hero fonts.

Note: Keep in mind, that there aren't many interesting icon choices for special font sets outside the range of CHAR(33) through Char(255).

Using Special Fonts in Formulas

Now that you have a character map, you can browse through the available icons and think about which ones you might want to use for your report. Let's start with a simple report showing unit sales by product line by month.

	A	B	C	D	E	F	G
1							
8		*Jan*	*Feb*	*Mar*	*Apr*	*May*	*Jun*
9							
10	Guns	401	500	425	400	350	300
11	Germs	300	85	202	241	117	84
12	Steel	200	305	301	300	350	400
13							

Next, choose the icons you want to apply by browsing through your CHAR() character map. You can see that when you use a Webdings font, CHAR(246) will give you a cat and CHAR(33) will give you a spider. Cool!

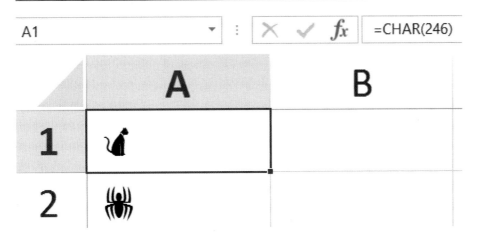

Just like with conditional formatting, you're going to need some rules to tell Excel when to display each icon. So you come up with a plan based on the notes you took in that last department meeting.

3

Dashboard notes

IF units >= 300 then
CATS

IF units >=200 then
SPIDERS

All others, blank / no icon

Note to self- delete Tweets I sent out last night after 3rd PowerPivotini

Back at your desk, you open up your report in Excel. You add some placeholder columns to the left of each month column to make room for your icons. Next, you look at those notes and translate them into Excel formulas. Recall that you want to display a *cat* for each value greater than or equal to 300, a *spider* for each value greater than or equal to 200, and no icon for all others. This sounds like a job for an IF() function. Recalling that the CHAR() codes for you chosen icons are 246 (for cats) and 33 (for spiders), you have:

```
=IF(C10>=300,CHAR(246),If(C10>=200,CHAR(33),""))
```

Note: Remember when creating nested IF() statements, you should use descending order for each logical test. Notice here that you start by testing whether your value is >=300, then you perform the >=200 test, and so on. If you don't use descending order, you will eventually get erroneous results.

Note that at this point, you are still using a "regular" style font *while you're typing* the initial formula. Of course, you're not going to see any cats or spiders as long as you are still using Arial, Verdana, or any other familiar font. But if you can wait until *after* you've constructed your formula to apply the correct font, you can avoid having to see this weird and unreadable-looking thing in B10 as you type. (Yes, you could always just look at the formula bar, but it's nice to be able to see what you are typing in-cell also.)

| B10 | ▾ | ⋮ | ✕ ✓ *fx* | =IF(C10>=300, |

	A	B	C	D	E	F	G	H
8			Jan	Feb	Mar	Apr	May	Jun
9								
10	Guns	[icons]	401	500	425	400	350	300
11	Germs	*whaaat?*	300	85	202	241	117	84
12	Steel		200	305	301	300	350	400

Finishing Touches

Now that your formula is done, you can apply the Webdings font and copy the formula to the remaining placeholder columns D, F, H, J, and L. You should also resize these columns to be narrower, since they only need to hold a single icon in each cell. 19 pixels seems about right.

| B10 | ▾ | ⋮ | ✕ ✓ *fx* | =IF(C10>=300,CHAR(246),IF(C10>=200,CHAR(33),"")) |

	A	B	C	D	E	F	G	H	I	J	K	L	M	N	O	P
1																
8			Jan		Feb		Mar		Apr		May		Jun			
9																
10	Guns	✓	401	✓	500	✓	425	✓	400	✓	350	✓	300			
11	Germs	✓	300		85	✳	202	✳	241		117		84			
12	Steel	✳	200	✓	305	✓	301	✓	300	✓	350	✓	400			

You're nearly there. Just add a report header plus a few more cosmetic finishing touches to your final report design. I like to add a left margin spacer column to the left of A. You can also:

Remove gridlines. This is often a nice choice for reports that need to have a clean look because they will be viewed on a monitor (as opposed to being viewed on old school paper only). Removing gridlines is simple. In the Home tab, Show group, uncheck the box next to Gridlines.

☑ Ruler	☑ Formula Bar
☐ Gridlines	☑ Headings

Show

Apply conditional formatting to the icons. Wait. Didn't I just spend the last two pages complaining about conditional formatting? Yes. But this has nothing to do with the conditional formatting icon sets. In this case you use conditional formatting to modify the font colors, so your cats will always be orange, and your spiders will be black.

To do this, select all the cells that contain your icons. Press the Ctrl key while you make your selections to select noncontiguous ranges. Just before you launch the conditional formatting menus, make sure you have selected all the cells where your cat and spider icons appear.

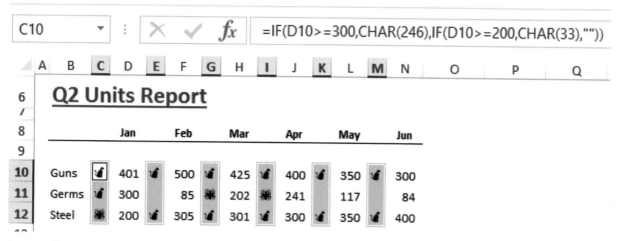

Notice that even though you're selecting multiple cells at once, Excel considers C10 your "active" cell. This becomes obvious when you glance up in the Name box. This is important to keep in mind as you create your conditional formatting rules.

With the cells still highlighted, from the Home tab, click Conditional Formatting. Click New Rule…. From the list of rule types, choose Use a Formula to Determine Which Cells to Format. Then type your rules in the rules description box. This is where you will create a logical test to determine which font colors to use. Because C10 is your "active" cell, that is the cell reference you use in your logical test formula.

New Formatting Rule

Select a Rule Type:

- ► Format all cells based on their values
- ► Format only cells that contain
- ► Format only top or bottom ranked values
- ► Format only values that are above or below average
- ► Format only unique or duplicate values
- ► **Use a formula to determine which cells to format**

Edit the Rule Description:

Format values where this formula is true:

=C10=CHAR(246)

Returns TRUE if the value in C10 equals CHAR(246). But really, the same logic will apply to all cells in your selection.

You don't want to use any absolute references in your conditional formatting formula here. You want the conditional formatting rules to apply *relatively* to each cell in your selection so Excel evaluates each cell individually and decides which format to apply, if any.

Next, you must tell Excel what kind of format to apply for each cell where the test returns TRUE. CHAR(246) gives you cats, and you love orange cats, so you choose an orange font. In the New Formatting Rule dialog, you click Format…, and choose the font color you want.

Format Cells

Number | **Font** | **Border** | **Fill**

Font:

Cambria (Headings)
Calibri (Body)
Agency FB
Aharoni
Aldhabi
Algerian

Font style:

Regular
Italic
Bold
Bold Italic

Size:

8
9
10
11
12
14

Underline:

Color:

Automatic

- Automatic

Theme Colors

Standard Colors

Orange, Accent 6, Darker 25%

Recent Colors

More Colors...

Effects

- Strikethrough
- Superscript
- Subscript

For Conditional Formatting you can set Font Style, U... h.

Clear

OK | Cancel

You click OK twice to exit all conditional formatting menus. At this point, your conditional formatting "all cats in orange" rule is done. In fact, you don't need to create a separate rule for spiders, because you are already using a standard black font.

Your report is done. Neat!

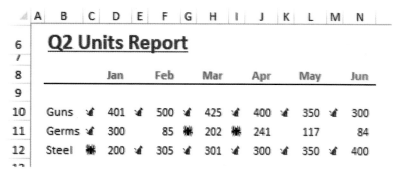

	Jan	Feb	Mar	Apr	May	Jun
Q2 Units Report						
Guns	401	500	425	400	350	300
Germs	300	85	202	241	117	84
Steel	200	305	301	300	350	400

Thanks to Olga Kryuchkova for suggesting Conditional Formatting.

#2 In-Cell Charting with REPT()

File this tip under "charts without charts." The wonder that is Excel offers many ways you can creatively display data using methods that in many cases are much faster and easier than creating and maintaining charts. One of these is a little-known function called REPT().

About REPT()

REPT() takes two arguments: text, a character to repeat, and num_times, a number that tells Excel how many times to repeat `text`. So, this formula:

```
=REPT("HAPPY BIRTHDAY, EXCEL!",4)
```

spells out the lyrics to the Happy Birthday song (You'll have to supply the melody, or just check out "Bonus Tip: A Great April Fool's Day Trick" on page 133 for the "Speak Cells" feature. Then let "Microsoft Anna" take her best stab.)

Maybe dancing is more your thing. You've had a few Jitterbug Jelens and are ready to get on the floor. Here's one for you:

REPT() for In-cell Charts

Let's see how you can use REPT as a no-charts-required data visualization technique. The trick here is to use a special character for you first argument. When that character is stacked side by side and repeated enough times, your REPT formula will basically mimic the look of a horizontal bar chart.

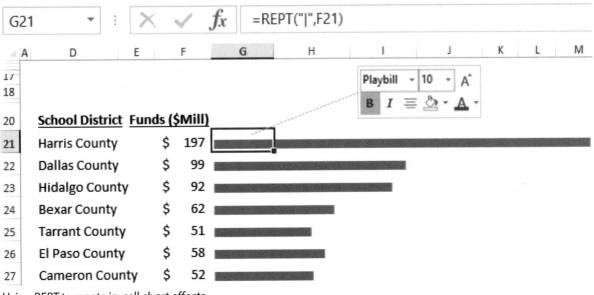

Using REPT to create in-cell chart effects

There are a couple things to notice on the previous illustration. First, notice the character you use in the first argument. It might look like a lowercase "L" but in fact it is the vertical bar character (typically on your keyboard just above the Enter key). Apply the Playbill font, size 10 or higher.

#HT to Jordan Goldmeier for pointing this out to me. I had been using lowercase L, which never looked as good as the vertical slash character.

Let's look at the formula again:

```
=REPT("|",F21)
```

Recall that the second argument is your number_of_times argument. In the previous example, the highest value, 197, happens to be in F21. You can see that the REPT function still produces a reasonably sized bar chart. But sometimes it might make sense to scale down the number_of_times argument. In cases where you are dealing with much larger numbers, or only have limited column width sizes to work with, this helps reduce the amount of screen real estate your REPT function takes up. As long as you use apply a consistent scaling factor, the end result will be the same, just more compact. Let's see what happens in the same example when you scale down by one-third.

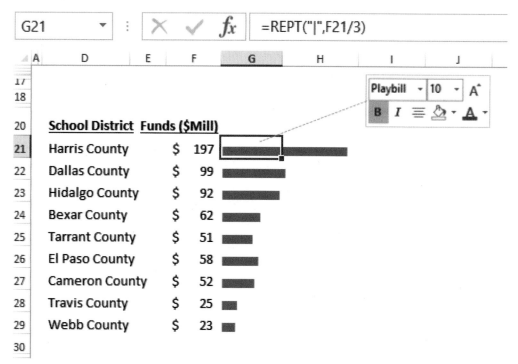

Scaling down by one-third. Same proportions, but your bar charts are no longer spilling over into column I like they were before.

#3 AutoSum on a Matrix

OMG. WHY DIDN'T THIS TIP DAWN ON ME UNTIL I HAD ALREADY BEEN USING EXCEL FOR TEN YEARS?

After all, I *have* known for quite some time that Excel is very good at working with more than one cell at a time, even when it comes to *noncontiguous* ranges. Just press the Ctrl key while you click, click, click away on individual worksheet cells to select them. Then enter a formula or value and press Ctrl+Enter to populate all selected cells at once.

	A	B	C	D	E	F	G	H
1								
2	Jan		Feb		Mar		Apr	
3	38		34		13		13	
4	20		15		44		29	
5	=A3+A4							
6								

Pressing Ctrl+Enter will populate all the highlighted cells in row 5. This is the same result as if you had entered the Jan formula in A5 and used Copy and Paste to repeat the formula logic for Feb, Mar, and Apr.

So why I did not make the mental leap and extend this same concept to Autosum until recently? I don't know. Go ahead, judge me all you want. Now, let's move on.

Let's say you have a matrix with regions going down a column and months going across the top row. You need monthly totals in row 13 and YTD totals in column K.

	B	C	D	E	F	G	H	I	J	K
8										
9			JAN	FEB	MAR	APR	MAY	JUN	JUL	
10		Easteros	123	310	313	246	467	253	308	
11		Westeros	477	353	402	265	355	246	135	
12		Redmond	124	382	341	138	152	170	217	
13		**TOTAL**								
14										

Select all the numbers in the matrix to include in the totals. Be sure to also include in your highlighted area the empty cells just below the final row and the empty cells to the immediate right of the final column.

D10	▼	:	✕	✓	*fx*	123				

	B	C	D	E	F	G	H	I	J	K
8										
9			JAN	FEB	MAR	APR	MAY	JUN	JUL	
10		Easteros	123	358	182	256	364	152	263	
11		Westeros	477	163	394	320	343	345	232	
12		Redmond	124	470	411	200	162	426	480	
13		**TOTAL**								
14										

3

Now, from the Formulas tab, Function Library group, click the AutoSum button.

The formulas all populate beautifully, all the way across row 14 and down column K.

| D13 | ▼ | ⋮ | ✕ ✓ | *fx* | =SUM(D10:D12) |

	B	C	D	E	F	G	H	I	J	K
8										
9			**JAN**	**FEB**	**MAR**	**APR**	**MAY**	**JUN**	**JUL**	
10		Easteros	123	411	310	220	199	325	354	1942
11		Westeros	477	232	241	359	363	497	467	2636
12		Redmond	124	259	184	448	258	357	294	1924
13		**TOTAL**	724	902	735	1027	820	1179	1115	6502
14										

File under, "H*ow the heck did I miss this before?*"

#4 Retrieve the Intersection Value – From Space!

The Great Looking-Stuff-Up Debate

Excel community insiders are keenly aware of this ongoing "VLOOKUP versus INDEX/MATCH" rivalry. As a professional contrarian, I refuse to pledge allegiance to either camp. I also just never got the extent of the hype. For one thing, what is wrong with using VLOOKUP *with* MATCH? But I digress. There is yet another method for accomplishing the same things these two camps continue to debate. That *thing* we are really talking about is getting a value from a certain row and column intersection.

The following technique does just that by combining range-naming techniques and the intersection operator. The intersection operator is nothing more than an empty space.

Huh?

Let's start with an example to illustrate. You have three employees, and three activities you want to track.

	A	B	C	D
1		PlanetsSaved	BabiesRescued	VilliansFoiled
2	Batman	93	23	32
3	Aqua Man	83	11	29
4	Steve	12	14	3
5				

How can you ask Excel how many babies Aqua Man has rescued on a given day? Or how many villains Steve has foiled? All such questions are ultimately asking Excel to *retrieve the value from a row/column intersection*.

Armed with this understanding, let's look at a new way to do this outside the realm of VLOOKUP or INDEX/MATCH.

The Empty Space Operator

Whether you even realize it, you already know a lot about operators. If you didn't, you probably would not have read this far. Common operators we use in Excel include * for multiplication, + for addition, / for division, and so on. But here's the crazy thing: The empty space is also an operator. Yes, space. As in the Spacebar. As in the extra spaces I'm using right now.

Using the previous Superhero employees example, let's say you type the following formula somewhere on the same worksheet:

    =A3:D3 C1:C4

Excel will retrieve the value that intersects the range A3:D3 and C1:C4. Looking at this on the grid makes it easier to see: This intersection is cell C3.

B6		▾	⋮	✗ ✓ ƒx	=A3:D3 C1:C4	

	A	B	C	D
1		PlanetsSaved	BabiesRescued	VilliansFoiled
2	Batman	93	23	32
3	Aqua Man	83	11	29
4	Steve	12	14	3
5				
6		=A3:D3 C1:C4		

B6 will return 11 – that is the value at the intersection of A3:D3 and C1:C4.

Admittedly, it is not a very intuitive formula on the surface. This is easily solvable if you apply range names to the three rows and three columns in the matrix.

Creating a Friendly Name for Each Range

If you are unfamiliar with named ranges, you can simply think of them as "friendly" names. For example, instead of referring to the BabiesRescued column as C2:C4, you can create a friendly name instead, like BabiesRescued. Then you can use that name in any formulas you might create that need to point to C2:C4. Once you've done that, these two formulas will mean the same thing, but one is perhaps easier to read:

    =SUM(C2:C4)   =SUM(BabiesRescued)

Naming a range is as simple as highlighting the cells you want to include in the name and typing the name you want in the Name Box, located to the left of the Formula Bar.

BabiesRescued	▾	⋮	✗ ✓ ƒx	23	

Name Box

	A	B	C	D
1		PlanetsSaved	BabiesRescued	VilliansFoiled
2	Batman	93	23	32
3	Aqua Man	83	11	29
4	Steve	12	14	3
5				

When you have multiple rows and columns for which you want to create names, there is a much faster way.

Start by highlighting the entire range, including both the row labels and column labels.

	A	B	C	D
1		PlanetsSaved	BabiesRescued	VilliansFoiled
2	Batman	93	23	32
3	Aqua Man	83	11	29
4	Steve	12	14	3
5				

From the Formulas tab, Defined Names group, click Create from Selection. Because you're already selected a proper range, the dialog that appears will have check boxes configured correctly for you.

Create Names from Selection ? ✕

Create names from values in the:
- ☑ Top row
- ☑ Left column
- ☐ Bottom row
- ☐ Right column

OK   Cancel

Excel will automatically use the top row and left column values as range names.

Click OK. Now you have 6 new names you can use in any formula you create, such as:

    =SUM(BabiesRescued)

which would return 48, just as if you had typed:

    =SUM(C2:C4)

Putting It All Together

You can combine the "friendly" named ranges with the empty space/intersection operator method. If you want to know how many babies Aqua Man has rescued, you can now use the named ranges instead of the standard A1-style referencing.

As soon as you start typing a range name, Excel's fabulous AutoComplete feature is already guessing what you are trying to say before you finish.

As soon as you see this pop up, you can press the Tab key to finish it rather than typing the entire word.

Now just add the empty space and finish the second half of the formula.

B6	▾	: ✕ ✓ *fx*	=BabiesRescued Aqua_Man

	A	B	C	D
1		PlanetsSaved	BabiesRescued	VilliansFoiled
2	Batman	93	23	32
3	Aqua Man	83	11	29
4	Steve	12	14	3
5				
6		=BabiesRescued Aqua_Man		

B6 will return 11. Note that Excel added an underscore to Aqua_Man to make it a legal name.

Thanks to Meni Porat for suggesting intersection. Olga Kryuchkova and John Lythe suggested various Name techniques.

#5 How to Lose Your VBA-V (VBA-Virginity)

Readers of this book are a diverse bunch. If you are in the "been there, done that" camp when it comes to macros, you can feel free to gloss over this tip. However, if you are a newbie and are VBA-curious, or if you want to know how I got into macros, stay with me.

On the Subject of Macros

One thing I will say at the very start: Learning VBA is like learning a brand-new language. Particularly if your general computer programming education comes primarily from the school of hard knocks, like mine did.

The topic of macros and VBA is far too vast to cover in one tip in a book. Indeed, the subject could be its *own book* or, rather, many books and indeed, it is! Numerous books, blogs, and training courses have attempted to tackle this challenge of learning VBA. Those books and blogs speak to a wide range of skill levels, needs, and learning styles. I encourage you to explore on your own as much as possible. In the meantime, I'll share with you how I got started, in the hopes that this one Excel developer's perspective – mine – might resonate with some of you.

Before You Attempt to Read any Book

I've heard fellow Ohioan and Microsoft MVP Jordan Goldmeier tell some tall tales about he when read *Professional Excel Development: The Definitive Guide to Developing Applications Using Microsoft Excel.* He says he read it without even having Excel open. He. Just. Read. It. The way one might read *Valley of the Dolls*: on vacation, poolside, DAX on the Beach in hand, just indulging in unapologetic amusement.

I am not sure I totally buy Jordan's claim, but he really knows his stuff, so feel free to try his approach. I dare you to get through an entire chapter of *Professional Excel Development* or any other VBA book without opening Excel and tinkering around. I also dare you to absorb it all in one sitting. It's never worked for me this way.

In my case, before I even cracked open a single book, I played around a lot with the macro recorder. The macro recorder is just like an old school tape recorder. I clicked Record. I did some stuff in Excel. I clicked Stop Recording. Then I looked at the *code* – written in the VBA language - that was automatically generated behind the scenes. I was able to start making associations between my actions and the VBA language.

The key was to look at the code as soon as possible after I hit the Stop Recording button, while things were still fresh in my mind.

You can actually learn a lot this way, and it is quite exciting at the beginning when simple things start working. But if the recorder is the *only* thing you use to create macros, you'll soon discover some limitations. You might even discover this immediately, the first time you record a macro. Even when you find ways to work around those limitations, you'll find some new ones. For me, it was running into these limitations that made me curious enough to crack open some books and focus. Or, maybe it was just stubborn determination to figure out how this thing works. I was ready, and after all that practice with the macro recorder, I found the books were an easier read. The concepts were sinking in.

Danny Moon Esq enjoying Power Programming with VBA.

Favorite Books

There are definitely more books and blogs out there today than when I was starting out. Starting with books, there are a couple that were instrumental in my initial learning.

John Walkenbach's *Power Programming with VBA* books were a prominent influence. Looking at his book on my shelf, it is in the top five in terms of visible creases on the paperback spine, so that says something. His chapter called "Introducing Visual Basic for Applications" includes a subsection called "The Basics of VBA". I found this in particular to be a great overview of all the most important terms a newbie developer needs to grasp, like objects versus methods versus properties and the like. Interestingly, despite that heading, "The Basics of VBA", it was only *after* I had been playing around with the macro recorder for a while that it really made any sense to me. Think of it as learning to speak before learning the rules of grammar.

In addition, my coauthor ~~blackmailed me into saying his books are totally superior to everyone else's~~ has some excellent published works on the subject, including *VBA and Macros for Microsoft Excel* by Bill Jelen and Tracy Syrstad. I really liked the grammar analogies there: Objects are like nouns, methods are like verbs, and so on. That was quite helpful.

Favorite Online Resources

By the time this book goes to print, more Excel websites and blogs will have be born. After all, it is a revolutionary time for Excel right now. Some sites will be great, others less so. Even these opinions will vary from reader to reader. Excel bloggers themselves will blog about other blogs and debate which are the most helpful blogs, and which are the amazing blogs, and blah de blah de blah. So get out there and *explore* what resonates best with you rather than just relying on my advice. Remember, ~~Google~~ Bing is your best friend for quick and free advice.

Next Steps

Enough deliberating for now. In the next tip, I will actually show you how to record your first macro.

#6 Recording Your Very First Macro

As I confessed in tip #5, when it comes losing VBA virginity, many developers (including me) start with the macro *recorder*. But don't worry. It's not *that* kind of recording.

Put as simply as possible: You hit the Record button, you do some stuff, and you hit the Stop Recording button. Like an old school tape recorder.

3

Starting Your (Macro) Recording Career

There's got to be something very easy that you can do in Excel just to see the mechanics of the macro recorder. I know you can record a macro that will "print" your name onto a worksheet:

1. Click inside any cell. I'll use A1 in this example.

2. Click the Developer tab. Click Record Macro.

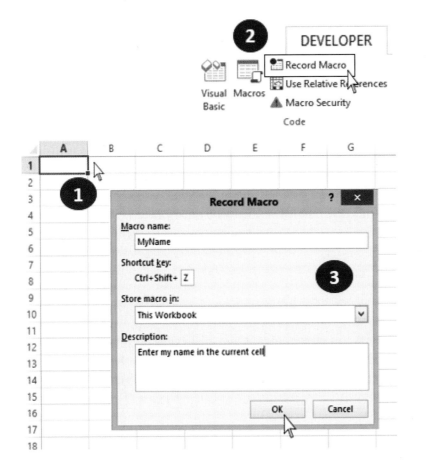

Note: If you don't have a Developer tab visible, click File, Options, Customize Ribbon. In the Customize Ribbon section on the right, check the box next to Developer. Click OK. You should see a Developer tab on your Ribbon now.

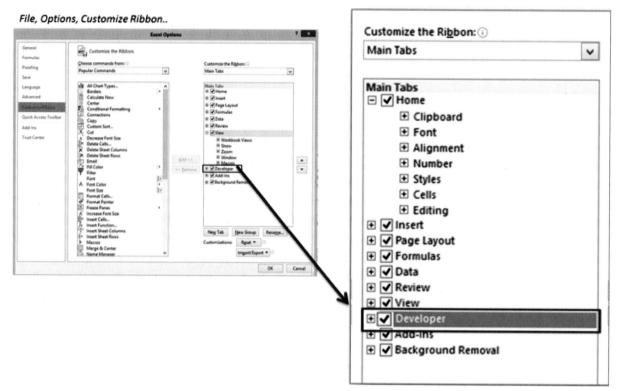

File, Options, Customize Ribbon..

3. In the Record Macro dialog that appears, use the following settings:

- **Macro Name (Required)**: Call this one MyName. (No spaces or special characters allowed in a macro name.)

- **Shortcut Key (Optional)**: If you want to assign a specific keyboard shortcut to run your macro later, enter a letter or number here. To avoid overwriting existing Excel shortcuts (like Ctrl+C for copy), incorporate the Shift key into the keystroke to help reduce the risk. (It's a pain to get it back once you overwrite!!!)

- **Store Macro in (Required)**: Choose This Workbook for this exercise.

- **Description (Optional)**: Any comments you add here will be stored along with the macro code for future reference.

4. Type your name in the cell you're in.

5. Press the Enter key and notice that Excel moves down to row 2. (This will be important when we examine the code later.)

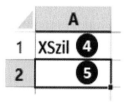

6. On the Developer tab, click the Stop Recording icon. You're ready to test the macro and then examine the VBA code that was generated by the recorder.

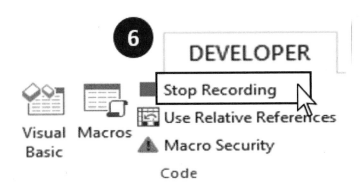

Playback and Inspection

Before you run your new macro, try clicking in a different cell first. To run the macro, use the shortcut you assigned in step 3 above. You should notice the macro "prints" your name in the active cell.

How *does* it do that?

To find out, you need to inspect the code that got generated while you were still in Recording mode. You should do this ASAP. Why ASAP? Because whatever you were doing while you were still recording is still fresh in you mind at this point, so making those associations between action and code will be much easier.

Backstage, Where the Code Resides

Welcome to the VB Editor. This "backstage" area is where all of your code hangs out. Here's how to get in:

1. Click the Developer tab.

2. Click the Visual Basic icon. The Visual Basic Editor windows opens. In the Project Explorer on the left, there is a list of VBA projects, including your current file's.

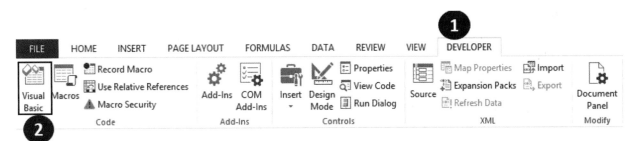

3. Click the + sign next to the filename and then one next to Modules. Double-click on Module1.

4. Study the code in the code window to start learning how the macro recorder "translates" your Excel actions into the VBA language.

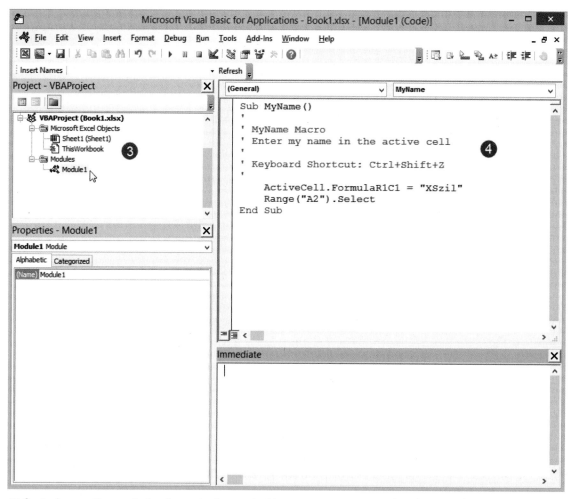

At first glance, the code looks sort of cryptic. How are we supposed to know what all of this means? Remember, this is like learning a language.

First things you will observe: At the very beginning of your code, you have Sub, followed by the name of the macro we entered earlier, and an opening and closing parentheses. You also have End Sub at the very end of the code. Sub and End Sub are in a blue font and are the standard opening and closing lines for any macro you record. You will also notice any comments you entered in the Description field are in green. This is another standard thing you will see with every macro you record.

Moving on to the first line of recorded code: ActiveCell is what the macro recorder interprets as the active cell position. This is not too hard to grasp. The .FormulaR1C1 bit is unfortunately a bit less intuitive. FormulaR1C1 is a property of the ActiveCell *object*. It is the way that the macro recorder likes to describe the "formula" of the active cell. (Never mind that this isn't even a formula since you've just entered text!) Welcome to the oddities of the macro recorder.

These two lines of code accomplish the same thing:

```
ActiveCell.FormulaR1C1 = "XSzil"
ActiveCell = "XSzil"
```

Moving on to the next line of code, you see that the recorder also generated this bit:

```
Range("A2").Select
```

This happened because, after you were done typing in A1, you pressed Enter. When you press Enter in Excel, your cursor moves down to the next row, and therefore you have just selected that cell. So, regardless of your intent, the recorder interpreted this action as "select the next row."

Here's another oddity with the macro recorder: With VBA, you never really need to *select* anything. Unlike "regular" Excel, VBA can perform an action on a cell without actually *selecting* it. Known in the VBA language as *methods*, these actions can be just about anything you do in Excel, including entering text, entering formulas, applying fonts or other format styles, cutting, copying, pasting, etc.

So as you can see by now, the macro recorder is both helpful and confusing at the same time! It is helpful for learning some basic mechanics. But it also produces a lot of extra stuff you don't need. Put bluntly, it doesn't always interpret your intention.

So what can you do? For one, you can modify the code right in the VB Editor window to delete stuff you don't need. As you experiment more, you will become more familiar with what you can remove and what you need to keep to make your code work.

Welcome to the VBA Jungle

I don't blame you if you are already frustrated with VBA. It seems very illogical at first, and isn't Excel supposed to be a supreme ruler of all things logical? I feel your pain, I really do. Sometimes I even wonder what possessed me to keep tinkering with macros for so long. Maybe I am a masochist. Happily there are many great resources out there to guide you past this initial stage. If you didn't read my other tip "#5 How to Lose Your VBA-V (VBA-Virginity)" on page 151, go ahead and check it out for some additional advice on getting started.

Several readers suggested Macros as their favorite Excel tip: Pete Doyle, Chris Jones, @theexcelclub

#7 Turn Your QAT into Your Personal Laugh Track

Talking Spreadsheets

If you're reading this book cover to cover, you've already enjoyed "#40 Avoid Whiplash with Speak Cells" on page 132. If you have not seen it, turn there now! Bill walks you through how to get Excel to "talk back" to you by reading the contents of your worksheet to you - out loud. Bill describes one practical use of this feature and one that fits into a category I like to call "Excel hijinks."

Just as you can use VBA to work with Windows Speech Recognition, you can use VBA to play sounds from any .wav or .mp3 sound files. You can play these files automatically with the click of a button. In the next example, I'll show you how to use your QAT (Quick Access Toolbar) to store these buttons and play sound effects any time you want right from Excel.

Hat Tip

I am very grateful to have stumbled upon the macros used in this tip years ago, on John Walkenbach's old j-walk.com site. It opened my eyes to all sorts of new ways to ~~annoy~~ amuse my co-workers and friends at the office.

BONUS tip: Set Up Your Personal Macro Workbook

One thing you'll need for your sound effects toolbar is a *personal macro workbook*. A personal macro workbook, unlike regular Excel workbooks, is one that, once created, will open each time you start Excel but stays hidden in the background. You don't really use it like a regular workbook but rather like a backend storage place for any macros you want to store and make available globally, meaning available to more than one workbook.

To create a personal macro workbook:

1. Click the Developer tab.

2. Click Record Macro.

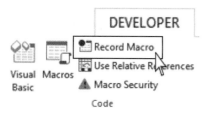

3. The Record Macro dialog appears. From the Store Macro In dropdown, choose Personal Macro Workbook. Leave all other settings as-is.

4. Click OK.

5. From the Developer tab, click Stop Recording. Your personal macro workbook has just been created.

Notice you didn't really *do* anything while you were recording. But by choosing Personal Macro Workbook in Step 2, you've essentially created your personal macro workbook. This was a one-time thing. Going forward you can store any macros you want in your personal macro workbook, so they are available to run regardless of the Excel file you have open at the time.

Your New Personal Macro Workbook

Now let's explore what happened behind the scenes. From the Developer tab, click Visual Basic (or press Alt+F11). You are now backstage at the Visual Basic Editor.

You will notice in the Project Explorer section that there is a new file listed called Personal.xlsb. Click the + symbol next to the filename, then click the + sign next to the Modules folder. Double-click Module1. You now see the (mostly empty) code for Macro1 you just recorded in the code window.

Since the purpose of recording Macro1 was to create a personal macro workbook only, you won't need the code for Macro1 anymore. So for now, you will simply delete the code. You can highlight everything from Sub Macro1() all the way to End Sub, right-click, and delete.

Put all Your Favorite Sound Files in a Folder

Next, you will add the VBA code to play your sound effects. Before you do that, you might want to collect all your sound effects in one place – ideally in one folder. You'll need the folder pathnames and filenames for your macros to work properly.

As you browse for sound files (.mp3 or .wav), use your own music collection or any clips that you find online and build your collection over time. Here is an early-days look at the folder I used to start building my sound effects toolbar (I have a few more now, a bit of an addiction).

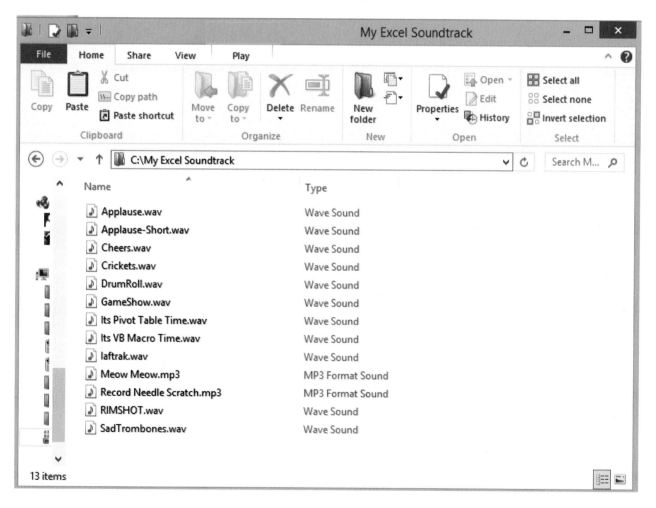

Add new PlaySound Macro to Your Personal Macro Workbook

Since this macro is not one that can be recorded, you need to type it directly into the Visual Basic Editor. From Excel, get back into the Visual Basic Editor by clicking Visual Basic from the Developer tab or using the keyboard shortcut Alt+F11. Navigate back to Module1 in the Personal.xlsb file, as described in the previous section.

Type the code shown in the next figure in the Module1 code window. Notice the modifications you will have to make; I've added comments to guide you on the specific lines you will have to modify to make it run in your environment.

Here is the code:

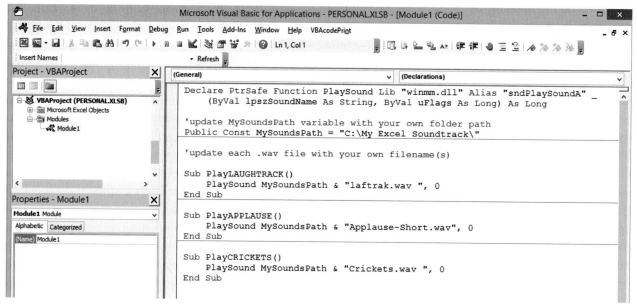

Let's examine this code.

The first line, which starts with Declare PtrSafe, sets up the main function, which I've assigned to the name PlaySound.

> **Note**: I should point out that this line of code starts with Declare PtrSafe and ends with As Long. Even though it may look like two lines, the underscore character (preceded by a space) adds a line break. This is a macro writer's technique to enhance readability for very long lines of code. This way you are avoiding having a single line of code that stretches across so far you have to keep scrolling right to see it all.

In the next line, which starts with Public Const, sets the default folder. Here you should replace the folder path with the one you have set up to store all your sound files.

Next, there are three subroutines: Sub PlayLAUGHTRACK(), Sub PlayAPPLAUSE(), and Sub PlayCRICKETS(). These are individual macros to play specific sounds. Again, you'll need to update the filenames with whatever you have. You can also change each macro name to something intuitive to match the specific file you are going to play. You can also replicate as many times as you need for new sound files as your collection grows. To do this, just copy any one of the existing Subs and paste it right into the same module. Then just update the macro name and the filename.

> **Tip**: If you are not working in a 64-bit operating environment, you might notice that the first line of code suddenly turns red, VBA starts complaining, and your code won't run. If this happens to you, try deleting PtrSafe from the first line of code. The red font should go away, and your code will now work properly.

Create Icons on Your QAT

Sound files organized in one folder? Check. Code added to Personal.xlsb? Check. It's finally time to set up the QAT shortcuts to Excel-hilarity! You'll want to add one icon per sound effect. I like to use several, to suit different moods.

Your QAT sits just above or just below your Ribbon. It has a few default icons on it when you first install Excel, but you can add or remove any icons you want. The icons can be used for your personal macros, as well as any built-in Excel commands you want to be able to access quickly and easily without navigating around the Ribbon.

To customize your QAT and create your personal Excel sound effects toolbar:

1. Right-click on the QAT and choose Customize Quick Access Toolbar.

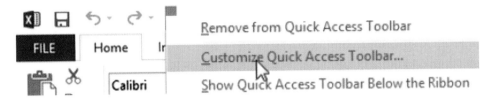

2. In the Excel Options dialog select Macros from Choose Commands From dropdown.

3. Click on the first sound effect macro in the list. Click the Add button. The macro will now be added to the Customize Quick Access Toolbar list on the right.

The next two steps are optional but recommended if you plan to have more than a few personal macro icons on your QAT.

4. Select one of the macros in the Customize Quick Access Toolbar list on the right and click Modify. The Modify Button dialog appears.

5. Change the symbol and display name to your liking. The symbol will be the icon that actually appears on the QAT, and the display name will appear as you hover over the icon. Click OK when you're done.

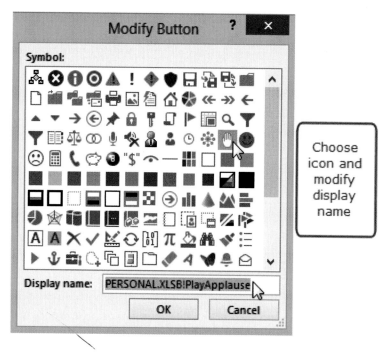

Choose icon and modify display name

Have Fun with Your New QAT

Are you presenting your latest Excel model to your whole department? Are you an Excel trainer facing a tough crowd? Sass it up with some sound effects. Make sure your speakers are on. At the appropriate moment, click the icon for the sound effect you want on your QAT. You will instantly change the energy in the room. Whether that is a good or bad thing remains to be seen. Good luck!

Bonus Tip: Add Icons to the Quick Access Toolbar

The Quick Access Toolbar is great for collecting commands that you use frequently. Hate to go to the Data tab just to click the AZ sort button? Right-click the button and choose Add to Quick Access Toolbar. Other useful commands can be found by selecting All Commands in the top-left dropdown in the Customize Quick Access Toolbar section. Try some of these useful icons:

- Select Visible Cells - see "Bonus Tip: Copying the Subtotal Rows" on page 40
- AutoFilter to do Filter by Selection. See "#2 Filter by Selection" on page 4
- Print Preview Full Screen to bring back the old style Print Preview
- Camera Tool - see "#18 Smile for the Excel Camera!" on page 190
- New (but not New...). See "My Rant About New and New..." on page 22
- Quick Print to print without stopping at the Backstage.

Thanks to Matt Atkins for New. Chris Jones for suggesting adding Select Visible Cells. @K_Tizy55 for Quick Print.

#8 VBA For Troublemakers

Continuing with our VBA hijinks theme, there are a few ways I like to use Excel's Text to Speech functionality.

VBA Events

In Excel VBA programming, there is this concept known as an *event*. An event can trigger a macro to fire. Examples of events include clicking on a button, activating a worksheet, deactivating a worksheet, recalculating a worksheet, changing the selection, changing the active sheet, and clicking on a specific cell.

Storing Code for VBA events

There are two ways we can embed VBA code in a workbook. Double-click on any of these to access its corresponding code window:

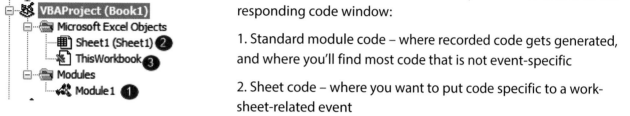

1. Standard module code – where recorded code gets generated, and where you'll find most code that is not event-specific

2. Sheet code – where you want to put code specific to a worksheet-related event

3. ThisWorkbook code – where you want to put code specific to a workbook-related event

MrExcel on April Fool's

In his tip "#40 Avoid Whiplash with Speak Cells" on page 132, Bill has already explained how to use Excel's Text to Speech feature. He even described a "harmless prank" you can pull on your co-workers that looks like this:

```
Worksheet                          ▼   Change

Private Sub Worksheet_Change(ByVal Target As Range)
    Application.Speech.Speak "Damn Straight!  " & Target.Value
End Sub
```

Now, let's try a few more variations on this hilarity.

Excel for Narcissists

Let Excel greet you each day with Workbook_Open. Pick a file you work with frequently. Open it. Get into the VB Editor. In the Project Explorer, navigate to that file. Double-click on ThisWorkbook and add this little bit of code:

```
Workbook                       ˅   Open                              ˅

Private Sub Workbook_Open()
    Application.Speech.Speak Application.UserName & ", you look amazing."
End Sub
```

Pretty soon, you will start to believe it.

Always Know Where You Are with Worksheet_SelectionChange

One of the many VBA events with lots of practical uses is the selection change event. Here is a not-so-practical and super-annoying way to use it. Pick another victim and get your hands on their file. Get into the VB Editor. In the Project Explorer, navigate to that file. Find the sheet name where you want to make a little trouble. Double-click on it to access that Sheet code window. Then add this little bit of code:

| Worksheet | ⌄ | SelectionChange | ⌄ |

```
Private Sub Worksheet_SelectionChange(ByVal Target As Range)
    Application.Speech.Speak Target.Address(0, 0) & " is a nice place to be"
End Sub
```

Target Your Message with Worksheet_Activate

Another handy property of the Application object in VBA is the UserName property. What that means is, you can get VBA to read the name associated with the user of a particular computer. This is usually the same name that immediately follows C:\Users in your My Documents folder, for example:

C:\Users*YourName*\Documents

Anyway, you can have more fun with this in VBA. Find out the username associated with a particular co-worker, or even your boss if you are feeling really foolish. Then pick a file you all use. Get into the VB Editor. In the Project Explorer, navigate to that file. Double-click on the sheet where you want your message to be heard each time it's activated. Then add this little bit of code:

| Worksheet | ⌄ | Activate |

```
Private Sub Worksheet_Activate()
  If Application.UserName = "Pat" Then    'Pat is your boss
     Application.Speech.Speak "Isn't is time you gave XSzil a raise?"
  ElseIf Application.UserName = "DannyMoon" Then 'DannyMoon is your crush
     Application.Speech.Speak "Someone in accounting loves you"
  End If
End Sub
```

#9 Absolute, Relative, and Multiplication Tables

After you have reached a certain level of Excel prowess, absolute and relative referencing is something you do in your sleep. This probably includes many of those reading this book. But can you *explain* it to someone else? If there is one thing I have learned as a professional Excel instructor, it is that the ability to *do* and the ability to *teach* can be two entirely different animals.

This tip is one tried-and-true Excel instruction technique, and it's particularly handy if you have a mixed crowd. It is a quick way to figure out how to pace the instruction for the rest of the day. If everyone can do this in 20 seconds or less, I slam another double espresso and brace myself for an advanced crowd. If I have a bunch of frightened, deer-in-headlight looks, I know we'll need to dial it back and focus on fundamental, Excel 101 kind of stuff.

Back to School

Here is how the exercise works. Start creating a multiplication table mockup of sorts. Enter the numbers 1-10 in B1:K1, then do the same in A2:A11. Of course, you can click and drag the Fill Handle to do the first set of 10, then copy, paste, and transpose for the second set. At this point, it should look like this:

⬓	A	B	C	D	E	F	G	H	I	J	K
1		1	2	3	4	5	6	7	8	9	10
2	1										
3	2										
4	3										
5	4										
6	5										
7	6										
8	7										
9	8										
10	9										
11	10										
12											

Now, ask your audience to see if they can figure out how to create a single formula in cell B2 that can be copied all the way across to column K and all the way down to row 11 and return the correct answer for each cell. If the cell referencing was correctly applied in B2, you should see all other cells returning the correct answer.

3

⬓	A	B	C	D	E	F	G	H	I	J	K
1		1	2	3	4	5	6	7	8	9	10
2	1	1	2	3	4	5	6	7	8	9	10
3	2	2	4	6	8	10	12	14	16	18	20
4	3	3	6	9	12	15	18	21	24	27	30
5	4	4	8	12	16	20	24	28	32	36	40
6	5	5	10	15	20	25	30	35	40	45	50
7	6	6	12	18	24	30	36	42	48	54	60
8	7	7	14	21	28	35	42	49	56	63	70
9	8	8	16	24	32	40	48	56	64	72	80
10	9	9	18	27	36	45	54	63	72	81	90
11	10	10	20	30	40	50	60	70	80	90	100

Word to the Excel gurus out there seeking to help out their friends: This multiplication table exercise is not always a cinch for many people who don't use Excel 24/7. It's been a while since fifth grade, so yes, people will forget things like *multiplication is commutative*, and therefore these two formulas return the same result:

```
=C$1*$A4    =$A4*C$1
```

B2	▼	⋮	✕ ✓ *fx*	=$A2*B$1

⬓	A	B	C	D	E	F	G	H	I	J	K
1		1	2	3	4	5	6	7	8	9	10
2	1	$A2*B$1	2	3	4	5	6	7	8	9	10
3	2	2	4	6	8	10	12	14	16	18	20
4	3	3	6	9	12	15	18	21	24	27	30
5	4	4	8	12	16	20	24	28	32	36	40

The "Answer" for Those Learning Excel

For the new Excel learners, the short answer is to put the following formula in B2:

    =$A2*B$1

Or, alternatively =B$1*$A2 will also work. Once you've done that, you can copy this same formula all the way across to column K and down to row 11.

The "Answer" for Those Teaching Excel

The other fun part of this exercise is discovering that even with a seemingly simple example such as this, there are quite a few opportunities to showcase Excel timesavers and shortcuts like:

- Using the Fill Handle to create a series of numbers
- Using copy, paste, transpose to transform a vertical range to a horizontal one or vice versa
- Using Ctrl+Enter to populate a matrix of cells simultaneously

and perhaps a few more that I've missed, to be sure.

In short, there is no single "right" answer on how to approach this problem. But it is a great way to illustrate how important the correct mix of references can be in our Excel formulas!

#10 From Outline to Flat Table

Hat Tip to Bob Umlas

Here is yet another one of those *"now why didn't I think of that?"* moments in my Excel life. I read this tip on a plane from Atlantic City to LA a few years ago, when I read *This Isn't Excel, It's Magic* by Bob Umlas. Thanks Bob! Why didn't I think of that?

You Have an Outline, but That's It

Somebody put this together and thought they were very clever. But now you can't sort it, or filter it, or make it into a pivot table, because it has all these blanks in it.

	C	D	E	F
7				
8		**State**	**Region**	**Sales**
9		PA	North	274
10				615
11				871
12				491
13			South	976
14				140
15				348
16			East	723
17				230
18		WA	North	993
19				513
20			South	376
21				601
22				617
23		NY	North	522
24				97
25			South	927

The Solution

Just Go To it:

1. Highlight the entire outline area, including empty cells that need to be filled.

2. Press the F5 key.

3. From the Go To dialog, choose the Blanks option and press Enter.

4. Type an equals sign.

5. Tap the Up arrow key.

6. Type Ctrl+Enter. Your outline is now filled.

	C	D	E	F	G	H	I
7							
8		**State**	**Region**	**Sales**			
9		PA	North	274			
10		PA	North	615			
11		PA	Nor				
12		PA	Nor				
13		PA	Sou				
14		PA	Sou				
15		PA	Sou				
16		PA	Eas				
17		PA	Eas				
18		WA	Nor				
19		WA	Nor				
20		WA	Sou				
21		WA	Sou				
22		WA	Sou				
23		NY	Nor				
24		NY	Nor				
25		NY	South	927			
26							

Menu shown: Cut, Copy, Paste Options:, Paste Special..., Insert Copied Cells..., Delete..., Clear Contents, Quick Analysis, Filter, Sort, Insert Comment, Format Cells..., Pick From Drop-down List..., Define Name..., Hyperlink...

Submenu: Paste, Paste Values, Other Paste Options, Paste Special...

An optional final step is recommended if you need to sort, filter, or create a pivot table. Convert all the formulas to values. Either just highlight D9:F27, then press Ctrl+C, and select Paste Dropdown, Paste Values. *Or* use one of the methods Bill described in "#25 The Fastest Way to Convert Formulas to Values" on page 90.

This technique was the most-suggested tip for this book. Thanks to Matt Allington, Ray Hauser, Chris Hicks, Barbara Johnston, Laura Lewis, Paul Martinez, Michael A. Rempel, Rene Sprebitz, Darrell Wade, Steven White, @AuditExcel.

#11 Goal Seek for Renters and Shoe Lovers

When You Must Blow Your Whole Wad

Sometimes the Jimmy Choos just beckon and you are compelled to spend every last penny in your pocket. It happens. Fortunately Goal Seek can help you through it. Goal Seek allows you to back into a question when you already know the answer. For example, "What is the maximum retail price I can afford in order to spend exactly $450, including tax?" This analysis could be accomplished with Algebra, of course. But who needs Algebra when you have Excel (and a sweet pair of Italian leather slingbacks)?!

Illustration: Michelle Routt

Setting Up the Problem

In Excel, this starts out as a simple math problem: Retail price plus tax equals what I must pay:

	A	B	C
1			
2	**Retail Price**	$ 365.00	*Changing cell*
3	**9.75% Sales Tax**	$ 35.59	*=B2*0.0975*
4	**Total**	$ 400.59	*=B2+B3*
5			

I have one variable I can play around with here, which is the retail price in B2. Am I right? Of course I am, because the other two cells are both formulas that are "set" in the sense that I can't really change their logic. In B3, I cannot change the amount of sales tax I must pay, because it's required by law, so that formula must remain. B4, the total amount, must also stay because retail+tax = amount due is a fact of life beyond my control. *Changing cells* and *set cells* are important concepts to understand when you are learning to use Goal Seek.

Recall that the original goal was to spend all the money I have in my pocket, $450. Using the setup shown in the figure above, I can change the value in B2 as many times as I want and observe how close the total gets to $450. But that might take a while, and I'm not very good at Algebra, so I turn to Goal Seek.

Goal Seek to the Rescue

Here is how you use Goal Seek to solve this problem:

1. Click the total cell, B4.

2. Click the Data tab, Data tools group, What-If Analysis, Goal Seek.

3. In the Goal Seek dialog, enter the following settings:

- B4 for the Set Cell
- 450 for the To Value
- B2 for the Changing Cell

4. Click OK to see what Goal Seek is proposing for a solution. Notice that it puts the proposed value into B2 for you.

5. Click OK to accept the proposed solution or click Cancel to return to the original value you had.

Buying, Renting, or Living in a Shoebox

Indeed, life can be more complicated than having $450 to blow on shoes. In most real-world problems, things are often more complicated, and Goal Seek is therefore not always the best choice. For more complex analysis, complete with multiple changing set cells, multiple fixed cells, and constraints, check out Goal Seek's over-achieving cousin, Solver. See "#37 Find Optimal Solutions with Solver" on page 124.

You can still use Goal Seek to analyze questions of slightly higher complexity, but you have to frame the problem so there is only one variable and one set cell at a time. For example, a question like "how much can I afford to take out as a loan, given a fixed interest rate and a fixed term in months?" could be analyzed with Goal Seek, using the set up here:

	C	D	E	F	G
40					
41		*Changing Cells*			
42		Loan Amount	$ 279,422.00		
43		Term in Months	360		
44		Rate	5.0%		
45					
46		*Set Cells*			
47		Monthly Payment	$ 1,500	=PMT(E44/12, E43, -E42)	
48		Total Payments	$ 539,999	=E47*E43	
49		Total Interest	$ 260,577	=E48-E42	

Goal seek only allows for one changing cell at a time.. take your pick!

Let's say you have $2,000 to spend each month on housing, and you want Goal Seek to help you do some analysis on what size loan you might take out. Because you have a fixed amount you can spend each month, you would choose the monthly payment cell, E47, as the set cell. You can then pick one of the three changing cell options. For example, if you assume that the term is a fixed 360 months, and the interest rate is a fixed 5%, then the loan amount becomes your changing cell (by process of elimination).

Once you have chosen one set cell and one changing cell, you are ready for Goal Seek. You click the set cell, E47 and click the Data tab, What-If Analysis, Goal Seek. You use the following parameters:

	C	D	E
40			
41		*Changing Cells*	
42		Loan Amount	$ 279,422.00
43		Term in Months	360
44		Rate	5.0%
45			

Goal Seek   ?   ✕

Set cell: $E$47

To value: 2000

By changing cell: $E$42

OK   Cancel

When you click OK, Goal Seek lets you know that assuming your term is 360 months, and your interest rate is 5%, and you want to spend no more than $2,000 each month, you can take out a loan of $372,563.

#12 Controlled Lists with Data Validation

When building interactive Excel models, you want to keep your end user in mind. Data validation is a great, no-macros way to control the acceptable values for a given cell. For example, you can limit entries to a fixed list of choices, a value in a range, text of a certain length, and more.

This tip focuses on the dropdown list option you have with Excel's data validation feature. It's pretty easy to create a dropdown list. Unfortunately, it can also get screwed up easily if you don't pay attention to the "gotcha" caveats, so I will comment on those also.

Restrict Entries to a List of Values

Let's say that you want your end user to enter a company name in C2, but you want to make sure the company is one from your approved vendors list.

	A	B	C
1	Company		
2	Access Analytic	Select Company:	
3	adaept information management		
4	All Systems Go Consulting		
5	Analytic Minds		
6	Areef Ali & Associates		
7	Association for Computers & Taxation		
8	Berghaus Corporation		
9	Bits of Confetti		
10	Blockhead Data Consultants		
11	bradedgar.com		
12	Budget Wand		
13	California Blazing Chile Farms		
14	Calleia Company		
15	Cambia Factor		
16			

This is one of the easiest types of data validations to create:

1. Click on C2

2. From the Data tab, Data tools group, click Data Validation, Data Validation again.

Note: In real life, you would click the top of the Data Validation icon to choose Data Validation. I added the extra click in this case to show the Circle Invalid Data choices. They aren't discussed in this book, but you might want to check them out. In the future, the book will describe clicking only the top half of the Data Validation icon.

3. In the Data Validation dialog, select List from the Allow dropdown.

4. Click inside the Source box and select the range where your list values are stored.

5. Click OK.

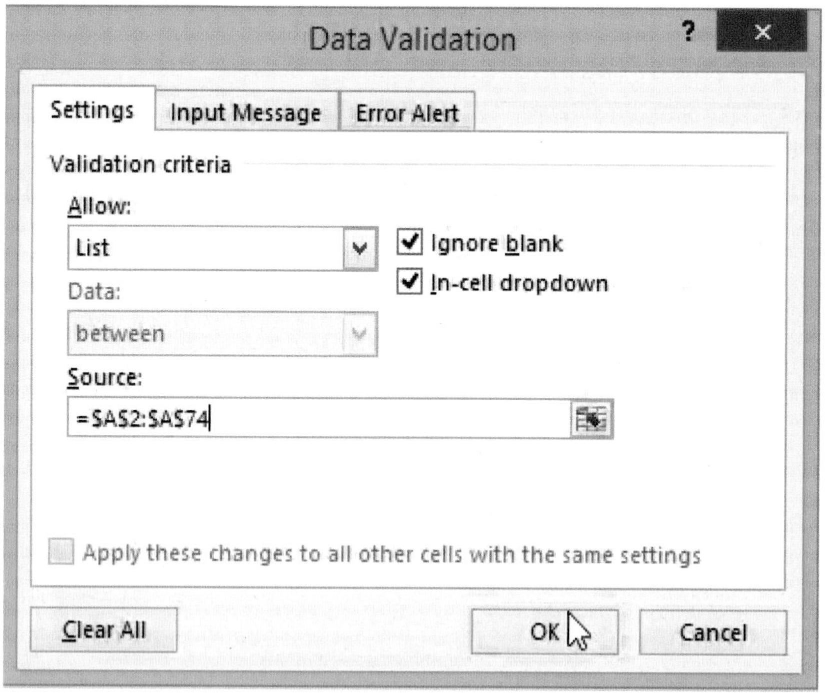

Now when the user clicks on C2, Excel immediately presents a dropdown list of acceptable choices.

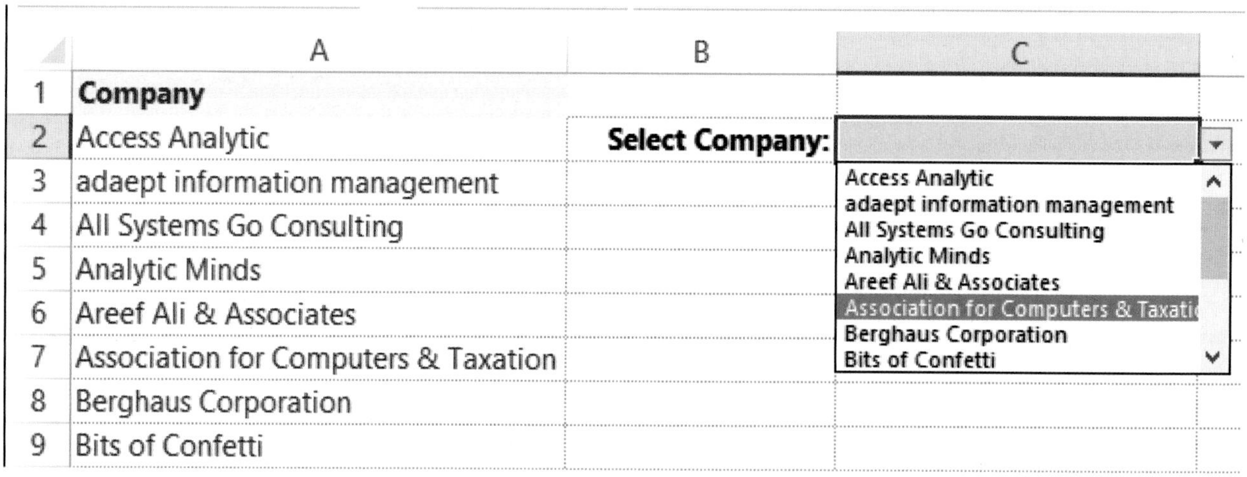

Note that the source range that populates your list need not be visible to the end user. The previous figures show the easiest variation of this technique, but in practice, you can define the source in a variety of other, more practical ways:

Option 1. Put your list in a hidden column on the same worksheet. Caveat: Unless you implement some clever sheet protection schemes (sometimes even requiring VBA), the user can easily mess things up.

Option 2. Use a named range. Your named range can refer to names on other worksheets. For example, I can create a new named range called CompanyList:

Then I can use that name as my source in the Data Validation dialog:

Tip: When you click inside the Source box, press the F3 key. You will get a Paste Name dialog. Double-click any range name that shows up in the Paste Name list to automatically transfer that name into the Data Validation Source box.

Option 3. If you have a short list, typing a comma-separated list directly in the Source box will do the trick also.

The Problem with Static Lists

One problem with using regular, A1-style range definitions in your data validation source is that the list will not be dynamic. Like Excel formulas, however, you can sort of work around this by remembering to insert new values *above* the last row in your defined range. For example:

```
=SUM(A1:A15)
```

This will easily pick up new rows past row 15 as long as those new values are inserted *above* row 15 after you've created the initial formula. Similarly, the source for any data validation lists will expand to pick up new list values as long as those new values are inserted somewhere between the first and last rows of the range. But in practice, somebody always appends rather than inserting, and things get screwy.

To work around this, you can use your favorite dynamic range naming technique, then use those defined names as your list source. The OFFSET function is one such technique, but since Excel tables came onto the scene, I find I use OFFSET a lot less. So, for this tip, let's focus on the easier one: tables.

A Solution with Dynamic Tables

Creating a table is simple: Click inside a list and click OK on the Create Table dialog. You now have a table.

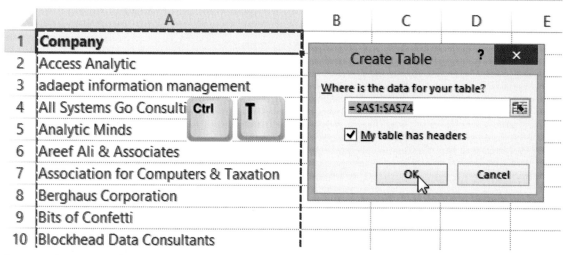

Among the many advantages of using Excel tables (they extend well beyond the scope of this tip), one of the big ones is built-in dynamic ranges. The next illustration shows two ways of counting the number of companies I have in my list. In C1, I have the old, A1-style cell referencing we are all used to with "regular" Excel. C2 shows the newer, structured referencing syntax used by Excel tables. Of the two, only the structured referencing style is dynamic.

	A	B	C	D	E
1	Company		73	=COUNTA(A2:A74)	
2	Access Analytic		73	=COUNTA(Table1[Company])	
3	adaept information management				
4	All Systems Go Consulting				
5	Analytic Minds				
6	Areef Ali & Associates				
7	Association for Computers & Taxation				
8	Berghaus Corporation				

Note: Creating the formula in C2 was as simple as typing =COUNTA(and then clicking just above cell A2 to select the entire column. Excel then puts in the table name, Table1, and column name, Company, for you, using the correct syntax.

Once the table is created, you can use another trick with the INDIRECT function to bring it all together for the data validation list source. For more details on INDIRECT, check out Bill's "#30 Cure Triskaidekaphobia with a Killer Formula" on page 102. In this example, we'll use the INDIRECT function in a data validation list source, to specify a reference to a table range. You know the table name is Table1. You know the field name is Company. So, armed with all this information, the winner for dynamic validation list sources looks like this:

3

Bonus Tip: Other Data Validation Settings

You have seen by now that the Data Validation dialog contains two other tabs besides Settings.

The Input Message tab allows you to offer people additional guidance, in "real time," as soon as they click on the validated cell.

The Error Alert tab allows you to deliver another message to end users if they try to type in something that is not on the list. Error Alert offers three styles of alerts of varying tones, ranging from polite to stern.

After the user tries to enter an unapproved vendor, this Stop-style error alert kicks in.

While you can have some fun with these…

…don't be fooled. These settings, like data validation in general, do not offer very robust protection against mistakes. In fact, in the absence of fairly well-thought-out protection schemes, sometimes even requiring passwords and VBA, a casual end user could easily screw up your validation with a simple copy and paste action. All someone has to do is copy another cell, paste over the validated cell, and poof! Validation gone.

Therefore, you should use data validation with the intent of guiding cooperative, well-meaning end users. For this it is still very effective. For the rest, unless you are prepared to spend some time implementing a more sophisticated VBA solution, it is likely to get screwed up.

Thanks to Wilde XL Solutions for suggesting Data Validation.

> **Note**: I am often asked about my thoughts on sheet protection, passwords, and the like. For more information on that, read my next tip, "The XSzil Guide to Excel Protection"

#13 The XSzil Guide to Excel Protection

Should you protect your Excel model or not? I am often asked this question. It's hard to offer a concise answer. Excel offers many types of protection: protect an entire workbook, protect a worksheet, protect certain cells within a worksheet, and more. Each type can involve a password, or not. But in reality, none of it is high-security stuff. So my answer usually starts with "It depends…"

I do not come from an official computer programming background. However, I have experimented with Nassi-Shneiderman diagrams. You know, for fun. Also, I found that this technique offers an interesting, "visual" way of solving complex problems. I sometimes use this technique for approaching Excel problems as well, VBA or non-VBA subjects. A Nassi-Shneiderman diagram looks sort of like a flowchart, but with simpler rules.

> **Note**: From Wikipedia: "A Nassi–Shneiderman diagram (NSD) in computer programming is a graphical design representation for structured programming."

So, here you go. A Nassi-Shneiderman lover's guide to whether you need to worry about protecting your Excel model.

You're welcome, America!

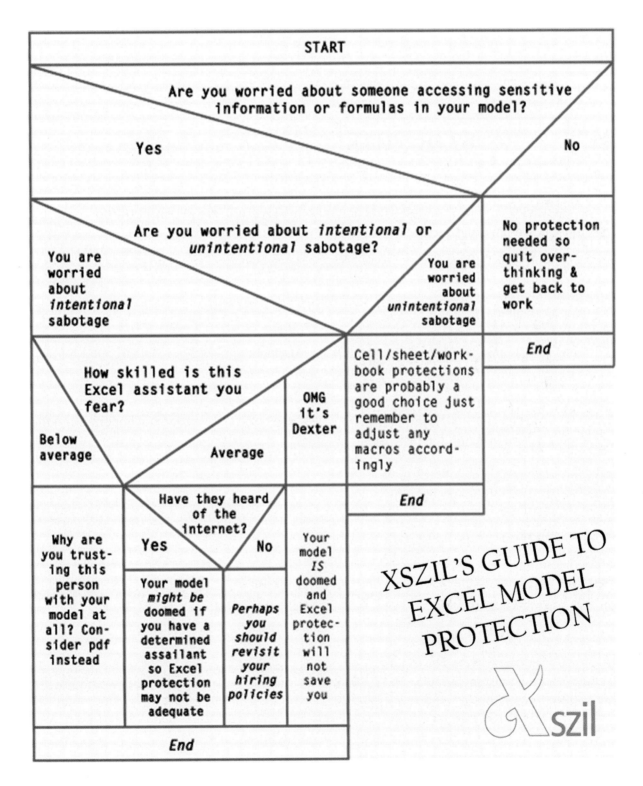

#14 Named Formulas: Yesterday and Tomorrow

Another sneaky tip on using names in Excel: They're not just for ranges! They are, in fact, great tricks to include in your Excel modeling toolkit.

In Excel There Is Only TODAY()

There is no YESTERDAY(). There is no TOMORROW(). If you think this profound opening line is just another cheap segue to an Excel cocktail pairing, you are right! I recommend an Excel Libre, in celebration of the TODAY() function's beautiful simplicity:

A1	▼	× ✓ *fx*	=TODAY()

	A
1	6/28/2015

This figure was created on June 28, 2015.

However, there is no similar YESTERDAY() function built into Excel (Cheers, Microsoft!). So for our first named formula, we can make our *own* YESTERDAY.

From the Formulas tab, Defined Names group, click the Name Manager icon. Then click New.

The New Name dialog appears. Type YESTERDAY in the Name box (capitalization not important). In the Refers To box, type =TODAY()-1. Click OK.

New Name ? ×
Name: YESTERDAY
Scope: Workbook ⌄
Comment:
Refers to: =TODAY()-1
OK   Cancel

You now have a new custom formula, =YESTERDAY, that you can type in any cell in your workbook. It will always return the current day's date minus one day.

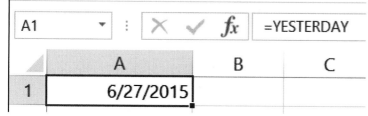

| A1 | ▾ | ⋮ | ✕ | ✓ | *fx* | =YESTERDAY |

	A	B	C
1	6/27/2015		

This figure was created on June 28, 2015.

You could repeat the above steps to create your own TOMORROW: just change the -1 to +1:

New Name   ?   ✕

Name: TOMORROW

Scope: Workbook ▾

Comment:

Refers to: =TODAY()+1

#15 Named Formulas: VLOOKUP Without the Sausage

Let's look at an example, with a bit more complexity. I know you're ready for it!

You have an Excel model where you want the end user to enter shipping information for customer orders. There are two tabs, Input and Customer Table.

On the Customer Table tab, you are storing customer shipping information for your frequently contacted customers. You create a table (Ctrl+T) so you can use the built-in advantages of Excel tables.

	A	B	C	D	E
1	**Bill-to Name** ▾	**Address** ▾	**City** ▾	**State** ▾	**Zip** ▾
2	Awesome Computers	615 76 Street	Brooklyn	NY	11209
3	Baldwin Museum of Science	1121 Rossi Rd	Templeton	CA	93465
4	City Power & Light	IL Northbrook	Northbrook	IL	60062
5	Coho Vineyard & Winery	3546 Meeker Ave.	El Monte	CA	91731
6	Consolidated Messenger	10255 York Rd.	Cockeysville	MD	21030
7	Contoso Pharmaceuticals	611 W. 9 Mile Rd.	Ferndale	MI	48220-1234
8	Electronic, Inc.	136 S. Industrial Rd	Tupelo	MS	38801
9	Graphic Design Institute	511 Canal St	New Smyrna	FL	32168
10	Itexamworld.com	1413 W. Grace St	Chicago	IL	60613
11	Margie's Travel	PO Box 2678	Chapel Hill	NC	27515
12	Northridge Video	803 Broadway	West Plains	MO	65775
13	Southbridge Video	117 N. Kickapoo St	Lincoln	IL	62656
14	TailSpin Toys	1305C East Airline	Victoria,	AA	77901
15	Tasmanian Traders	47 King St.	St. Augustine	FL	32084
16	Shabby Sheik	6313 East 400th St.	Martinsville	IL	62442
17	A. Datum Corporation	600 US 31-W Bypass	Bowling Green	KY	42101
18	Alpine Ski House	11039 B Manchester Rd	Kirkwood	MO	63122

◂ ▸ | Input | **Customer Table** | ⊕

On the Input tab, you want to create dropdown menus to speed up data entry where possible. The first input field, Bill-to Name, reads the Customer Table tab's Bill-to Name field and uses that for its data validation source list. You can use the INDIRECT technique to make the data validation source list dynamic (For more information on dynamic lists and data validation, check out "#12 Controlled Lists with Data Validation" on page 171.*)

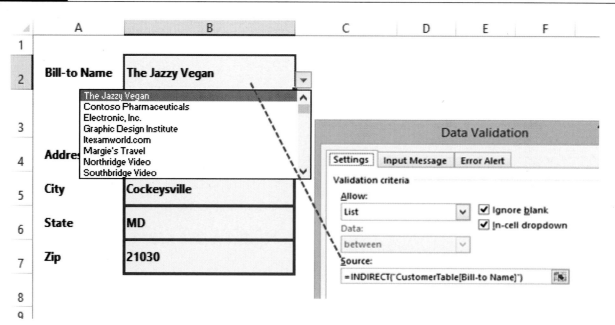

VLOOKUP Without the Sausage

Now you can move on to the other four input fields: Address, City, State, and Zip. Once the user selects a customer from the Bill-to Name dropdown, how will you get these four fields populated? I can hear team VLOOKUP out there, already crying out: *We get it! We know how to do this with VLOOKUP, using Bill-to Name as our Lookup value...*. Let me stop you right there and say it: Good for you. But recall that this tip is about providing a solution for *end users* who are not you – and who might be terrified of VLOOKUP. These people don't need to see the sausage being made.

So here's the plan: Let's separate the sausage-making process from the end user. You can take if off of the Input sheet and into the back end room where you create a named formula. All the logic built into your VLOOKUP will be embedded in the name.

First, create the VLOOKUP formula in the Address cell B4, just like you were going to do in the first place. Recall that the lookup range is a table named CustomerTable, and the Address field is the second column, so you would have this:

Inevitably, at some point there will be a one-off address change. You can let your end user overwrite the default formula, but after that you're back to square one (A1?). You must either re-create the formula for the users or rely on them to reconstruct it. Neither is a good option. But a named formula *is* a good option. Here's how to do it:

1. Click on B4.

2. Click in the formula bar and then highlight the text of the formula you just created.

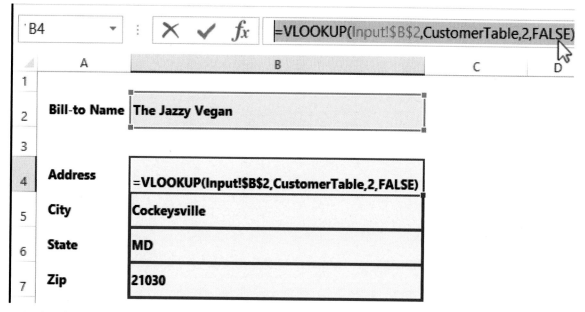

3. Right-click your selection and choose Copy.

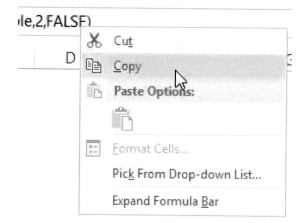

4. Press Enter to exit the formula bar.

5. From the Formulas tab, click Name Manager. The New Name dialog appears.

6. Click inside the Refers To box and press Ctrl+V to paste the clipboard contents.

7. In the Name box, type AddressLookup and then click OK.

3

8. Click on cell B4 again. Clear the contents (by right-clicking and selecting Clear Contents).

9. Click the Data tab, Data tools group, Data Validation. The Data Validation dialog appears.

10. From the Allow tab, choose List.

11. Click inside the Source box. Enter a + sign and press F3. Double-click AddressLookup to send it to the Data Validation dialog's Source box.

12. Click the Error Alert tab and uncheck Show Error Alert After Invalid Data is Entered.

This essentially allows you to create an either/or-style input field.
Either use the default address dropdown or fill-in your own address.

13. Click OK to close the Data Validation dialog.

Your Address field is now ready for prime time.

You can choose the "default" address using the dropdown or enter an alternate.

Replicating for the remaining fields

Now that you've done the first input field, AddressLookup, you can repeat exactly the same steps for City, State, and Zip. You could go straight to the Name Manager and create additional named formulas for each of these. Be sure to update each VLOOKUP with the correct column index references. From the Formulas tab, Defined Names group, Name Manager:

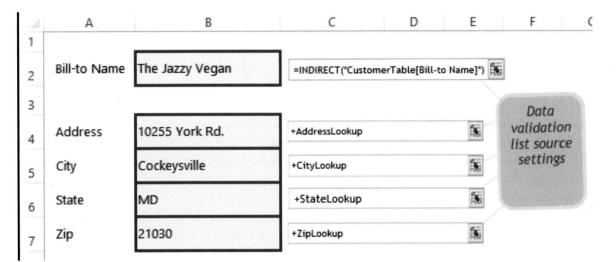

You now have a fully functioning input worksheet in your model, with data validation:

#16 Controlled Formula Lists with Data Validation

Just now, in tip #15 we explored some advanced techniques for using data validation lists. You added *named formulas* to a data validation list. However, you might recall that each of these lists used only a single formula.

Let the record show that you need not limit yourselves to *one* formula *per* Data Validation dialog Source box. You can have, well, a *list* of them.

Data Validation and Dates

It's true that data validation already offers a way to restrict input to a limited range of dates. Click the input cell where you want to apply date restrictions and then from the Data tab click Data Validation. In the Settings tab, choose Date from the Allow list. In the Data dropdown you see all the usual suspects for setting date parameters:

But you may still encounter problems if/when your end users are not very skilled at entering dates in Excel properly.

So here is another way. Let's say you want your end user to have the ability to choose from a few key dates, including the current day. The TODAY() function, discussed in "#14 Named Formulas: Yesterday and Tomorrow" on page 178, is a built-in Excel function. Like custom functions, it too can be added as an item in a Data Validation dialog's Source box:

Today, Tomorrow, Yesterday Recap

Note the syntax in the previous figure. Remember that TODAY() is a built-in function in Excel, with no arguments. When you add TODAY to the Data Validation dialog's Source box, make sure to use the + sign at the start and the opening and closing parentheses at the end, as shown in the previous figure. Otherwise, when your end users select it from the dropdown list, they may receive a #NAME error.

Unlike the built-in function TODAY, there is no similar YESTERDAY or TOMORROW function in Excel. So you created one in tip #14. To refresh your memory, here they are again, shown in action on a worksheet. Notice that I've also fired up the Name Manager to show the definitions for TOMORROW and YESTERDAY.

Restrict Choices to a Short List of Date Functions

With YESTERDAY, TOMORROW, and Excel's built in TODAY(), you have all the functions you need to build a nifty data validation dropdown list. You pick the input cell and set up a data validation rule to allow a list, where the choices are typed directly into the source box, like this:

Source:

+YESTERDAY,+TODAY0,+TOMORROW

Putting it all together:

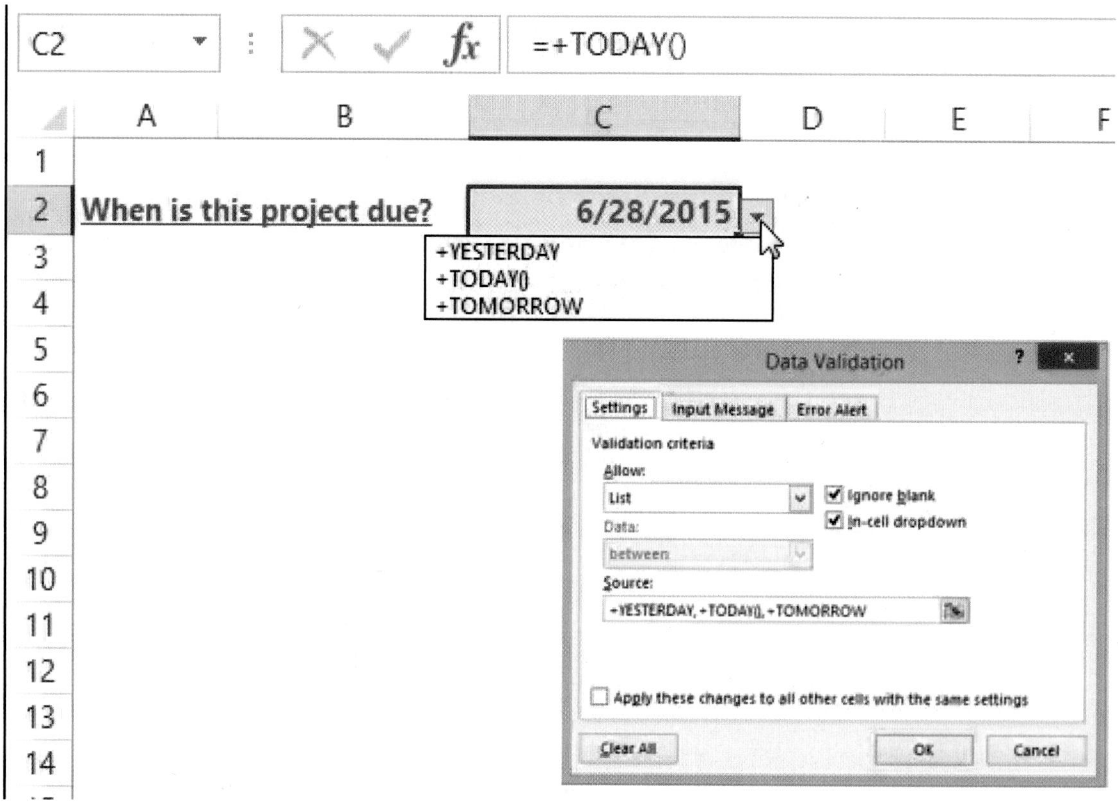

#17 Dependent Data Validation Lists

More tips in our data validation series! In the last few tips, you've learned how to use several types of data validation controlled lists, including choosing from a list of values, and choosing from a list of built-in or even named formulas you can create.

One aspect we have yet to explore: What happens when you have more than one list to consider, and these lists are *related* to each other in some way? For example, let's say you are creating a sign-up form to collect subscriber information. It has a dropdown list for state and then a second dropdown list for city. It would make sense to somehow filter the city dropdown list *dynamically*, based on the first selection made, in the state list.

By combining data validation list techniques with Excel's INDIRECT function, you can address these types of challenges.

For example, let's say you are planning on having an Excel-inspired cocktail party. You are creating a model to help you with your planning. You are building your ingredient lists by drink. You want two dropdown lists – one for your drink choice, and one for ingredients related to the drink choice. So far it looks like this:

	A	B	C	D
1	**BrokenLink**	**DAXOnTheBeach**	**PowerPivotini**	**JitterbugJelen**
2	Amaro	Lemon / Lime Soda	Angostura Bitters	Aged Rum
3	Angostura Bitters	Lime Juice	Egg White	Angostura Bitters
4	Aperol	Mango Nectar	Elderflower Liqueur	Falernum
5	Rye Whiskey	Vodka	Honey	Lime Juice
6	Sweet Vermouth		Lime Juice	Pomegranate Grenadine
7			Navy Strength Gin	
8				
9				
10	**Choose drink:**			
11				
12	**Choose ingredient:**			
13				

In B10 you want a dropdown to choose from the list of drinks you might serve at your party. This one is a straightforward data validation list. Click on B10, click the Data tab, then click Data Validation. In the Settings tab, Allow dropdown, click List. Click in the Source box and then highlight the horizontal range A1:D1, where you have your drink names.

Source:
| =$A$1:$D$1 | |

The next dropdown list, for ingredients, should depend on the drink selection made in B10. You can start tackling this problem by creating named ranges, one for each of the drinks listed in A1:D1. You can do this in just a few clicks:

1. Click A1 and drag down to the end of the ingredients list (that is, A6).

2. Press and hold the Ctrl key until the end of this series of steps.

3. Click B1 and drag down to the end of the ingredient list (that is, B5).

4. Repeat step 3 (still holding the Ctrl key) for the remaining two columns, C and D.

When you've selected all drinks and ingredients, your selection should look like this:

	A	B	C	D
1	**BrokenLink**	**DAXOnTheBeach**	**PowerPivotini**	**JitterbugJelen**
2	Amaro	Lemon / Lime Soda	Angostura Bitters	Aged Rum
3	Angostura Bitters	Lime Juice	Egg White	Angostura Bitters
4	Aperol	Mango Nectar	Elderflower Liqueur	Falernum
5	Rye Whiskey	Vodka	Honey	Lime Juice
6	Sweet Vermouth		Lime Juice	Pomegranate Grenadine
7			Navy Strength Gin	
8				

5. Click the Formulas tab. In the Defined Names group, click Create from Selection.

Define Name ▾
Use in Formula ▾
Name Manager · Create from Selection
Defined Names

6. In the Create Names from Selection dialog, ensure that Top Row is checked. Click OK.

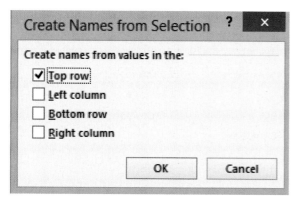

You have just created four new names. You can check the Name Manager to make sure. From the Formulas tab, click Name Manager to see them:

Name	Refers To	Scope
BrokenLink	=Drinks!$A$2:$A$6	Workbook
DAXOnTheBeach	=Drinks!$B$2:$B$5	Workbook
PowerPivotini	=Drinks!$C$2:$C$7	Workbook
JitterbugJelen	=Drinks!$D$2:$D$6	Workbook

INDIRECTly Speaking.

Now it's time for our INDIRECT trick. The INDIRECT function in Excel is one of those oddballs that is hard to explain without going straight to an example. One way to think of INDIRECT: it lets you change up the range arguments you might supply in a formula. You can type the name of a range in a cell and then use INDIRECT to grab that information and pop it into a formula. For instance, look at these wacky examples of the INDIRECT function:

In this figure, all the range definitions being supplied to the various INDIRECT functions are standard A1-style references. But you can also use named ranges as well. This is the key to implementing the dependent data validation list in this next example.

B8   =INDIRECT("B6")

	A	B	C
1	Drinks Sold		
2		*April*	*May*
3	Power Pivotini	10	12
4	Chandoo's Condition	12	16
5	Jitterbug Jelen	10	12
6		**32**	**40**
7			
8		32	=INDIRECT("B6")
9		40	=INDIRECT("C6")
10	B6	32	=INDIRECT(A10)
11	B3:B5	32	=SUM(INDIRECT(A11))
12	C3:C5	40	=SUM(INDIRECT(A12))
13	A3	Power Pivotini	=INDIRECT(A13)
14			

Creating the List Dependencies

To create a dependent dropdown list in B12:

1. Click on cell B12.

2. Click the Data tab, Data tools group, Data Validation. The Data Validation dialog appears.

3. From the Allow tab, choose List.

4. Click inside the Source box and enter the following:
=INDIRECT($B$10)

5. Click OK.

▲	A	B	C	D	E
1	**BrokenLink**	**DAXOnTheBeach**	**PowerPivotini**	**JitterbugJelen**	
2	Amaro	Lemon / Lime Soda	Angostura Bitters	Aged Rum	
3	Angostura Bitters	Lime Juice	Egg White	Angostura Bitters	
4	Aperol	Mango Nectar	Elderflower Liqueur	Falernum	
5	Rye Whiskey	Vodka	Honey	Lime Juice	
6	Sweet Vermouth		Lime Juice	Pomegranate Grenadine	
7			Navy Strength Gin		
8					
9					
10	**Choose drink:**	BrokenLink			
11					
12	**Choose ingredient:**	▼			
13		Amaro			
14		Angostura Bitters			
15		Aperol / Rye Whiskey / Sweet Vermouth			

Data Validation dialog:

Settings | Input Message | Error Alert

Validation criteria
Allow: List
☑ Ignore blank
☑ In-cell dropdown
Data: between
Source: =INDIRECT($B$10)
☐ Apply these changes to all other cells with the same settings
Clear All | OK | Cancel

You now have a dependent ingredients list. It bears mentioning once you select an item in B12, if you change the item in B10 you now have something invalid in B12. The way around this is a small piece of VBA to clear the item in B12 when B10 changes. In a Worksheet_Change module you could use this:

Worksheet | Change

```
Private Sub Worksheet_Change(ByVal Target As Range)

'Each time B10 changes, clear the contents of B12

If Not Intersect(Target, [B10]) Is Nothing Then
    [B12].ClearContents
End If

End Sub
```

Cheers!

Thanks to Todd Schulz and Shirlene Wilkin for naming this technique as one of their favorites.

#18 Smile for the Excel Camera!

Excel is all about straight lines. While this is great, it can also be a pain to make everything look *good* when you are trying to line up disparately sized elements onto a single page. Fortunately, the Excel camera tool is here to help.

First, Get Yourself a Camera

The camera tool doesn't automatically appear on your Ribbon, but you can add it to your QAT:

1. Right-click on the QAT and choose Customize Quick Access Toolbar.

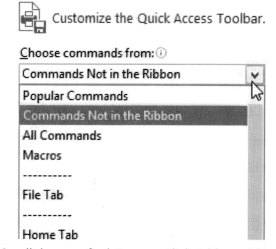

2. The Excel Options dialog appears. In the Choose Commands From dropdown, choose Commands Not in the Ribbon.

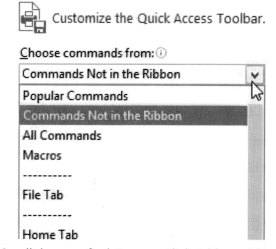

3. Scroll down to find Camera. Click Add to add it to your QAT.

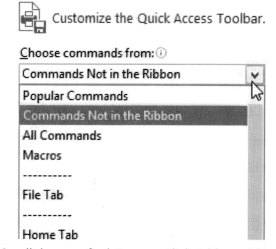

When Your Data Is Not Camera Ready

Say that you want to show a quarterly payroll report below a budget table. But the payroll account numbers are too long, and if you make the columns wide enough to display them, you've made your budget report look ugly again. The solution is to move the payroll report somewhere offscreen to make it look nice.

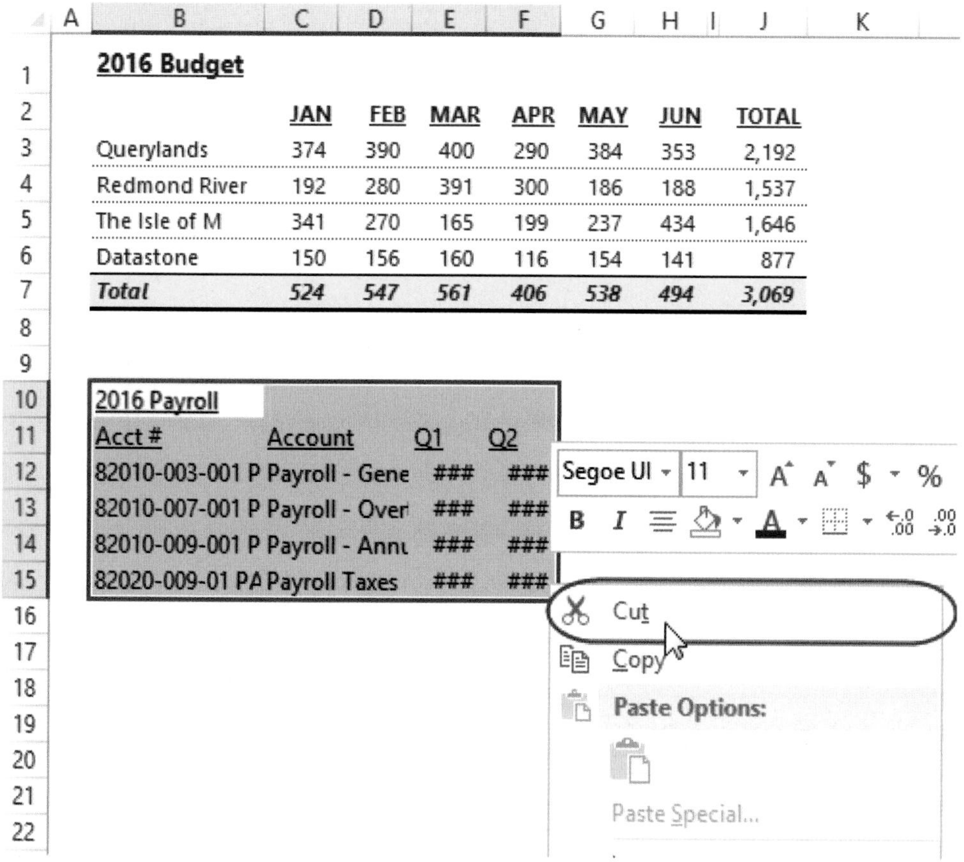

Once your payroll data is off in faraway lands in column Y, you can give it the makeover it desperately needs!

Here's the before shot:

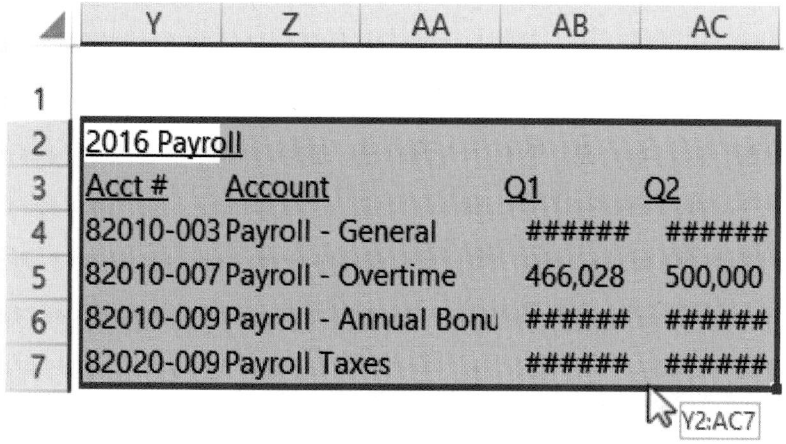

Here's a recap of what I did to make it look better: I started by removing the 2016 Payroll title in Y2 and moved that over to B9, where the rest of the payroll information will eventually appear. I applied the same formatting to B9 as I had in B1.

	2016 Budget							
		JAN	FEB	MAR	APR	MAY	JUN	TOTAL
	Querylands	374	390	400	290	384	353	2,192
	Redmond River	192	280	391	300	186	188	1,537
	The Isle of M	341	270	165	199	237	434	1,646
	Datastone	150	156	160	116	154	141	877
	Total	524	547	561	406	538	494	3,069

2016 Payroll

payroll data will go here once it's ready

Back to the Makeup Chair

Back over to column Y. For the remaining data, to get the alternate-row shading effect quickly, I used Ctrl+T to temporarily turn Y3:AC7 into a table and then I converted it back into a standard range by selecting Table Tools, Tools group, Convert to Range. I adjusted column widths so everything is visible, and at this point I am pleased with the look of it:

	X	Y	Z	AA	AB
3		Acct #	Account	Q1	Q2
4		82010-003-001 PAGEN	Payroll - General	2,000,000	1,080,930
5		82010-007-001 PAOVT	Payroll - Overtime	466,028	500,000
6		82010-009-001 PABNS	Payroll - Annual Bonus	1,631,098	1,513,302
7		82020-009-01 PATAX	Payroll Taxes	1,165,070	1,080,930

Ready for an Excelfie!

All that is left to do is snap the picture and place it somewhere on the worksheet. At this point, you just highlight the now beautifully formatted payroll data and then click the new camera icon on your QAT. You will see the "marching ants" around your selection, just like when you copy something into the clipboard.

Camera

Y3   ✕ ✓ *fx*   Acct #

	X	Y	Z	AA	AB
1					
2					
3		Acct #	Account	Q1	Q2
4		82010-003-001 PAGEN	Payroll - General	2,000,000	1,080,930
5		82010-007-001 PAOVT	Payroll - Overtime	466,028	500,000
6		82010-009-001 PABNS	Payroll - Annual Bonu:	1,631,098	1,513,302
7		82020-009-01 PATAX	Payroll Taxes	1,165,070	1,080,930
8					

Now go back over to where your original report is, in column B. You'll notice that your cursor has turned into a small black cross, which means you are ready to *draw*.

Position your cursor just below B9, under your payroll report header.

Now just click once. The picture appears! It's an object that "floats" above your worksheet so you can move it around and adjust sizing just as you would with a text box or shape.

5	The Isle of M	341	270	1
6	Datastone	150	156	1
7	*Total*	*524*	*547*	*5(*
8				
9	**2016 Payroll**			
10	+			
11				

Design tip: Don't stretch it too much in any direction, or the resolution will start to look off.

The best part is, the picture is a *linked* object, as you might notice by looking at the formula bar, which shows the source range when the object is selected. So when you make a change in the source range, the changes will be reflected in your linked picture object.

| Picture 6 ▼ | ⋮ | ✕ ✓ *fx* | =$Y$3:$AB$7 |

2016 Budget

	JAN	FEB	MAR	APR	MAY	JUN	TOTAL
Querylands	374	390	400	290	384	353	2,192
Redmond River	192	280	391	300	186	188	1,537
The Isle of M	341	270	165	199	237	434	1,646
Datastone	150	156	160	116	154	141	877
Total	*524*	*547*	*561*	*406*	*538*	*494*	*3,069*

2016 Payroll

Acct #		Account	Q1	Q2
82010-003-001	PAGEN	Payroll - General	2,000,000	1,080,930
82010-007-001	PAOVT	Payroll - Overtime	466,028	500,000
82010-009-001	PABNS	Payroll - Annual Bonus	1,631,098	1,513,302
82020-009-01	PATAX	Payroll Taxes	1,165,070	1,080,930

Now there is something to smile about!

Joerg Decker, Gerald Strever and Bernard Vukas suggested the Camera tool

Illustration: Walter Moore

#19 VLOOKUP – to the Left!

Go West, Young Man

You've all heard it before. VLOOKUP can only "look right". It's a myth, but a very popular one. It's not surprising this is such an ingrained fact of life. In his Excelcampus blog, Excel MVP Jon Acampora reminds us just how often we do VLOOKUP in our heads, following exactly the same motion that Excel does:

VLOOKUP Explained

Scan down to find item

1

CLASSIC FAVORITES	TALL	GRANDE	VENTI
Café Latte	$2.95	$3.75	$4.15
Cappuccino	$2.95	$3.65	$4.15
Caramel Macchiato	$3.75	$3.95	$4.25
Café Mocha	$3.25	$3.95	$4.40
	$3.45	$4.15	$4.55
Caffe Americano	$2.00	$2.40	$2.75
Cinnamon Dolce Latte	$3.95	$4.75	$5.15
Steamer	$2.25	$2.50	$2.75
Drip Coffee	$1.75	$1.95	$2.05

2 *Look across to find price* **3**

Courtesy of Jon Acampora. Logos modified here to protect the innocent.

So we reinforce our familiar VLOOKUP mindset every time we order coffee?? Apparently so!

But data isn't always arranged in the way we need it. So what if we wanted Excel to look to the left?

When Going Right Just Won't Work..

Let's say you're back at Excelicious Café again, and it's trivia night! You fire up Excel to check the scores from last week. Here's a partial view of the first 19 teams:

	A	B	C	D	E
1	Best Week	Team Captain	Team name	Number of players	Last week's score
2	9	Matt A.	Power Pivot Pit Stop	5	83
3	4	Mike G.	Excel Dragon Slayers	6	90
4	4	Ken P.	M Kay?	6	84
5	1	Marco R.	DAX The Way I Like It	2	85
6	1	Rick G.	The What-Ifs	2	87
7	5	Anne W.	Copy, Paste, Craic	3	92
8	12	Kevin L.	Canadians Excel Too	4	85
9	2	Kris S.	Hungarian Notation	3	97
10	2	Jordan G.	Cambia Slackers	7	89
11	4	Jon P.	The Chart Legends	6	88
12	4	Dan F.	The (Problem) Solvers	6	84
13	6	Melissa E.	Grand Theft Autofilter	3	98
14	5	XSzil	Tequila Text Box	2	99
15	10	Zack B.	Blue Screen Of Death Match	7	83
16	6	Oz D.	Sparklines & Sriracha	3	85
17	2	Mynda T.	Excel Assassins	2	98
18	1	Ryan W.	Holy Balance Sheet	5	83
19	7	Yesenia G.	Index Match Attack	2	97
20					

Highest possible score of 100; Excel people are to be feared.

You can use VLOOKUP to find the number of players or last week's score by team captain or by team name, because directionally both of those questions "look right." But what if you want to look up team captain based on team name? Or how about best week by team captain?

CHOOSE to Go Left

It turns out you can "trick" VLOOKUP into going left by incorporating the CHOOSE function with VLOOKUP. On its own, CHOOSE will choose an item from a list, based on an index number. The official Excel syntax is:

```
=CHOOSE(index_num, value1, [value 2]…)
```

You can have up to 254 values. CHOOSE will return the value based on the index_num. For example:

```
=CHOOSE(1,"Excel","Tableau","Babylonian Clay Tablet")
```

will return Excel because that is first in the list of values. Now, buckle up. Here is the crazy part. Array formula fans will love this trick, one that I learned from Mynda Treacy (thanks, Mynda)!

If you surround the index_num argument with some curly brackets {} you can specify more than one index number. You can also specify *ranges* instead of values, so CHOOSE will return a range *reference*. So this formula:

```
=CHOOSE({1,2},$C$2:$C$15,$B$2:$B$15))
```

is basically saying, C is the first column, and B is the second column. What does all this mean for VLOOKUP? *It means you can replace the entire table_array argument VLOOKUP with a CHOOSE function like this anytime you want VLOOKUP to go left.*

A Whole New Syntax

Now let's compare the "old" VLOOKUP – looking only right – with our "new" VLOOKUP that can look left.

To look right, the old familiar syntax:

```
=VLOOKUP(lookup_value, table_array, col_index_num, [range_lookup])
```

To look left, the new syntax:

```
=VLOOKUP(lookup_value,CHOOSE({1,2},lookup_array,return_array), 2,
FALSE)
```

where

lookup_value is the value you seek, lookup_array is the column containing your lookup value , and return array is the column containing the return value.

Let's try an example. Say that you're back at trivia night, and the competition is still fierce! You want to know who the team captain of *Hungarian Notation* is because those people worry you. You break down the arguments using the "look left" syntax:

- lookup_value is "Hungarian Notation".

- lookup_array is C2:C19.

- return_array is B2:B19.

Plugging these into a look-left-style VLOOKUP function:

```
=VLOOKUP("Hungarian Notation",CHOOSE({1,2}, C2:C19, B2:B19), 2, FALSE)
```

returns *Kris*. I knew it!

And Now, with Structured Referencing

Now, if you've turned the data into Excel table (Ctrl+T), you will of course wind up with structured references in your formulas. Assume that you've done this and that you've named your table TriviaTable. The final example shows how your new VLOOKUP-LEFT* technique lets Excel find the team captain in C24 and the best performance week in C26 based on a team name selected from a dropdown list in C22.

Neat!

*Dear Microsoft, can we please have a simpler way to do this now? Maybe just allow negative numbers for the column_index_num argument? Thanks!

Illustration: Walter Moore

	A	B	C	D	E	F	G	H
1	Best Week ▼	Team Captain ▼	Team name ▼	Number of players ▼	Last week's score ▼			
2	9	Matt A.	Power Pivot Pit Stop	5	83			
3	4	Mike G.	Excel Dragon Slayers	6	90			
4	4	Ken P.	M Kay?	6	84			
5	1	Marco R.	DAX The Way I Like It	2	85			
6	1	Rick G.	The What-Ifs	2	87			
7	5	Anne W.	Copy, Paste, Craic	3	92			
8	12	Kevin L.	Canadians Excel Too	4	85			
9	2	Kris S.	Hungarian Notation	3	97			
10	2	Jordan G.	Cambia Slackers	7	89			
11	4	Jon P.	The Chart Legends	6	88			
12	4	Dan F.	The (Problem) Solvers	6	84			
13	6	Melissa E.	Grand Theft Autofilter	3	98			
14	5	XSzil	Tequila Text Box	2	99			
15	10	Zack B.	Blue Screen Of Death Matcl	7	83			
16	6	Oz D.	Sparklines & Sriracha	3	85			
17	2	Mynda T.	Excel Assassins	2	98			
18	1	Ryan W.	Holy Balance Sheet	5	83			
19	7	Yesenia G.	Index Match Attack	2	97			
20								
21								
22	**Select team:** Holy Balance Sheet ▼							
23								
24	**Captain =** Ryan W.							
	=VLOOKUP(C22,CHOOSE({1,2},TriviaTable[Team name],TriviaTable[Team Captain]),2,FALSE)							
25								
26	**Best week =** Week 1							
27	="Week "&VLOOKUP(C22,CHOOSE({1,2},TriviaTable[Team name],TriviaTable[Best Week]),2,FALSE)							
28								

Mark Ford, Jeremy Trebas and @InfiniteDrifter suggested this technique.

#20 Data Shaping (Unpivot) with Power Query

A good portion of this book is dedicated to the amazing powers of the pivot table, and now I'm suggesting you *un*pivot? Yes!

If you are a regular Excel user and have not used Power Query, you should get on that ASAP. It is a free add-in, easily found online via a quick ~~Google~~ Bing search. It works with Excel 2010 or higher.

So what does Power Query do? In a nutshell, it is a hugely powerful program that lets you do all kinds of data cleansing, aggregating, and *reshaping* in a much simpler way than ever before. The total scope of its powers is far greater than what can be covered in the next pages here. Nevertheless, I suspect you will be hooked and will want to know more. If so, you should check out the great resources Ken Puls and Miguel Escobar have to offer: http://mrx.cl/pqtraining.

One for the Pivot Table Users

If you use pivot tables, you know that creating a pivot table is the easy part. Even on the reporting side, you can do quite a bit without a ton of effort. But challenges arise before any of this happens, in particular when the source data is not in the format you need. For example, if you try to pivot this, it will basically suck:

	A	B	C	D	E	F	G	H
1	Product	6/30/2015	6/23/2015	6/16/2015	6/9/2015	6/2/2015	5/26/2015	5/19/2015
2	Guns	227	381	275	165	473	298	230
3	Germs	102	124	439	455	248	324	207
4	Steel	233	198	335	429	499	270	262
5	Popsicles	251	472	359	171	143	231	249
6	Floor Wax	326	428	273	365	151	432	390
7								

You might *think* it looks like a flat table – even pivot table data source-esque. Close, but no dice. It might be just fine as a pivot table *report* but not as *source data*. The official reasons for the eventual suckitude have to do with database theory and data normalization forms. But let's not ~~put ourselves to sleep~~ digress. Suffice it to say: *if the column headers in your source data can double as values within a field, you need to re-shape your data before you pivot*. In this case, the column headers (6/30/2015 and so on) *could* double as *values* - for a field called *week*. That's why it won't work as a data source, and that's why you need Power Query.

Power Query to the Rescue

You've downloaded Power Query. It shows up as a new tab on your Ribbon. Now:

1. Click anywhere inside your data table that needs to be fixed. In your new Power Query tab, click From Table.

Power Query helpfully reminds you of your data range and confirms that your table has headers.

2. Click OK to accept this.

▲	A	B	C	D	E	F	G	H
1	**Product**	**6/30/201**	**6/23/201**	**6/16/201**	**6/9/2015**	**6/2/2015**	**5/26/201**	**5/19/201**
2	Guns	227	381	275	165	473	298	230
3	Germs	102	124	439	455	248	324	207
4	Steel	233	100	225	420	400	270	262
5	Popsicles	251						
6	Floor Wax	326						
7								
8								
9								
10								
11								
12								
13								
14								

From Table

Where is the data for your table?

$A$1:$H$6

✓ My table has headers

OK　　Cancel

3. In the Power Query Editor dialog, click the column header for the Product field to highlight the Product column.

4. Click the Transform tab on the Power Query ribbon. In the Any Column group, find Unpivot Columns icon. Choose Unpivot Other Columns from the dropdown list.

Table1 - Query Editor

File　　Home　　Transform　　Add Column　　View

Data Type: Any ▾　　Statistics ▾　　Trigonometry ▾
Replace Values　　Standard ▾　　Rounding ▾
Table　　Replace Errors　　Text Column ▾　　Scientific ▾　　Information ▾

Any Colum　　Unpivot Columns　　Number Column　　Date &

Unpivot Other Columns

▦▾	Product ▾	6/30/2			▾ 6/9/2015	▾ 6/2/2015
1	Guns	227	381	275	165	
2	Germs	102	124	439	455	
3	Steel	233	198	335	429	
4	Popsicles	251	472	359	171	
5	Floor Wax	326	428	273	365	

3

Your data now looks like this:

5. Clean up the columns: Right-click the Value column, choose Rename, and change Value to Units. Right-click on the Attribute column, choose Rename, and change Attribute to Week.

6. With the Week column highlighted, click the Transform tab and change the Week column's Data Type from Any to Date.

7. In the Query Settings pane on the right change the name of your data table to Units (optional, but good practice). Also notice that Power Query has been recording your steps for you all this time, in the Applied Steps list.

The Query Settings pane, with Applied Steps. It's like a modern Excel version of the VBA macro recorder!

8. In the Power Query Home tab, click Close & Load (or it might be Apply & Close).

Power Query creates a new worksheet and loads your reshaped data into an Excel table. Best of all, it's "normalized" – that is, pivot table friendly!

Product	Week	Units
Guns	6/30/2015	227
Guns	6/23/2015	381
Guns	6/16/2015	275
Guns	6/9/2015	165
Guns	6/2/2015	473
Guns	5/26/2015	298
Guns	5/19/2015	230
Germs	6/30/2015	102
Germs	6/23/2015	124

Modern Excel. You've come a long way, baby!

Alaeddin Badran and David Rosenthal both suggested unpivoting for this book.

#21 XSzil Design Tips for Excel for Presenters and Trainers

By popular demand, this tip is just for presenters and Excel trainers. Following are some "outside the gridlines" ideas I've used over the years to design fun, engaging Excel classes and takeaway materials.

Use FORMULATEXT()

If you want to show a formula in your onscreen or printed materials so the reader can easily see both a formula and the result at the same time, use FORMULATEXT.

E5		f_x	=FORMULATEXT(D5)

	A	B	C	D	E
1					
2	SUMIFS()				
3			Name	Cat Pie	
4			Category	Cat Nip	
5			Amount	$ 24.10	=SUMIFS(D8:D21,A8:A21,D3,C8:C21,D4)
6					
7	Name	Date	Category	Amount	
8	Meowz'Bub	12/27	Cat Nip	$36.80	
9	Meowz'Bub	12/21	Accessories	$22.00	
10	Fluffy Pants	12/6	Cat Nip	$25.00	
11	Cat Pie	12/28	Boarding	$320.00	
12	Cat Pie	12/15	Cat Nip	$6.30	
13	Danny Mewn	12/29	Cat Nip	$17.80	
14	Danny Mewn	12/18	Accessories	$25.00	
15	Danny Mewn	12/11	Accessories	$32.50	
16	Lucky	12/16	Boarding	$96.00	
17	Cat Pie	12/11	Cat Nip	$17.80	
18	Cat Pie	12/25	Accessories	$25.00	
19	OC (Original Cat)	12/24	Accessories	$32.50	
20	OC (Original Cat)	12/29	Boarding	$96.00	
21	OC (Original Cat)	12/18	Cat Nip	$32.50	
22					

*Adapted from a Mike Girvin example, except he used dogs. I am team **both**, personally.*

Yes, FORMULATEXT will save your life, especially for printed materials.

Trainers, take note! If you distribute any files to others, remember that there are still people in this world who do not have Excel 2013. FORMULATEXT was introduced in 2013. Here is a simple VBA function you can use that will work for all versions:

```
Public Function FT(MyCell As Range)
    FT = MyCell.Formula
End Function
```

Using this approach will ensure that pre-Excel 2013 users won't get a bunch of #NAME errors when they open your file:

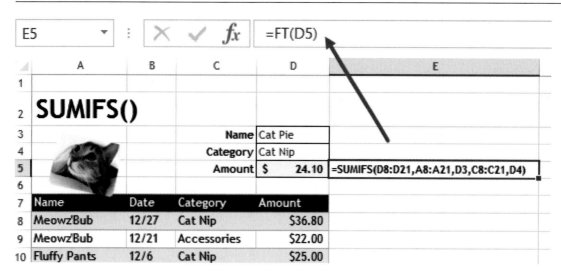

Excel for Presentations at the Office

Even for non-training purposes, you can make Excel more presentation friendly by minimizing the Ribbon, hiding gridlines, hiding the formula bar, and hiding row and column headers. With enough creativity, people won't even realize you're in Excel! Aesthetics count. This is increasingly important these days, with more and more Excel "competitors" capitalizing on the beautiful look and feel of their products, forever comparing themselves to Excel.

Excel for Excel Training

For training sessions, of course I like to stay in Excel as much as possible rather than doing the constant Alt+Tab between Excel and PowerPoint (no offense, PowerPoint, I love you, too). So, I create Excel/PowerPoint hybrids. How do I do it without sacrificing the intent of an Excel training session with too much silliness?

Make Use of Pictures and Shapes

In the previous figure, you can see my cat's beautiful headshot. Hard to believe, but that handsome image adds more than incredible cuteness to a presentation. As you know, we can assign macros to shapes and pictures with a simple right-click:

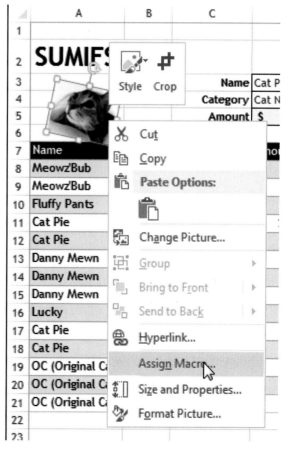

This opens up all kinds of possibilities. Here are some of the macros that I've used in training presentations:

- Toggle font color between black and white for anything I don't want attendees to see on screen until I'm ready to show them. This macro will do that trick:

```
Sub ToggleFontColor()

'Toggle FORMULATEXT cell (or any other cell's)
'font color between white and black

With [E1].Font

    If .Color = vbBlack Then
       .Color = vbWhite
    ElseIf .Color = vbWhite Then
     .Color = vbBlack
    End If

End With

End Sub
```

- Toggle the formula bar on/off (to hide the formula bar until you are ready to show it):

```
Sub ToggleFormulaBar()

'Show / hide the formula bar

With Application
    .DisplayFormulaBar = .NotDisplayFormulaBar
End With

End Sub
```

- Toggle a specific row or column to show/hide:

```
Sub ToggleSpecificColumn()

'Show / hide a specific column
'Could also be modified for .EntireRow
'to show / hide a specific row

With [E1].EntireColumn
    .Hidden = .NotHidden
End With

End Sub
```

"Worksheet Within a Worksheet" Effect

This effect is kind of like those Russian nesting dolls. It looks like this:

FILE	HOME	INSERT	PAGE LAYOUT	FORMULAS	DATA	REVIEW	VIEW	DEVELOPE

C8   ▾   ⁝   ✕   ✓   *fx*   =LEFT(ADDRESS(1,COLUMN(),2),1+(COLUMN()>26))

1.3 Auto Sum, Many Columns

<u>Challenge</u>: Create monthly and YTD totals - in 2 steps!

	C	D	E	F	G	H	I	J
9		Jan	Feb	Mar	Apr	May	Jun	Jul
10	North	123	396	165	330	128	271	237
11	East	477	264	499	420	115	193	140
12	West	124	251	100	117	225	180	383
13	South	194	412	152	404	127	201	490
14	TOTAL							
15								
16								
17								

The "fake column" effect is created with the formula you see in the formula bar. COLUMN() won't work because it returns a number. For "fake rows" it's easier: use ROW().

Why all the fuss? For one thing, when you convert the Excel file to PDF, poof! Instant e-book that you can distribute to attendees. The Excel file is then a practice file and book, all in one.

Final Word

There are certainly many other ways to approach designing course materials, and I am sure many of them are far more efficient than mine. Using Excel for course materials is probably every serious graphic artist's nightmare. I know. I've seen the raised eyebrows. But to me, it's a labor of love and further proof that Excel is truly the world's most versatile software, ever.

XSzil evangelizing

#22 Fill in a Flash

Excel 2013 added a new data-cleansing tool called Flash Fill. In the figure below, you see full names in column A. You want to get the person's first initial and last name in column B. Rather than try to puzzle out =PROPER(LEFT(A2,1)&" "&MID(A2,FIND(" ",A2)+1,50)), you simply type a sample of what you want in B2.

	A	B
1	Name	First Initial Last Name
2	ALEX PILAR	A. Pilar
3	GARY KANE	
4	DENNIS P. JANCSY	
5	ALLAN MATZ	
6	MIKE GIRVIN	
7	CAROLINE BONNER	
8	GRAHAM STENT	
9	MARTHA K. WENDEL	
10	PETER SUSEN	
11	BRIAN CANES	

Type the first initial in B3. Excel sees what you are doing and "grays in" a suggested result.

	A	B
1	Name	First Initial L
2	ALEX PILAR	A. Pilar
3	GARY KANE	G. Kane
4	DENNIS P. JANCSY	D. Jancsy
5	ALLAN MATZ	A. Matz
6	MIKE GIRVIN	M. Girvin
7	CAROLINE BONNER	C. Bonner
8	GRAHAM STENT	G. Stent
9	MARTHA K. WENDEL	M. Wendel
10	PETER SUSEN	P. Susen
11	BRIAN CANES	B. Canes

Press Enter to accept the suggestion. Bam! All of the data is filled in.

Look carefully through your data for exceptions to the rule. Two people here have middle initials. Do you want the middle initial to appear? If so, correct the suggestion for Dennis P. Jancsy in cell B4. Flash Fill will jump into action and fix Martha K. Wendel in B9 and any others that match the new pattern. The status bar will indicate how many changes were made.

	A	B	C
1	Name	First Initial Last Name	
2	ALEX PILAR	A. Pilar	
3	GARY KANE	G. Kane	**Type**
4	DENNIS P. JANCSY	D. P. Jancsy	
5	ALLAN MATZ	A. Matz	
6	MIKE GIRVIN	M. Girvin **Flash**	
7	CAROLINE BONNER	C. Bonner **Fill**	**on grid**
8	GRAHAM STENT	G. Stent	**menu**
9	MARTHA K. WENDEL	M. K. Wendel	
10	PETER SUSEN	P. Susen	

Sheet1 Sheet2 (+)

Ready   Flash Fill Changed Cells: 1

An on-grid dropdown menu appears. Open this, and you can select the cells that were just changed. Change the font color and the filter by color to inspect them.

In the above case, Excel gurus could have figured out the formula. But Flash Fill is easier. In the following case, it would be harder to write a formula to get the last word from a phrase that has a different number of words and more than one hyphen.

	A	B
1	Customer	Type
2	900 bradedgar.com - consulting	Consulting
3	1164 Frontline Systems - applications	
4	1156 California Blazing Chile Farms - retail	
5	1175 Safety Elements Ltd. - services	
6	918 Hybrid Software - applications	
7	947 IMA Houston Chapter - associations	
8	1048 Fintega Financial Modelling - consulting	
9	1001 Roto-Rooter - services	
10	1103 MN Excel Consulting - consulting	
11	1145 Open Sky Martial Arts - training	

Flash Fill makes this easy. Go to cell B3. Press Ctrl+E to invoke Flash Fill.

	A	B
1	Customer	Type
2	900 bradedgar.com - consulting	Consulting
3	1164 Frontline Systems - applications	Applications
4	1156 California Blazing Chile Farms - retail	Retail
5	1175 Safety Elements Ltd. - services	Services
6	918 Hybrid Software - applications	Applications
7	947 IMA Houston Chapter - associations	Associations
8	1048 Fintega Financial Modelling - consulting	Consulting
9	1001 Roto-Rooter - services	Services
10	1103 MN Excel Consulting - consulting	Consulting
11	1145 Open Sky Martial Arts - training	Training

Note that Flash Fill will not automatically fill in numbers. If you have numbers, you might see Flash Fill temporarily "gray in" a suggestion but then withdraw it. This is your signal to press Ctrl+E to give Flash Fill permission to fill in numbers.

Thanks to Chad Rothschiller at Microsoft for building this feature. Thanks also tto Olga Kryuchkova.

#23 Suppress Errors with IFERROR

Formula errors can be common. If you have a data set with hundreds of records, a divide-by-Zero or a #N/A are bound to pop up now and then.

In the past, preventing errors required herculean efforts. Nod your head knowingly if you've ever knocked out =IF(ISNA(VLOOKUP(A2,Table,2,0)),"Not Found",VLOOKUP(A2,Table,2,0)). Besides being really long to type, that solution requires Excel to do twice as many VLOOKUPs. First, you do a VLOOKUP to see if the VLOOKUP is going to produce an error. Then you do the same VLOOKUP again to get the non-error result.

Excel 2010 introduced the greatly improved =IFERROR(Formula,Value If Error). I know that IFERROR sounds like the old old ISERROR, ISERR, ISNA functions, but it is completely different.

This is a brilliant function: =IFERROR(VLOOKUP(A2,Table,2,0),"Not Found"). If you have 1,000 VLOOKUPs and only 5 return #N/A, then the 995 that worked only require a single VLOOKUP. It is only the 5 that returned #N/A that need to move on to the second argument of IFERROR.

Oddly, Excel 2013 added the IFNA() function. It is just like IFERROR but only looks for #N/A errors. One might imagine a strange situation where the value in the lookup table is found, but the resulting answer is a division by 0. If you wanted to preserve the divide-by-zero error for some reason, then IFNA() will do this.

| B4 | | | f_x | =IFNA(VLOOKUP(A4,Table,4,0),"Not Found") |

	A	B	C	D	E	F	G
1	Handle	Average					
2	Bluefeather8989	539		Handle	Qty	Revenue	Avg Price
3	MikeAsHimself	582		aBoBoBook	895	521785	583
4	MrExcel	#DIV/0!		Bluefeather8989	989	533071	539
5	ExcelisFun	Not Found		INDZARA	1124	611456	544
6	Bluefeather8989	539		Kazmdav	1019	507462	498
7	McGunigales	527		McGunigales	921	485367	527
8				MikeAsHimself	843	490626	582
9				MrExcel	0	0	#DIV/0!
10				Symons	972	562788	579

Of course, the person who built the lookup table should have used IFERROR to prevent the division by zero in the first place. In the figure below, the "n.m." is a former manager's code for "not meaningful."

| | | f_x | =IFERROR(F9/E9,"n.m.") |

D	E	F	G
Handle	Qty	Revenue	Avg Price
aBoBoBook	895	521785	583
Bluefeather8989	989	533071	539
INDZARA	1124	611456	544
Kazmdav	1019	507462	498
McGunigales	921	485367	527
MikeAsHimself	843	490626	582
MrExcel	0	0	n.m.
Symons	972	562788	579

Thanks to Justin Fishman, Stephen Gilmer, and Excel by Joe.

#24 Plural Conditions with SUMIFS

Did you notice the "S" that got added to the end of SUMIF starting in Excel 2007? While SUMIF and SUMIFS sound the same, the new SUMIFS can run circles around its elder sibling.

The old SUMIF and COUNTIF have been around since Excel 97. In the figure below, the formula tells Excel to look through the names in B2:B22. If a name is equal to the name in F4, then sum the corresponding cell from the range starting in D2. (I realize that most people would use $D$2:$D$22 as the last argument, but you only have to specify the top cell.)

| G4 | | | f_x | =SUMIF($B$2:$B$22,F4,$D$2) |

Summary Table

	B	C	D	E	F	G
1	Rep	Product	Quantity			
2	Richard Oldcorn	Widget	267			
3	Allen Matz	Widget	221		Name	Qty
4	Rob Collie	Widget	371		Allen Matz	1543
5	Rob Collie	Gadget	354		Lorna Banuilos	799
6	Lorna Banuilos	Widget	236		Richard Oldcorn	1940
7	Allen Matz	Widget	237		Rob Collie	1688
8	Richard Oldcorn	Widget	292			

SUMIF and COUNTIF were great when you only had one condition. But if you had two or more things to check, you had to switch over to SUMPRODUCT. (I realize most people would replace my multiplication signs with commas and add a double-minus before the first two terms, but mine works, too.)

| G4 | | | f_x | =SUMPRODUCT(($B$2:$B$22=$F4)*($C$2:$C$22=G$3)*($D$2:$D$22)) |

Summary Table

	A	B	C	D	E	F	G	H	I	J
1	Invoice	Rep	Product	Quantity						
2	1001	Richard Oldcorn	Widget	267						
3	1002	Allen Matz	Widget	221		Name	Widget	Gadget		
4	1003	Rob Collie	Widget	371		Allen Matz	1290	253		
5	1004	Rob Collie	Gadget	354		Lorna Banuilos	799	0		
6	1005	Lorna Banuilos	Widget	236		Richard Oldcorn	1355	585		
7	1006	Allen Matz	Widget	237		Rob Collie	1334	354		
8	1007	Richard Oldcorn	Widget	292						

SUMIFS allows for up to 127 conditions. Because you might have an indeterminate number of conditions in the function, the numbers that you are adding up move from the third argument to the first argument. In the following formula, you are summing D2:D22, but only the rows where column B is Allen Matz and column C is Widget.

| G4 | | | f_x | =SUMIFS($D$2:$D$22,$B$2:$B$22,$F4,$C$2:$C$22,G$3) |

Summary Table

	A	B	C	D	E	F	G	H	I
1	Invoice	Rep	Product	Quantity					
2	1001	Richard Oldcorn	Widget	267					
3	1002	Allen Matz	Widget	221		Name	Widget	Gadget	
4	1003	Rob Collie	Widget	371		Allen Matz	1290	253	
5	1004	Rob Collie	Gadget	354		Lorna Banuilos	799	0	
6	1005	Lorna Banuilos	Widget	236		Richard Oldcorn	1355	585	
7	1006	Allen Matz	Widget	237		Rob Collie	1334	354	
8	1007	Richard Oldcorn	Widget	292					

Excel 2007 also added plural versions of COUNTIFS and AVERAGEIFS. All of these "S" functions are very efficient and fast.

Thanks to Nathi Njoko, Abshir Osman, Scott Russell, and Ryan Sitoy.

#25 Formatting as Façade

Excel is amazing at storing one number and presenting another number. Choose any cell and select Currency format. Excel adds a dollar sign and a comma and presents the number rounded to two decimal places. In the figure below, cell D2 actually contains 6.42452514. Thankfully, the built-in custom number format presents the results in an easy-to-read format.

	A	B	C	D
1	Rep	Qty	Revenue	Avg Price
2	Andrew Spain	26,850	172,498.50	$6.42
3	Geoffrey G Lilley	24,458	157,921.10	$6.46
4	Kevin J Sullivan	24,754	160,180.30	$6.47
5	Peter Polakovic	24,090	143,880.50	$5.97

The custom number format code in D2 is $#,##0.00. In this code, 0s are required digits. Any #s are optional digits.

However, formatting codes can be far more complex. The code above has one format. That format is applied to every value in the cell. If you provide a code with two formats, the first format is for non-negative numbers, and the second format is for negative numbers. You separate the formats with semi-colons. If you provide a code with three formats, the first is for positive, then negative, then zero. If you provide a code with four formats, they are used for positive, negative, zero, and text.

Format
Format >=0;Format<0
Positive;Negative;Zero
Positive;Negative;Zero;Text

Even if you are using a built-in format, you can go to Format Cells, Number, Custom and see the code used to generate that format. Here is the code for the Accounting format:

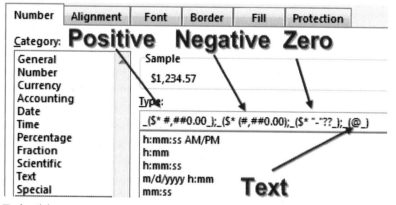

To build your own custom format, go to Format Cells, Number, Custom and enter the code in the Type box. Check out the example in the Sample box to make sure everything looks correct.

In the following example, three zones are used. Text in quotes is added to the number format to customize the message.

	Format in C: "Please Remit "$0.00;"Credit Balance of "$0.00" (Do not pay)";"No Balance"		
3	Customer	Balance	Formatted
4	Wag More Dog Store, San Antonio	-18.03	Credit Balance of $18.03 (Do not pay)
5	How To Excel At Excel.Com	192.28	Please Remit $192.28
6	SurtenExcel.com	27.72	Please Remit $27.72
7	University of North Carolina	-187.38	Credit Balance of $187.38 (Do not pay)
8	Yesenita	120.15	Please Remit $120.15
9	Lake Local School District	147.49	Please Remit $147.49
10	Resource Optimizer	-78.33	Credit Balance of $78.33 (Do not pay)
11	GL Wand	-178.59	Credit Balance of $178.59 (Do not pay)
12	The Salem Historical Society, Salem, Ohio	-110.53	Credit Balance of $110.53 (Do not pay)

If you create a zone for zero but put nothing there, you will hide all zero values. The following code uses color codes for positive and negative. The code ends in a semi-colon, creating a zone for zero values. But since the zone is empty, zero values are not shown.

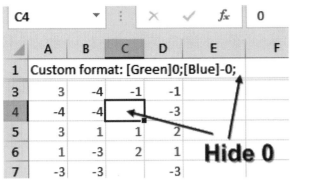

Walter Moore

You can extend this by making all zones blank. A custom format code ;;; will hide values in the display and printout. However, you'll still be able to see the values in the formula bar. If you hide values by making the font white, the ;;; will stay hidden even if people change the fill color. The following figure includes some interesting formatting tricks.

	A	B	C
1	Value	Display	Format Code
2	123.45	********** 123.45	**0.00
3	123.45	!!!!!!!!!!!!!! 123.45	*!0.00
4	123456	123K	0,K
5	4565789	4.6M	0.0,,"M"
6	One	Enter a number!	0;-0;0;"Enter a number!"
7	62	62	[Red][<70]0;[Blue][>90]0;0
8	85	85	[Red][<70]0;[Blue][>90]0;0
9	99	99	[Red][<70]0;[Blue][>90]0;0
10	1234	1 2 3 4	0_W_W0_N0_i0

In B2 and B3, if you put ** before the number code, it will fill to the left of the number with asterisks like the old check writer machines would do. But there is nothing that says you have to use asterisks. Whatever you put after the first asterisk is repeated to fill the space. Row 3 uses *! to repeat exclamation points.

In B4 and B5, each comma that you put after the final zero will divide the number by 1,000. The code 0,K shows numbers in thousands, with a K afterward. If you want to show millions, use two commas. The "M" code must be put in quotes, since M already means months.

In B6 put a stern message in the fourth zone to alert anyone entering data that you want a number in the cell. If they accidentally enter text, the message appears.

In B7 to B9 the normal zones Positives, Negatives, and Zero are overwritten by conditions that you put in square brackets. Numbers under 70 are red. Numbers over 90 are blue. Everything else is black.

In B10, those odd _(symbols in the accounting format are telling Excel to leave as much space as a left parenthesis would take. It turns out that an underscore followed by any character will leave as much white space as that character. In B10, the code contains 4 zeroes. But there are different amounts of space between each. The space between the 1 and 2 is the width of 2 WW characters. The space between 2 and 3 is the width of an N. The space between 3 and 4 is the width of a lowercase letter i.

The following figure shows various date formatting codes.

	A	B
1	Display	Format Code
2	7/3/18	m/d/yy
3	7/3/2018	m/d/yyyy
4	07/03/2018	mm/dd/yyyy
5	20180703	YYYYMMDD
6	Jul	mmm
7	July	mmmm
8	J	mmmmm
9	Tue	ddd
10	Tuesday	dddd
11	Tuesday the 3 of Jul	dddd" the "d" of "mmm

Note that the mmmmm format in row 8 is useful for producing J F M A M J J A S O N D chart labels.

Thanks to Dave Baylis, Brad Edgar, Mike Girvin, and @best_excel for suggesting this feature.

#26 Extract Uniques with a CSE Formula

This example is way beyond the scope of this book. There is a secret type of formula in Excel that requires you to press Ctrl+Shift+Enter in order to unlock the powers of the formula.

If you or I needed to get a unique list of values from column B, we would do something such as use an advanced filter or a pivot table or copy the data and use Remove Duplicates. These methods take five seconds and are easy for you or me.

	A	B
1	Invoice	Customer
2	1001	Excel-Translator.de
3	1002	St. Peter's Prep
4	1003	www.ExcelTricks.de
5	1004	SpringBoard
6	1005	www.ExcelTricks.de
7	1006	www.ExcelTricks.de

The problem rears its head when you need your manager's manager to use the spreadsheet. You cannot hope that the VP of Sales is going to master doing a Copy and Remove Duplicates. You need a way to have live formulas that will always be extracting unique lists of values.

The formulas to do this are absolutely insane. But they work. In the figure below, a long formula in D2 figures out how many unique values are in the list. An even longer formula in D5 that is copied down extracts the unique list.

	D
1	Unique Count
2	8
3	
4	Unique List of Customers
5	Excel-Translator.de
6	St. Peter's Prep
7	www.ExcelTricks.de
8	SpringBoard
9	WSLCB
10	NetCom Computer
11	MAU Workforce Solutions
12	F-Keys Ltd

Here is the formula. I won't try to explain it to you.

```
{=IF(ROWS(D$5:D5)>$D$2,"",
INDEX($B$2:$B$146,
SMALL(IF(FREQUENCY(IF($B$2:$B$146<>"",
MATCH($B$2:$B$146,$B$2:$B$146,0)),
ROW($B$2:$B$146)-1),
ROW($B$2:$B$146)-1),
ROWS(D$5:D5))))}
```

But I will do the next best thing. I will introduce you to someone who can explain it to you. Mike Girvin has

produced thousands of Excel videos on YouTube under the ExcelisFun channel. He has also written a few Excel books, including *Ctrl+Shift+Enter* – the complete guide to these amazing formulas. In the book, Mike explains this formula and many other formulas in detail so you can understand how they work and write your own. If you are ever about to give up on a formula because it can't be done, there is a good chance the formulas in Mike's book will solve it.

Thanks to Mike Girvin, Olga Kryuchkova, and @canalyze_it for suggesting this feature.

While I am promoting Mike Girvin's book, I should mention that you should check out is ExcelisFun YouTube channel where he has thousands of free amazing videos. Mike and I have done a series of fun Dueling Excel videos, where we show various ways to solve problems in Excel.

3

Illustration credit: Szilvia Juhasz

You could say that Mike is the Elvis of Excel.

Illustration: Michelle Routt

#27 Consolidate Quarterly Worksheets

There are two ancient consolidation tools in Excel.

To understand them, say that you have three data sets. Each has names down the left side and months across the top. Notice that the names are different, and there are a different number of months in each data set.

Name	Jan	Feb	Mar
James WSLCB Tallman	75	75	69
Michael Seeley	98	90	83
David Colman	62	53	88
P B Rayudu	71	86	93
Fr. Tony Azzarto	71	84	70
Erik Svensen	62	91	81

Name	Apr	May	Jun	Jul	Aug
Michael Seeley	62	56	83	78	98
David Colman	92	58	83	81	67
P B Rayudu	84	97	69	58	60
Erik Svensen	71	69	65	91	68
Michael Karpfen	52	80	89	83	73
Victor E. Scelba II	93	70	54	90	81
Emily Mathews	80	57	51	62	69

Name	Sep	Oct	Nov	Dec
Michael Seeley	94	79	86	92
P B Rayudu	75	83	85	90
Erik Svensen	81	79	87	97
Michael Karpfen	78	86	93	91
Emily Mathews	64	93	92	90
Robert Mika	99	84	93	99
David Ringstrom	71	80	93	94

You want to combine these into a single data set. Turn the page for a discussion of the two methods.

Illustration: Cartoon Bob D'Amico

The first tool is the Consolidate command on the Data tab. Choose a blank section of the workbook before starting the command. Use the RefEdit button to point to each of your data sets and then click Add. In the lower left, choose Top Row and Left Column.

When you click OK, a superset of all three data sets is produced. The first column contains any name in any of the three data sets. Row 1 contains any month in any data set.

▲	A	B	C	D	E	F	G	H	I	J	K	L	M
1		Jan	Feb	Mar	Apr	May	Jun	Jul	Aug	Sep	Oct	Nov	Dec
2	James WSLCB Tallman	75	75	69									
3	Michael Seeley	98	90	83	62	56	83	78	98	94	79	86	92
4	David Colman	62	53	88	92	58	83	81	67				
5	P B Rayudu	71	86	93	84	97	69	58	60	75	83	85	90
6	Fr. Tony Azzarto	71	84	70									
7	Erik Svensen	62	91	81	71	69	65	91	68	81	79	87	97
8	Michael Karpfen				52	80	89	83	73	78	86	93	91
9	Victor E. Scelba II				93	70	54	90	81				
10	Emily Mathews				80	57	51	62	69	64	93	92	90
11	Robert Mika									99	84	93	99
12	David Ringstrom									71	80	93	94

In the above figure, notice three annoyances. Cell A1 is always left blank. The data in A is not sorted. If a person was missing from a data set, then cells are left empty instead of being filled with 0.

Filling in cell A1 is easy enough. Sorting by name involves using Flash Fill to get the last name in column N. Here is how to fill blank cells with 0:

1. Select all of the cells that should have numbers: B2:M11.

2. Select Home, Find & Select, Go To Special.

3. Choose Blanks and then click OK. You will be left with all of the blank cells selected.

4. Type 0 and then Ctrl+Enter.

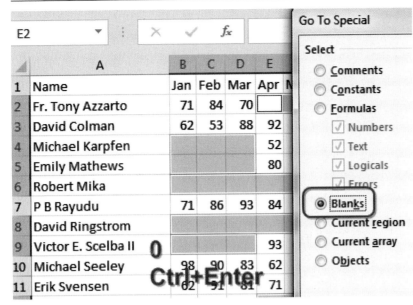

The result: a nicely formatted summary report.

Name	Jan	Feb	Mar	Apr	May	Jun	Jul	Aug	Sep	Oct	Nov	Dec
Fr. Tony Azzarto	71	84	70	0	0	0	0	0	0	0	0	0
David Colman	62	53	88	92	58	83	81	67	0	0	0	0
Michael Karpfen	0	0	0	52	80	89	83	73	78	86	93	91
Emily Mathews	0	0	0	80	57	51	62	69	64	93	92	90
Robert Mika	0	0	0	0	0	0	0	0	99	84	93	99
P B Rayudu	71	86	93	84	97	69	58	60	75	83	85	90
David Ringstrom	0	0	0	0	0	0	0	0	71	80	93	94
Victor E. Scelba II	0	0	0	93	70	54	90	81	0	0	0	0
Michael Seeley	98	90	83	62	56	83	78	98	94	79	86	92
Erik Svensen	62	91	81	71	69	65	91	68	81	79	87	97
James WSLCB Tallman	75	75	69	0	0	0	0	0	0	0	0	0

The other ancient tool is the Multiple Consolidation Range pivot table. Follow these steps:

1. Press Alt+D, P to invoke the Excel 2003 Pivot Table Wizard.

2. Choose Multiple Consolidation Ranges in step 1. Click Next.

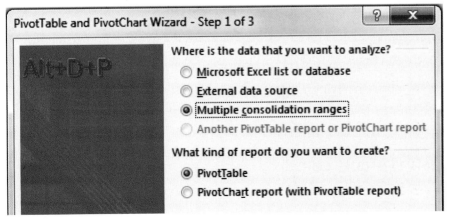

3. Choose I Will Create the Page Fields in step 2a. Click Next.

4. In Step 2b, use the RefEdit to point to each table. Click Add after each.

PivotTable and PivotChart Wizard - Step 2b of 3

Where are the worksheet ranges that you want to consolidate?

Range:

`'Q4'!$A$1:$E$8`

Add   **Delete**   **Browse...**

All ranges:

```
'Q1'!$A$1:$D$7
'Q2'!$A$1:$F$8
'Q4'!$A$1:$E$8
```

How many page fields do you want?

⦿ 0   ○ 1   ○ 2   ○ 3   ○ 4

5. Click Finish to create this pivot table.

Sum of Value	Column ▼			
Row ▼	Jan	Feb	Mar	Apr
David Colman	62	53	88	92
David Ringstrom				
Emily Mathews				80
Erik Svensen	62	91	81	71
Fr. Tony Azzarto	71	84	70	
James WSLCB Tallman	75	75	69	

Thanks to CTroy for suggesting this feature.

#28 A2:INDEX() Is Like a Non-Volatile OFFSET

This is a niche tip. There is an amazingly flexible function called OFFSET. It is flexible because it can point to a different-sized range that is calculated on-the-fly. In the image below, if someone changes the # Qtrs dropdown in H1 from 3 to 4, the fourth argument of OFFSET will make sure that the range expands to include four columns.

F2	fx	=AVERAGE(OFFSET(B2,0,0,1,$H$1))

	A	B	C	D	E	F	G	H
1	Name	Q1	Q2	Q3	Q4	Average	# Qtrs	3
2	Larry Vance	1376	1358	1403	1290	1379		
3	Anthony J. LoBello Jr.	1353	1518	1361	1341	1410.667		
4	Carl R Hooker	1629	1899	1372	1077	1633.333		
5	Will Riley	1053	1359	1545	1223	1319		
6	James N Johnson	1594	1243	1175	1836	1337.333		
7	Richard B Lanza	1740	1573	1373	1324	1562		

Volatile

Spreadsheet gurus hate OFFSET because it is a volatile function. If you go to a completely unrelated cell and enter a number, all of the OFFSET functions will calculate. Even if that cell has nothing to do with H1 or B2. Most of the time, Excel is very careful to only waste time calculating the cells that need to calculate. But once you introduce OFFSET, all of the OFFSET cells, plus everything downline from the OFFSET, starts calculating after every change in the worksheet.

Illustration Credit: Chad Thomas

3

I was judging the 2013 ModelOff finals in New York City when a few of my friends from Australia pointed out a bizarre workaround. In the formula below, there is a colon before the INDEX function. Normally, the INDEX function shown below would return the 1403 from cell D2. But when you put a colon on either side of the INDEX function, it starts returning the cell address D2 instead of the contents of D2. This is wild that it works.

| F2 | ▼ | : | ✕ | ✓ | *fx* | =AVERAGE(B2:INDEX(B2:E2,$H$1)) |

◢	A	B	C	D	E	F	G	H
1	Name	Q1	Q2	Q3	Q4	Average	# Qtrs	3
2	Larry Vance	1376	1358	1403	1290	1379		
3	Anthony J. LoBello Jr.	1353	1518	1361	1341	1410.667		
4	Carl R Hooker	1629	1899	1372	1077	1633.333		
5	Will Riley	1053	1359	1545	1223	1319		
6	James N Johnson	1594	1243	1175	1836	1337.333		
7	Richard B Lanza	1740	1573	1373	1324	1562		

Index returns D2

Why does this matter? INDEX is not volatile. You get all of the flexible goodness of OFFSET without the time-sucking recalculations over and over.

I first learned this tip from Dan Mayoh at Fintega. Thanks to Access Analytic for suggesting this feature.

#29 Sort and Filter by Color or Icon

Conditional formatting got a lot of new features in Excel 2007, including icon sets and more than three levels of rules. This allows for some pretty interesting formatting over a large range. But, once you format the cells, you might want to quickly see all the ones that are formatted a particular way. In Excel 2007, sorting and filtering were also updated to help you do just that!

This book analysis table has some highlighted rows to flag interesting books and an icon next to the price if the book is in the top 25% of prices in the list:

If you want to quickly view all the highlighted rows or cells that have icons, just dropdown the filter for the column and choose Filter by Color (or Sort by Color to bubble them to the top):

Then you can pick the formatting you want to sort or filter by! This doesn't just work for conditional formatting; it also works for manually coloring cells. It is also available on the right-click menu of a cell under the Filter or Sort flyout, and in the Sort dialog.

This tip is from Sam Radakovitz, a project manager on the Excel team. He is more fond of cats than dogs.

#30 Word for Excellers

Note: Sam Radakovitz from the previous tip is one of the coolest Excel Project Managers. For example, Sam actually enjoys hanging out with the Excel MVPs at the annual MVP Summit instead of seeing them annoying. Sam started bringing his fiancé, Katie Sullivan, to our gatherings. Katie is a Project Manager on the Microsoft Word team. For our last tip in the book, I turn the podium over to Katie.

While Excel fans sometimes tease that Word and PowerPoint are freeware apps that come on the Excel DVD, there are times when Microsoft Word offers a feature that Excel does not. In those cases, it makes sense to copy your data from Excel, paste to Word, do the command, then copy back to Excel. Here are some examples of techniques that are better handled in Word than in Excel.

Technique 1: Convert to Upper, Lower, Proper

If you have to convert from uppercase to lowercase or proper case, Word has a keystroke shortcut. Copy the data to Word and toggle the case using Shift+F3.

Technique 2: Add Bullets

If you want to add bullets to Excel cells, it is far easier in Word than in Excel. Copy the cells to Word and apply a bullet style. Copy from Word and paste back to Excel. You might have to use the Reduce Indent icon a few times.

Technique 3: Visualize and Color Formulas

If you have a massively long formula, say one with 10 nested IF statements, you can paste to Word and use colors and Shift+Enter to space the formula to help make sense of the formula. (One rebuttal from the Excel team: You can expand the formula bar and use Alt+Enter to split a formula into many lines. Or, use the great Ref Tree Analyser add-in from Jan Karel Pieterse; see http://mrx.cl/jkpformula.)

Technique 4: Faster SmartArt

Word offers the Convert Text to SmartArt option. While Excel offers SmartArt, too, it is not very handy there because you have to copy the entries one at a time into the SmartArt pane.

Technique 5: Extract Data from a PDF

Say that someone has an Excel workbook and saves that workbook as a PDF. They send it to you. This is annoying, and clearly they don't want you to reuse the data. If you open the PDF in Acrobat Reader, copy the data, and paste to Excel, it will unwind into a single column. But here is the secret: Paste that data to Word first. The rows and columns will paste properly. You can then copy from Word and paste back into Excel. (If you are stuck in a pre-2013 version of Office, I recommend Able2Extract: http://mrx.cl/pdftoxl.)

Here is the original data on the left and how it looks when you paste directly from PDF to Excel on the right. You can see that the data "unwinds," with B1:C1 going to A2:A3 and so on.

	A	B	C
1	Trait	Dogs	Cats
2	Protective instinct	Yes	No
3	Always happy to see you when return	Yes	No
4	Spit up hairballs	No	Yes
5	Big or small	Yes	Only small
6	Chase tennis balls	Yes	No
7	Herd small children	Yes	No
8	Swim with you	Yes	No
9	Do tricks	Yes	No

	A	B
1	Trait	
2	Dogs	
3	Cats	
4	Protective instinct	
5	Yes	
6	No	
7	Always happy to see you	
8	Yes	
9	No	

Paste that same data to Word (below left), then copy from Word and paste to Excel (below right). The data stays in the original order. You can unapply Word Wrap and adjust the column widths to get back to the original data.

Trait	Dogs	Cats
Protective instinct	Yes	No
Always happy to see you when	Yes	No

Trait	Dogs	Cats
Protectiv e instinct	Yes	No
Always happy to see you	Yes	No

Technique 6: Change Formatting of Words Within Excel

If you have sentences of text in Excel, it is possible to select one word while in Edit mode and change the color of that word. But globally change the color of all occurrences of the word in Excel is tedious. Instead, paste the data to Word and press Ctrl+H. Change dog to dog. Click More>> and then Format, Font. Choose Red. Click Replace All. Copy from Word and paste back to Excel.

Find and Replace

Find | Replace | Go To

Find what: dog
Format:

Replace with: dog
Format: Font color: Red

	A	B	C	D	E	F	G	H
1	Original							
2	A dog is always happy to see you when you return home.							
3	If you have children, a dog will be protective of the children. If it is a herding dog, i							
4	Certain breeds of dog love to swim. You can not keep my dog Bella from diving in t							
5	A dog has no problems chasing a tennis ball all day.							
6								
7	After doing Replace in Word and pasting back to Excel							
8	A dog is always happy to see you when you return home.							
9	If you have children, a dog will be protective of the children. If it is a herding dog, i							
10	Certain breeds of dog love to swim. You can not keep my dog Bella from diving in t							
11	A dog has no problems chasing a tennis ball all day.							
12								

Technique 7: Replace While Keeping Character Formatting

Word also handles a similar problem: replacing text but leaving the text formatting as it is. Below is a survey about the best pet. Someone has highlighted certain words within the text.

	A	B	C	D	E
1	Survey Results - Favorite Pet?				
2	Dog, dog, dog, dog, ~~eat~~, dog, dog, dog, ~~eat~~				
3	Dog, dog, dog, ~~eat~~, dog, dog, hamster, puppy				
4	Dog, dog, turtle, dog, dog, dog, puppy, dog, ~~eat~~				
5	*survey conducted at Wingfoot Lake dog park*				

Find and Replace

Find | Replace

Find what: puppy

Replace with: dog

Use Ctrl+H to do a Find and Replace. When you use Replace All, if a sentence was changed, your in-cell formats will be lost. In the figure below, the strikethrough remains in the first row because that row did not have an occurrence of the word *puppy* and thus was not changed.

Dog, dog, dog, dog, ~~eat~~, dog, dog, dog, ~~eat~~
Dog, dog, dog, cat, dog, dog, hamster, dog
Dog, dog, turtle, dog, dog, dog, dog, dog, cat

To keep the formatting in the original text, copy to Word. Do the Replace in Word. Copy from Word and paste back to Excel.

On behalf of the entire Word team, Katie invites all of you Excellers who still type your letters in Excel using Fill Justify to come on over and give Word a spin.

Bonus Tip: Merge Shapes

Here's a brief plug for PowerPoint: If you need to create a shape in Excel that is a combination of other shapes, create the shapes in PowerPoint. Select all the shapes. On the Drawing Tools Format tab, choose Merge Shapes. You can Union, Combine, Fragment, Intersect, or Subtract to combine the shapes. (The Subtract feature would let you cut a hole in a shape.) Then copy that shape and paste to Excel (or Word).

Bonus Tip: Eye Dropper

Another feature unique to PowerPoint is the eye dropper. If you want to use a particular color you can just click the eye drop on the color. When you open the Power Point color menu again. Choose More Colors and you can see the RGB colors. To use the eyedropper outside of the PowerPoint frame, hold down the left mouse button and pick from any website or picture you have visible on your desktop.

Thanks to Katie Sullivan (a project manager on the Word team!) for contributing this tip. Katie clearly prefers dogs to cats. Thanks to Glenna Shaw and Oz du Soleil for contributing ideas to this tip. Zack Barresse and Echo Swinford pointed out the Merge Shapes option in PowerPoint. Sam Radakovitz added the eye dropper tip and noted the subtract feature for shapes.

#31 40 Tips for the next MXL Book

More than 200 ideas were sent in for this book. While the following ideas did not get much press here, they are self-explanatory in a 140-character tweet. I will hang on to these for my 1040th (MXL) book!

- Quick Sum: Highlight a group of cells and see the sum, average, etc., on the status bar at the bottom of the screen. -Al Momrik
- To make Excel open full-screen, right-click the Excel icon and change the Run setting to Full Screen. -David Ringstrom, CPA
- Use a thin light border line to create useful scrollbar maximums when your worksheet contains charts that the scrollbars don't recognize. -Chris Mack
- Highlight duplicate records with Conditional Formatting, Highlight Cells, Duplicate Records. -@Leaf_xl
- If you want to color every other row, use this conditional formatting formula: =MOD(ROW(),2)=0. -Pedro Millers
- Save As CSV to get rid of all trailing spaces and merged cells. -Oz du Soleil
- Have a photo appear after a dropdown list in Excel http://t.co/TjbAtSkJ3t -Michael A. Rempel

- Select two (or more) columns, Find & Select, Go To Special, Row Differences. -Colleen Young
- Use Skip Blanks when pasting values. It skips any blanks in the target range. -Laura Lewis
- Use pictographs for charts (column and pie): Copy picture: select series, paste. -Olga Kryuchkova
- For a pie chart with too many slices: move small slices to second pie using Pie of Pie chart. -Olga Kryuchkova
- Use X/Y charts for drawing artwork. -Joerg Decker
- You can use a wildcard in =VLOOKUP("A*",Table,2,False). -Khalif John Clark
- Sort with a formula: =LARGE(A$1:A$10,ROW(1:1)). -Meni Porat
- INDEX can return an entire row/column and return a cell reference. -Sumit Bansal
- With year in A2, this formula calculates Easter Sunday: =DOLLAR(("4/"&A2)/7+MOD(19*MOD(A2,19)-7,30)*14%,)*7-6. sent by Matt Allington (author Thomas Jansen)
- Put an apostrophe in front of an Excel formula to stop it from being evaluated. -@DiffEngineX
- DATEDIF(A2,B2,"Y")&" years, "&DATEDIF(A2,B2,"YM")&" months, "&DATEDIF(A2,B2,"MD")&" days." -Paul Wright
- Insert rows without breaking formulas. Cell above is OFFSET(*thisCell*,-1,0) - Jon Wittwer, Vertex42.com
- The =NPV function does not calculate the Net Present Value of the investment. Always subtract one from the result. -Olen L. Greer
- Use EDATE to move the date out one month or year. -Justin Fishman
- When Excel says you have links, but you can't find them, check in the Name Manager. Ta-da! -Lisa Burkett
- Formulas created in Notepad, saved as CSV, & opened in Excel work. Example: mike,=proper(A1) will give Mike. -@mdhExcel
- Double-click a formula. Excel color codes the cells referenced in the formula. - Cat Parkinson
- Turn off Edit Directly in Cell. Then double-click a formula to show cells used in that formula, even if in external workbook. -Sean Blessitt, David Ringstrom
- Go To Special, Constants helps spot constants within a block of formulas where a formula is overwritten with a number. -@HowToExcel
- Select a random 5% of data using =RAND()<.05. -Olga Kryuchkova
- Format comments as funny shapes like a heart or smiley face. http://mrx.cl/commentshape -Olga Kryuchkova
- Highlight formulas using the Conditional Formatting formula =HASFORMULA(A1). Requires Excel 2013. -Justin Fishman
- Double-click a number in a pivot to get the detail behind that number. -@Sheet1
- Array formula to count without COUNT: =SUM(IF(ISNUMBER(MyRange),1,0)). -Meni Porat
- In the VBA window, you can set the property of a worksheet to xlVeryHidden to keep most people out of the sheet. -Sagar Malik
- In VBA, use Range("A1").CurrentRegion instead of RANGE(). It is like pressing Ctrl+*. -Arnout Brandt
- You can use hyperlinks to launch VBA macros. Smaller than buttons. -Cecelia Rieb
- Use a macro to color the heading cells that have filters applied. -Peter Edwards
- Use Environ("UserName") in VBA code for restricting workbook access. -Angelina Teneva
- Use a UDF in a hyperlink to change cells. http://mrx.cl/udfhyperlink -Jordan Goldmeier
- There are a variety of games written tin Excel (2048, MissileCommand, pleuroku, TowerDefense, Pac-Man, Rubic's Cube, Yahtzee, Tetris) -Olga Kryuchkova

THE EXCEL LOVER'S GUIDE TO COCKTAILS

Everything You Don't Need To Master Excel

By Szilvia Juhasz, aka XSzil
Featuring recipes by Eric Ho | Photography by BurkleHagen Studios

ACKNOWLEDGEMENTS

Dedicated to Excel addicts everywhere.

With special thanks to Excel-cutive producer Bill Jelen, mad scientist-mixologist Eric Ho, the photographer geniuses at BurkleHagen Studios, and XSzil creators John, the engineer, and Edith, the chef-artist. Thanks also to the additional "Excelebrities" mentioned in this book: Excel Is Fun host, Professor Mike Girvin, Mike the "Data Pig" Alexander, Excel MVP veteran Bob Umlas, Power Pivot guru Rob Collie, and the one and only, the great Chandoo. Thanks to the Excel TV team for having me on their show. Finally, thanks to all my creative supporters, idea contributors, taste testers, and XSzil believers: my own Jim Morrison, Helen Schneider, Valerie Peterson, Elle Brennan, Andrea and Jason Bour, Marik Daniel, Felicity Wood, and to my spiritual advisor, Danny Moon, Esq.

INTRODUCTION

Can I create a pivot table with VBA? Should I use a pie chart? When should I use VLOOKUP, and when should I use INDEX/MATCH? This book answers none of these questions. In fact, this is perhaps the first Excel book in history that can actually make you forget all the Excel tips you just read. Fortunately, you won't care, because your taste buds will be rejoicing when you sip your very first Excel inspired cocktail.

So what's an Excel cocktail anyway? The first of their kind, these cocktails are Excel "themed." Meaning, their recipes were inspired by, and carefully crafted with specific Excel concepts, ideas, truisms, or famous Excel personalities in mind. In short, the sort of stuff hardcore Excel nerds can truly appreciate. Only this time, served in a cocktail glass. The unveiling of this very special cocktail collection could not have been more appropriately timed. It was exactly 30 years ago when Microsoft Excel was released unto to the world. 30 years, especially in software years, really says something. For me personally, this book has been a true labor of Excel-love, a celebration, and my personal homage to Excel herself (oh yes I did).

Happy birthday, Excel! Cheers to you.

EXCEL LIBRE

Happy birthday, Excel! It's your big 3-0! Aww, you're so grown up! Why, I remember when I first installed you. Your tortured little 16-bit color palette, your adorable little pal Clippy (rest his soul), and those very first 3D charts of yours, they still make the data viz experts weep. Just look at you now: more than 50 new functions, Power BI, Excel Web App. Your power user fan base is over half a billion strong and still growing. Some might say you're the Coca-Cola of software. So here's a delicious modern variation on the classic Cuba Libre, in honor of your big day.

Main recipe yields 1 drink
Supporting recipes yield batches of 6-8

Ingredients
1 ½ oz. vanilla-infused aged rum*
¼ oz. roasted lime juice**
4 oz. Mexican Coke

Garnish
Lime wedge

Add all ingredients to a Collins glass filled with ice. Garnish with lime wedge.

* Vanilla-Infused Rum (make at least 24 hours in advance)
Yields approximately 6 1½-oz. portions
9 oz. aged rum
2½ vanilla beans
Split vanilla beans down the middle and place in a nonreactive container. Add rum. Let sit for at least 24 hours. Strain mixture through a fine-mesh strainer.

** Roasted Lime Juice (make at least 24 hours in advance)
Yields approximately 8 ¼-oz. portions
2 halved limes
Place limes, cut side up, on a baking sheet. Broil on low for 15–20 minutes, or until the limes are plump and moderately charred. Juice the roasted limes and strain through a fine-mesh strainer. Refrigerate in a nonreactive container.

SPARKLINE SWIZZLE

Do your data visualizations lack in sizzle? Try a Sparkline Swizzle! Those dull, sad little stacks of stats will go from drab to fab in just a few mouse clicks. But with so many colors and styles to choose from, you just might need a bit of help making your decisions. Meet my fabulous friends, vodka and Champagne. They're always ready to inspire your next great decision..

Main recipe yields 1 drink
Supporting recipe yields batches of 20

Ingredients
1 ½ oz. vodka
½ oz. green tea syrup*
½ oz. lemon juice
Champagne

Garnish
Lemon peel

Fill a cocktail shaker with ice and add all ingredients except the Champagne. Shake and strain into a champagne flute. Top with champagne. Garnish with lemon peel.

* Green Tea Syrup (Make up to 1 month in advance)
16 oz. sugar
8 oz. water
3 green tea bags

Heat sugar and water in a saucepan, stirring frequently. Once sugar has dissolved and syrup begins to boil, add green tea bags. Let steep at a simmer for 10 minutes. Turn off heat and let steep for an additional 20 minutes. Remove tea bags. Refrigerate syrup in a nonreactive container.

CORRUPT FORMULA

Sage advice for aspiring Excel analysts: Adding "just one more little column" of array formulas to a rickety old 40 MB Excel file probably isn't going to be "just fine." That would be like drinking alcohol to cure a hangover. Or would it?

This invigorating brew is a delicious descendant of the classic Corpse Reviver, which, according to cocktail historians, was a hair-of-the-dog formula devised precisely for the purpose of curing hangovers. So the next time you've blown your volatile functions wad and you've got some downtime while Excel hangs in "not responding" mode, enjoy a few of these little gems. You'll feel better in the morning, even if your spreadsheet doesn't.

Yields 1 drink

Ingredients
¾ oz. gin
¾ oz. Cointreau
¾ oz. Lillet Blanc
½ oz. lemon juice
1 bar spoon Crème Yvette

Garnish
Lime peel

Fill a cocktail shaker with ice and add all ingredients. Shake and strain into a chilled coupe glass. Garnish with lime peel.

BROKEN LINK

Science says our taste buds can detect up to 300 distinct types of bitterness. Thanks, Science, but can any of those truly compare to the bitterness of broken links in a spreadsheet? It's that dreaded scenario: Bob from Accounting has left the company. You've inherited his terrible Excel model, and now you're staring down hundreds of broken links pointing to a mysterious, nonexistent C: drive. Grab the whiskey, my friend, because you're about to spend your entire afternoon clicking the Change Source button, trapped in an inESCapable loop of Edit Links dialogs. You realize the other Bob (Umlas) is your best hope for salvation, so you wait for him to send you a solution, but it's coming by fax*. So in the meantime, this tasty, golden, orange-infused little gem has just the right amount of bitters to take the edge off. It's sweet yet strong, the perfect therapy to soothe your looming carpal tunnel syndrome. To (both) Bobs...

*DISCLAIMER: Bob Umlas is a "first wave" MVP. He does enjoy telling stories about the days when Microsoft used to actually fax people answers to their Excel questions. However, Bob has since moved on to embrace ListServs.

Yields 1 drink

Ingredients
1 ½ oz. rye whiskey
1 oz. Aperol
¾ oz. sweet vermouth
¼ oz. Amaro
3 dashes Angostura bitters

Garnish
Orange slice

Add all ingredients to a mixing glass filled with ice. Stir to chill and then strain into a double old fashioned glass. Add 1 large ice cube. Garnish with orange slice.

STACKED COLUMN SHOT

PARTY GAME! Can you make a stacked column chart in Excel faster than your bartender can make this Stacked Column Shot in your glass? No? Another shot for you, my friend... ♪♪♪ - Tequila! - ♪♪♪

Main recipe yields 2 shots (or 1 big one if you're down)
Supporting recipe yields batch of 20

Ingredients
1½ oz. Reposado tequila
¼ oz. Curaçao
½ oz. cinnamon syrup*
½ oz. lemon juice
1 oz. orange juice
1 dash Peychaud's bitters

Fill a cocktail shaker with ice and add tequila, cinnamon syrup, lemon juice, and orange juice. Shake and strain into 2 tall shot glasses. Next, gently pour blue curacao into shot glasses, taking care so the colors do not bleed together. Tilting the glass at an angle as you pour can help with this effort. Carefully add a dash of Peychaud's on top.

* Cinnamon Syrup (Make up to 1 month in advance)
16 oz. sugar
8 oz. water
4 cinnamon sticks

Heat sugar and water in a saucepan, stirring frequently. Once sugar has dissolved and syrup begins to boil, add cinnamon sticks. Let steep at a simmer for 10 minutes. Turn off heat and let steep for an additional 20 minutes. Remove cinnamon sticks. Refrigerate syrup in a nonreactive container.

DAX ON THE BEACH

Hey, single Excel lovers, do you remember when summer lasted forever? And do you remember how long it took you to finally figure out what the hell a DAX formula is? Well, you've done it, and it's time for some fun in the sun. While you download that Tinder-for-Excel add-in to speed up the search for your fresh new squeeze, keep sipping on this spin-on-the-original-sin. By the time that app finishes installing, this flirty formula will guarantee that everyone's "measures" look amazing! Before you know it, you'll be "swiping right" all day long.

Main recipe yields 1 drink
Supporting recipe yields batch of 20

Ingredients
1 ½ oz. vodka
½ oz. lime juice
*½ oz. simple syrup**
2 oz. mango nectar
1 small bottle or can lemon/lime soda

Garnishes
Lime wheel
Mint sprig

In a cocktail shaker filled with ice add all ingredients except the lemon/lime soda. Shake and strain into a goblet filled with ice. Top with lemon/lime soda. Garnish with lime wheel and mint sprig.

* Simple Syrup (Make up to 1 month in advance)
16 oz. sugar
8 oz. water
Heat sugar and water in a saucepan, stirring frequently. Once sugar has dissolved and syrup begins to boil, remove from heat. Refrigerate in a nonreactive container.

POWER PIVOTINI

Modern Excel has never tasted so good. This audience favorite (lucky focus group!) is powered by "Navy-strength" gin, which means it ranks 15 points higher on the alcohol proof scale than the more familiar varieties, like London dry style. It's like the 128-bit of gins! Industrial alcohol strength aside, it's hard to not notice the masterful presentation here, which, like a well-crafted PowerPivot model, takes a bit of patience and skill. Once you get there, you won't ever want to come back.

Main recipe yields 1 drink

Ingredients
1 ½ oz. Navy-strength gin
½ oz. lime juice
½ oz. honey
½ oz. elderflower liqueur
1 egg white

Garnishes
2-4 drops Angostura bitters

Add all ingredients to a cocktail shaker. Dry shake for 10 seconds to emulsify egg white. Add ice and shake for an additional 30 seconds. Strain into a coupe glass. Carefully tap bottle of Angostura bitters on top, allowing drops to form a PowerPivot-worthy design.

JITTERBUG JELEN

Fun fact about Mr. Excel: When he's not shaking his Excel moneymaker, he's shining up his boogie shoes then heading towards the world famous Tropical Haven Dance Hall in Melbourne, Florida. Sunday nights, it's "Don & Joy" bringing the live music, while Bill and his 93-years-young dad, Robert Jelen, captivate the crowd with their best ballroom shimmy shakes. Between cha-chas, Bill is often seen moonwalking towards his laptop to refresh his Excel based dance card decision model. Salud!

Yields 1 drink

Ingredients
1½ oz. aged rum
¼ oz. pomegranate grenadine
½ oz. lime juice
½ oz. falernum
3 dashes Angostura bitters

Garnishes
Lime wheel
Mint sprig

Fill a cocktail shaker with ice and add all ingredients. Shake well. Strain into a collins glass filled with crushed ice. Garnish with lime wheel and mint sprig.

CTRL+B

Next time you're discussing dashboards over Sunday brunch, go **bold** with this feisty take on the classic Bloody Mary. A dedication to self-professed bacon aficionado and "Data Pig" himself, Mike Alexander, the Ctrl+B is a surefire shortcut to some sizzling banter around the table. B is for breakfast. B is for bold. And now, B is for bacon-infused bourbon. Word to the wise: a formula this bacon-y delicious will require a bit of advance planning, like a finely tuned Excel dashboard with a generous helping of slicers. Fun for the whole Bloody Mary lovin' family!

Main recipe yields 1 drink
Supporting recipes yield approximately 6

Ingredients
1 ½ oz. bacon-infused bourbon*
½ oz. peppercorn & horseradish shrub**
1 large cube tomato water ice***
3 dashes celery bitters

Garnish
Salt rim (Eric suggests smoked sriracha salt)

Rim a double old fashioned glass with your salt. Add all ingredients to the glass and stir to chill.

* Bacon-Infused Bourbon (Make at least 12 hours in advance)
9 oz. bourbon
2 ½ oz. rendered bacon fat
Arrange approximately 9 bacon strips on a foil-lined sheet pan. Place the pan in a cold oven and set the temperature to 425°F. Bake for 15 to 20 minutes, or until crisp. Harvest all the rendered bacon fat. In a jar, mix together the bourbon and 2 ½ oz. of the rendered bacon fat. Close the jar and shake vigorously. Refrigerate for at least 12 hours. Skim the solidified bacon fat off the top of the mixture and strain the infused bourbon through cheesecloth or a fine-mesh strainer.

** Peppercorn & Horseradish Shrub (Make at least 30 minutes in advance)
2 oz. honey
2 oz. balsamic vinegar
1 tsp. whole black peppercorns
1 tsp. horseradish
Whisk all ingredients together and let rest for 30 minutes for flavors to meld. Strain mixture through a fine-mesh strainer.

*** Tomato Water Ice (Make at least 12 hours in advance, or long enough to freeze)
6 ripe vine-on tomatoes (OK if a bit over ripe, it will give it extra flavor)
Puree tomatoes in a food processor. Strain the pulp through cheesecloth. Fill an ice cube tray (a silicon one that makes larger cubes or orbs, if you have one) with the resulting tomato water. Freeze until solid.

RC COLUMNS( )

When modern Excel pioneer Rob Collie was interviewed about his preferred libational inspirations, he said he leans toward gin in order to "appear suaver than I really am." Indeed. RC's most impressive creation to date goes beyond the invention of the word "suaver." As a founding engineer of Power Pivot, Rob is a leading voice in the modern Excel revolution. His popular and entertaining blog PowerPivotPro is a great read on all things modern Excel, so it pairs perfectly with this modern twist (or shall we say "pivot"?) on the classic Tom Collins (or is it Tom Columns?)

Main recipe yields 1 drink
Supporting recipe yields batches of 20

Ingredients
1½ oz. gin (Rob prefers Hendrick's. Because suaver.)
½ oz. ginger syrup*
½ oz. lemon juice
Club soda

Fill a cocktail shaker with ice and add all ingredients except soda. Shake and strain into a collins glass filled with ice. Top with soda. Garnish with lemon wedge

* Ginger syrup (Can be made up to 1 month in advance)
16 oz. sugar
8 oz. water
8 oz. peeled, chopped ginger
¼ tsp. orange zest

Heat sugar and water in a saucepan, stirring frequently. Once sugar has dissolved, let syrup boil for 5 minutes. Pour the syrup and other ingredients into a blender and blend for 20 seconds. Strain mixture through cheesecloth. Refrigerate syrup in a nonreactive container.

DIRTY GIRVIN

XSzil: *"Hey, Mike, what do you like to drink?"*
Mike Girvin: *"Cheap Oakland beer [and a shot]!"*

Well, alrighty then. It's ON like a Dueling Excel smack down. Let's start with a fresh coffee bean infusion, because with over 2,500 Excel Is Fun video tutorials and counting, it would seem you've been pulling a few all-nighters this semester. Bottoms up, Professor!

Main recipe yields 1 drink
Supporting recipe yields batches of 6

Ingredients
1 can of your favorite Oakland beer, or classic American-style lager
1 ½ oz. vanilla espresso-infused bourbon*

Pop open the can and pour the beer into a frosty mug. Pour in a shot of vanilla espresso-infused bourbon. Throw one back every time Mike says, "Ctrl Shift Enter."

* Vanilla Espresso-Infused Bourbon (Make at least 24 hours in advance)
9 oz. bourbon
2 vanilla beans
2 oz. whole espresso beans (approximately 20 beans)

Split the vanilla beans down the middle and place them in a nonreactive container. Add bourbon and espresso beans. Let sit for at least 24 hours. Strain mixture through a fine-mesh strainer.

CHANDOO'S CONDITION

Oh, mighty Chandoo.
How DO you DO what you DO,
to make EXCEL DREAMS come TRUE( )..
by the thousands, the millions, or perhaps a BILLION times TWO??
If only I KNEW how to write an EXCEL HAIKU,
I'd do so for YOU.
Instead, I'll just sip this chocolatey BREW, so deliciously AWESOME, it's named after YOU.

Main recipe yields 1 drink
Supporting recipes yield batches of 6

Ingredients
1 ½ oz. vanilla-infused aged rum*
½ oz. chocolate syrup
½ oz. simple syrup**
1 oz. heavy cream
1 whole egg

Garnish
Ground cinnamon

Add all ingredients to an empty cocktail shaker. Dry shake for 10 seconds to emulsify egg. Add ice and shake for 30 seconds more. Strain into a goblet. Sprinkle top with ground cinnamon. Then write a Chandoo poem because a lot of words rhyme with Chandoo. Come on, you know you want TO...

* Vanilla-Infused Aged Rum (Make at least 24 hours in advance)
9 oz. aged rum
2 ½ vanilla beans

Split vanilla beans down the middle and place in a nonreactive container. Add rum. Let sit for at least 24 hours at room temperature. Strain mixture through a fine-mesh strainer.

** Simple Syrup (Make up to 1 month in advance)
16 oz. sugar
8 oz. water
Heat sugar and water in a saucepan, stirring frequently. Once sugar has dissolved and syrup begins to boil, remove from heat. Refrigerate in a nonreactive container.

ABOUT THE AUTHORS

Szilvia Juhasz, aka XSzil

Based on a True Story

Los Angeles-based Szilvia Juhasz, known in the Excel world simply as XSzil, hails from Cleveland, Ohio. As a young, aspiring spreadsheet artist, she ran away from home because her parents insisted that she would never make it as an Excel consultant. *"Why can't you focus on something practical...like acting or singing?!"* they would plead. But Szilvia had Sparklines in her eyes. One day, with nothing but her Windows 95 laptop, her tears, and the MrExcel poster she had torn down from her bedroom wall, she defiantly boarded a standby flight to Budapest to hang with fellow Excel bohemians and beg in the streets for unpaid Excel internships. Eventually she wound up in San Francisco, working as a nightclub singer to pay the bills while pursuing her ultimate dream of being an Excel consultant. Fast forward to present day, Szilvia is busy running XSzil Consulting. She helps businesses improve processes, leverage existing systems, and maximize their Excel potential. In her spare time, she enjoys relaxing at her beachside home office, making Excel-inspired parody music, jingles, and animation videos. Szilvia hopes this special cocktail collection will inspire creativity and passion in your own personal Excel journey. She'd also like to propose a toast, to Excel, on a milestone birthday!

Eric Ho, Master Mixologist & Unintentional Scientist

Also known as "Cleveland's greatest bartender," Brooklyn-born Ohio resident Eric Ho earned his aerospace engineering degree from Case Western University in 2009. So what did he do? Naturally, he sailed toward the boozier shores of bartending. In 2010, his original Beetnik's Tonic recipe was awarded top honors in the Tanqueray T&T Competition, a nationwide contest for the best twist on the classic Gin & Tonic. He has since had recipes published in numerous industry magazines, books, and periodicals. Currently Bar Manager and Principal Bartender at Melt Bar and Grilled in Cleveland, Eric has an insatiable passion for all things alcohol, from their origin to production practices to — most importantly — how they taste. While he says he's never really "looked back," his engineer's perspective still shines through in his inventive craft cocktail and menu creations, which he approaches with great attention to efficiency, accuracy, and balance. Eric also keeps busy running his new startup, Cantina Distillery. Eric loves to travel and explore the dining cultures and cuisines of lands both near and far away. His personal favorite libation is a shot of American whiskey and a good beer.

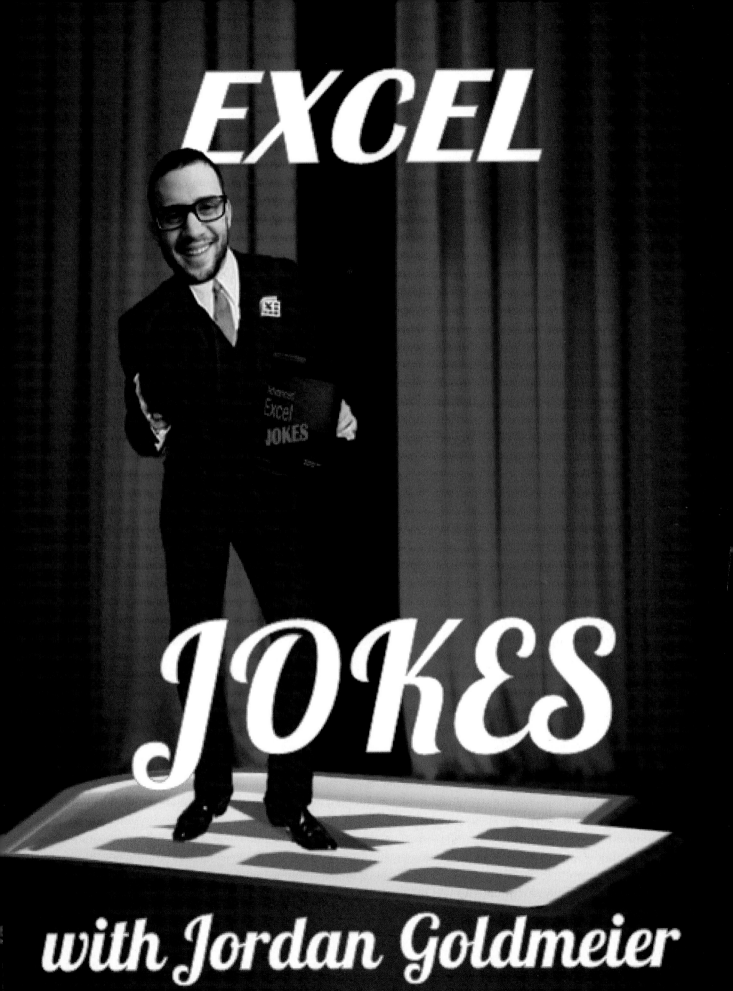

Part 4 - Excel Fun

Excel Jokes

Excel MVP Jordan Goldmeier is the Henny Youngman of Excel. He has written/collected 40 spreadsheet jokes. If the joke is not credited, it is by Jordan. Others: AG=Alex Guttman, LB = Liam Bastick , ODS=Oz du Soleil, and SJ=Szilvia Juhasz.

An analyst walks into a bar chart… Ouch?

Spreadsheet jokes are so formulaic. (-AG)

Q: What's the best way to ruin a spreadsheet? A: WordArt

Q: Why are spreadsheets like prison? A: So many cells

Q: Why can't spreadsheets drive cars? A: They crash too often

Walter Moore

Q: What happens when you insult an Excel application? A: It stops responding

Did you hear about the constipated spreadsheet? He couldn't budget. (-LB)

Q: Why was the spreadsheet arrested? A: For an illegal error

There once was a man named Dave,

Having worked for hours all day,

But then one fatal cell,

Sent his spreadsheet to hell,

Next time he'll remember to save

Q: What do spreadsheet developers order at McDonald's? A: A big macro

Calibri walks into a bar, and the bartender says, "Sorry, we don't serve your type in here"

Q: What do you call a broken spreadsheet? A: The new guy's problem

Q: What did the VLOOKUP say on his online dating profile? A: "Seeking an approximate match". It's True! (-SJ)

On Error Goto Excel Hell (-SJ)

The spreadsheet circus is in town: Circ du cell A

Best cell to store Excel error messages? FU2 (LB)

Accountants are now allowed to deduct jokes made at their expense.

When spreadsheets go on vacation, they go to Graceland, to see Excelvis (SJ)

Walter Moore

Please prepare a meta analysis to analyze the spreadsheet you use to analyze the spreadsheet you use to track all the spreadsheets you use… (-SJ)

Q: What happens when spreadsheets break up? A: They become Ex cells (-SJ)

SOLVER?! I barely know her! (-SJ)

Q: Kim Kardashian's favorite spreadsheet?
A: The #Excelfie (-SJ)

Walter Moore

Q: Why was the spreadsheet x-rated? A: Because of graphic content.

Q: What happens when a bar chart works out? A: It becomes stacked.

Q: What do you call a spreadsheet consultant who owns his own company? A: Cell-employed

Q: What happens when a spreadsheet gets sick? A: VTHROWUP()

Q: What do you call a spreadsheet philosopher? A: Excelstensial (-SJ)

Q: What do Excel users put in their hair? A: SUMPRODUCT()

Q: What does every newborn spreadsheet need? A: Formula

Q: What do statisticians look for in a spouse? A: A normal distribution

Q: What do you call an egotistical Excel user? A: Cell-centered

Q: Why were the data depressed? A: No validation.

Q: What do you call Excel users in contest to see who can fill up their spreadsheet the fastest? A: A drag-race

Q: How did the murderer get out of jail? A: He unselected View Gridlines (-ODS)

Q: Why did the spreadsheet hate his job? A: Too many functions

Q: How do you quickly take over a spreadsheet? A: By using Ctrl.

Q: Where do spreadsheets go to drown their errors?
A: The formula bar

Illustration: Chad Thomas

Q: Why can't you give an accountant a birthday gift? A: Because they'll want to know the present value!

Q: How do spreadsheets gain muscle?
A: Lots of REPTs

Illustration: Walter Moore

A pivot table walks into a bar and orders a beer and says, "Put me in the same tab, will ya?"
If I had a dollar for every time someone stuffed up my formulas by deleting a cell I'd have #REF! by now (LB)
Q: How many interns are required to fix a messed up spreadsheet? A: As many as you can blame

Q: Why can't spreadsheets tell stories? A: Too many circular references (-ODS)

Walter Moore

Excel Theatre

Debra Dalgleish

Excel Tweets

One of my favorite things about Friday is the collection of Excel tweets published by Excel MVP Debra Dalgleish. Check this out each Friday: http://exceltheatre.com/blog/. Here are 40 all-time favorite Excel tweets, courtesy of Debra.

- What kind of monster sets Workbook Calculation to Manual in Excel anyway?

- Today I wore my *VLOOKUP face* all day. It's a bit like my *Pivot Table face* crossed with my *I'm sure I can smell something nasty face*

- If I want to use an Excel worksheet on this computer today I have to open it last week.

- Oh, the joys of opening a 2+ year old Excel workbook and trying to remember how it was constructed.

- You know work changed you when you realize you are already using the so-called "Top 10 Excel Tips You Probably Don't Know".

- Put down the Excel slowly and step away from the chart…

- I totally just made Excel make a pie chart. It even included the right stuff. This is a breakthrough.

- I'm so crafty I've locked myself out of my OWN stupid Excel file!!!

- Kids - learn three things in Excel. Vlookup. Pivot tables. How to create a chart. The average office worker will think you're a GOD.

- Using a mouse in Excel is the work equivalent of wearing a lanyard when you first get to college.

- A blank Excel workbook - the world at your fingertips

- How does anyone work in Excel without visible gridlines. You're all barbarians

- OK, this is getting a little scary. My Excel VBA code is actually starting to work. I doubted this day would ever come.

- At some point, the pivot table that I was working on achieved sentience. Time for a beer.

- Sipping coffee while simultaneously making charts on Excel and reading Wall Street Journal articles. I'm adulting pretty hard today.

- It puzzles me why people "colour code" in Excel. Any good ideas why?

- Things I would rather do than work on an excel spreadsheet; 1; eat kale 2; bathe cats 3; get hit by a car

- There's a reason this Excel workbook is titled "Headache.xlsx"

- Guy in my class just asked me how to make a basic chart in excel…. *must not judge*

- How many engineers does it take to make a bar chart on excel? Apparently 5.

- I have an Excel file that contains 15 sheets and 108 charts. If I lose this file, I will die.

- Wondering how long I can stare at this same Excel sheet before boss realizes I haven't done any work since lunch

- They said, "You are gonna excel in life." What they really meant is, "I will be doing Excel my whole life." #FML

- never felt technologically challenged till I tried to graph on excel

- Intensive Excel-work can turn any day into a Monday really fast…

- I spend more time in Excel than I do in my bed. That is sad. #work #officelife #ctrlaltdelete

- Computer claims "It is impossible to close Excel." I pull the plug. — If I ever plug you back in, don't EVER forget who's boss! #Ineedadrink

- My grandfather swore he'd retire the day they made him use a computer. My Grandma uses Excel like a boss.

- Work is sending me to Excel school. Not sure if compliment… or punishment.

- I daydream about using my skills to save lives; "A monster is destroying the city! Can ANYONE make a pivot table in an Excel spreadsheet???"

- If you are asking yourself if now is a good time to save your #Excel workbook, the answer is 'yes'

- My husband is explaining a pivot table to our 7 year old, and she is in awe. #girlswhocode

- There is exactly one person on planet earth who will understand any given Excel worksheet; The person who created it.

- I can't work with human beings who hard code total amounts in excel files. Cannot.

- I judge people at the office by their ability to use a pivot table.

- Things I've learned to appreciate since starting work: free food, bathroom breaks, Excel formulas

- Always good to be friends with someone who can work Microsoft Excel!

- Well, turns out I don't know how to use a pivot table…

- Not everything I do at work revolves around Excel. Only the fun parts.

- Wrote a macro to save time. Closed Excel without saving it. #FML

4

Thanks to Debra Dalgleish for collecting thousands of funny Excel tweets and providing this list. Thanks to the tweeters: @28flyersfan, @aalannyse, @Adovy, @algaegirl328, @alliebp, @anarchival, @awellofcards, @beanbeannie, @BeingHanuman, @bethykins, @bouleg812, @cdhowe, @chiayilcy, @ChrisGriff87, @danieljayz, @DanielleHollyxx, @danmarsekapr, @DehvanM, @Dodslaw, @gilltuft, @gueroguerinche, @incurablehippie, @itsreallyerin, @KeithPulling, @leaflitter, @MarkBrooksVA, @mattyk21fb, @mdhExcel, @MMaxwellStroud, @MrPSB, @science_goddess, @Scrappy_INFP, @sethbaysinger, @sherrybearie, @shmouflon, @SWEDUN, @tarallodactyl, @thomasrafael, @ThriftyYinzr, @vndimitrova

Excel Art From The FrankensTeam

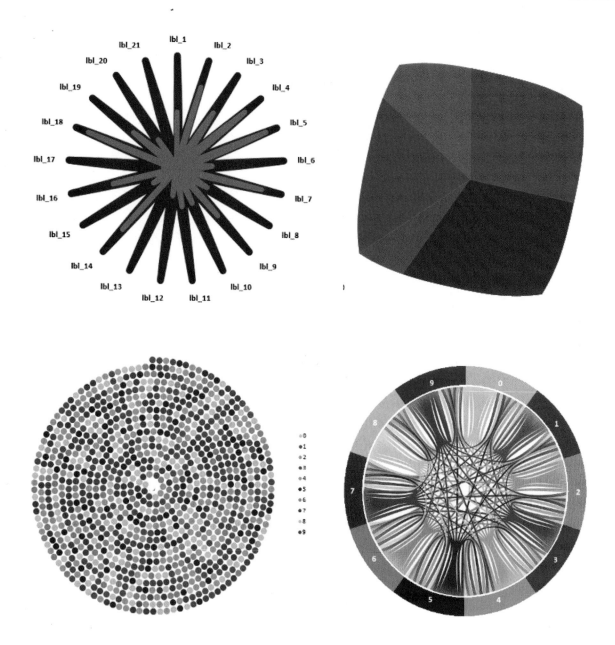

All of these are charts created in Excel by The FrankensTeam. https://sites.google.com/site/e90e50charts/

Clockwise From top right: Square Pie, Visualize the Digits of Pi 4, Visualize the Digits of Pi 6, Sun Chart

ADVENTURES

(TRUE AND ALMOST TRUE)

Excel Stories

How Did You Get So Good With Excel - Szilvia

It probably all started at birth. (Pardon me while I get comfortable on the therapist's couch.)

My dad is an engineer, and my mom is an artist and chef. I believe Excel is both art and science, so there is that. Also, I was born in the great state of Ohio. Every Excel community insider knows there is some serious Excel talent that flows through Ohio: my co-author Bill Jelen, MVP Jordan Goldmeier, bloggers like Chris Macro, and Power Pivot pioneer Rob Collie for a brief time. Even Chandoo stayed there for a summer. Although I'm in Los Angeles now, I make sure to get back to Ohio every so often to visit my family and to drink the Holy Excel water to stay on my game.

My first "serious" day job as an out-on-my-own adult was for one of those fancy "Big 6" consulting firms at their Budapest office. I think they must have hired me only because I could speak the local language, as I had no real accounting or audit experience to speak of. This is where I really cut my teeth on Excel, because those firms pretty much live and die by it. Spending most of my days cranking out spreadsheets, I soon realized there was just something about Excel. Somehow it came naturally to me, and I kept stumbling upon new little tricks and features by accident. I found it fascinating that there were so many things Excel could do. I didn't know at the time that most of the "normal" people around me did not share my fascination. But I kept going with it. I may have not understood all the ins and outs of debits and credits, but pivot tables and I were sure getting along great. I was finding Excel was making me more curious, and helping me understand a lot about business.

A few years and circumstances later, I wound up working for the Gap at their San Francisco headquarters. A finance manager there blew my mind when he walked me through me some VBA code that would help automate some reports I was doing. I never figured I would be able to decipher programming languages of any kind. I could not help myself, I just had to understand more about how it all worked. So began my foray into the Excel object model. It was addicting. I redesigned the entire payroll planning and reporting process for Old Navy finance with a VBA/pivot table-driven model. It was a solution used by corporate finance departments, and also by store managers out in the field across the country. I had to be mindful of the wide variety of skillsets of my end users so I found myself stepping in the role of accidental trainer as well. I believe I got one phone call asking me about the "foot pedal" (mouse).

A few years later San Francisco was no longer in the cards for me. The Gap was doing big-time layoffs, including most of their finance team, and including me. It wasn't a great job market up north, but I still loved California. So I moved down to LA and did what everyone else does there: "fake it till you make it." In other words, figuring things out without really committing to anything. Eager to try something different, I started to "fake" my way into a freelance consulting career by signing up with a bunch of temp agencies. So began a chapter I like to call the "Accidental Excel Consultant" years.

I would work for anyone needing anything remotely Excel related. Usually I didn't last long because I always wanted to rip apart then rebuild all the Excel spreadsheets instead of taking orders from someone who inevitably wanted things their old and inefficient way, which often made me cringe inside until I could no longer stand it. So for the most part, I was getting in trouble because I was doing a great job – a job that I wasn't hired to do. Other times my Excel habit would actually pay off, bosses were impressed, and would move me into more suitable roles. But typically, I was sent back out onto the streets (well, back to my small West Hollywood apartment, just off Melrose and across from a retired seniors/swingers community home, but that story is for another book), until the next sucker came along to help me pay rent.

Then another few years later as I got better at the whole game, I could afford to start getting pickier about my assignments. One lucky one was at Westfield, the retail and commercial real estate giant. I was brought in to help standardize and consolidate corporate overhead budgets for 40 departments – all in Excel! By this time I was getting really good, and realized that I had become that go-to Excel person in the office. A delightful, funny woman (and now friend), Nancy Kiriro, also worked there. One day she suggested we organize an afternoon training session for a few fellow finance employees "so you can show them how you do all that stuff in Excel." We did, and after a very successful day of tons of Excel demos and a few laughs, they wanted five more days. XSzil was born. And Westfield continues to be one of my favorite clients. They still bring me in for training and consulting gigs, almost a decade later.

There was one other day that stands out in my Excel-life as a turning point. Appropriately enough, it took place in Ohio. After several life-saver tips I picked up from the MrExcel.com message board over the years, I learned that Bill Jelen was doing a seminar in Ohio. I was due for a parental visit, so it made sense to co-ordinate the two trips (Okay, so maybe I also kind of wanted to meet MrExcel). So I showed up that day at the University of Akron and introduced myself. I learned some new stuff, and there was of course other stuff I already knew (*pats self on back*). But then, Bill learned something new too. Because in the middle of a longish demo he was doing on pivot tables, I piped up, "Are you going to show them that 'show pages' thing?" I asked casually. And then it happened. I don't even recall what he said exactly, but he had never heard of Show Pages. Bill was stumped. I. stumped. MrExcel. (Was I sitting in row 2? It's a blur, but I must have been.) Bill told me he was going to feature that tip on his next podcast. Since that day, I always chuckle at the shout-outs he gives me in his books whenever the subject of Show Pages comes up. We've become colleagues and friends over the years, so here I am co-writing this book.

Much has transpired since my "Accidental Consulting" days. These days it's quite on purpose. This golden era Excel is experiencing right now means I get to let my Excel [freak] flag fly high with each new business opportunity. I work with company leaders, managers, accountants, worker bees… all with the aim of better leveraging the world's most powerful business intelligence software system.

Life is good.

4

The Tech Intelligentsia in Leo's Green Room

A long time ago, in San Francisco, there was a cable channel called TechTV. Leo Laporte would do two shows, live, every afternoon: *The Screen Savers* and *Call for Help*. The latter was similar to the *Car Talk* show on National Public Radio, with people calling in with their tech problems and Leo Laporte troubleshooting their W-Fi network right on the air. Between calls, there were a number of interesting tech segments and two guests per show.

As a guest, you would get six minutes to show an interesting trick or technique. At the end of the six minutes, Leo would say something great about your book and hold it up for the camera. I made a total of 86 appearances on the show.

Leo Laporte and Bill Jelen on the set of The Lab with Leo Laporte. Photo Credit: Sean Carruthers, globalhermit.com.

My first two visits were at the San Francisco studio, where I met a very young Kevin Rose and Roger Chang. When the show moved to Toronto, Canada, Leo would film one week of shows a month. It was an easy 37-minute flight from Cleveland to Toronto, so I went up almost every month and would appear on two shows a month.

My favorite episode was my 26th, when I showed how to add subtotals to a data set. On the face of it, this had to be the most boring six minutes in the history of television. But the next day, viewer e-mail started streaming in. That segment was a hit. My favorite e-mail was from a woman who had been manually adding subtotals every morning, taking almost 2 hours each day. She saw the episode, tried the trick, and was done in one minute! She quipped, "The best part is that my manager doesn't watch your show!" She had just gained 1 hour and 59 minutes of "free" time to get other stuff done.

In Toronto, a co-host for many years was Amber MacArthur. Amber was always on the leading edge of technology. She was constantly in-the-know about what was new and upcoming. She is the one who advised me to grab the MrExcel handle on this new site called Twitter and introduced me to YouTube in the very early days.

This is also where I first heard about podcasting. Amber and Mike Lazazzera was doing a weekly *CommandN* video podcast. Leo was doing a weekly *This Week in Tech* audio podcast. Sean Carruthers and Andy Walker were doing *The Lab Rats*.

Leo is the one who suggested a 2-minute podcast every weekday. So, on July 23, 2006, I started producing the Learn Excel from MrExcel video podcast and putting it out on iTunes. Thanks to Amber and Leo and the gang, I had video content on iTunes even before the iPod could support video. A few months later, I found my podcast on the front screen of iTunes as a Top 10 tech video podcast. That was easy...since there were probably only 11 people doing video podcasts back then. Of course, the podcast later morphed into my YouTube channel, where I now have 1,900 Excel videos. It would be daunting to build that large of a collection of videos today, but by building them slowly, one at a time, it worked out.

Later, the show moved to Vancouver. Again, it was groundbreaking: *The Lab with Leo Laporte* was shot in HD before anyone had HD televisions. Matt Harris and Sean Carruthers made the move to Vancouver. Kate Abraham took over as co-host. Since Vancouver was a five-hour trek from Akron, producer Matt Harris let me do four shows each month.

Whether in Toronto or Vancouver, they were taping four shows a day. That meant I was hanging out in the green room with leading tech personalities. Security expert Steve Gibson was super-friendly. I remember asking Merlin Mann for life hacks. My favorite, though, was Dick DeBartolo, MAD Magazine's maddest writer. I've taken some improv classes, but Dick DeBartolo has the quickest wit of anyone I've met. Once I introduced myself as MrExcel, he pulled out his business card and autographed it, "To Mister Access...".

4

Leo Laporte, Bill Jelen, Amber MacArthur and Dick DeBartolo of GizWiz.biz on the set of Call for Help in 2006.

"Do You Want to Write a Book?"

Printed books are not dead!

I started MrExcel as a consulting firm, but I wanted to write a book. I was in a 2002 seminar listening to marketing maven Ivana Taylor, and she offered the advice that I needed a $20 product to sell at my website. Before Ivana, people had two choices: get their answer from the MrExcel Message Board for free or pay me a few hundred dollars for a custom Excel macro. Ivana pointed out that I needed to give people a chance to hand me a small amount of money. That idea worked well. Book sales outpaced consulting.

I hate rejection. I did not want to start trying to convince publishers that I could be the next J-Walk. So, I wrote my first book, *Guerilla Data Analysis Using Microsoft Excel*. My first print run was 10 copies at the CopyMax in Akron. I put them on my website and soon sold out. I took the $100 in profit from the first print run and printed another 10. Eventually, I found a place that would produce 100 copies with a real cover instead of the spiral binding. The Holy Macro! Books publishing company was born.

I was following advice from small-press guru Dan Poynter and reading Publishers Weekly magazine. I really wanted my book in the pages of Publishers Weekly, so I took a shortcut and bought an ad in the magazine. (Note: a few years later, Publishers Weekly (PW) did feature the cover of my book, *The Spreadsheet at 25* worth of a mention in the Upcoming Releases section.) The PW ad sales rep pointed me to Independent Publishers Group (IPG). This changed everything. Another small-ish publisher, Chicago Review Press, realized that small publishers could benefit from working together and formed IPG. More than 200 niche publishers are part of IPG. IPG handles selling my books into the book trade. They warehouse the books. They ship books. This is a beautiful relationship: I don't have to worry about storing books in my garage. I can focus on finding authors and producing interesting books.

As I travel around, my ears always perk up when I hear that someone wants to write a book. I've published books by a lot of Excel MVPs and Office experts but also some other books like a rasslin' memoir from the Reverend Billy C. Wirtz and *Harriers*, a book about running Cross Country in high school. It spent a few years in the top 10 for the Running category at Amazon. Amazingly, that book was written by cousins Joe and Paul Shivers, and they wrote the book in high school. Our next non-Excel project is *We Report Space*, a photo book written by a group of Social Media covering Florida rocket launches

I also write books for the QUE imprint at Pearson, the world's largest publishing house. I appreciate that relationship. But I have fun with the books produced here at Holy Macro! Off-the-wall titles like *M is for (Data) Monkey* are par for the course here. Good-quality content on the inside allows for a bit of light-heartedness on the cover.

Here is a list of books that I hope to write and publish one day. Thanks to Marie Leone, my former editor at CFO Magazine who brainstormed many of these!

- *Excel for Human Resources, Excel for the Hospitality Industry, Excel for Call Centers*, and so on.
- *27 Minutes to Excel*: The Concise Guide for that Job Interview where you have to "Know" Excel
- *Excel for Search Engine Marketing*
- *Option Explicit?* A Cage Match with Jordan
- Beginning Excel Book in Spanish (clearly, I need to learn more Spanish, or find a co-author)
- *25 Excel Projects* - a book detailing start-to-end projects without VBA
- *Household Excel* - from high school to retirement. Schedules. Budgets. Grocery Lists
- *Elementary Excel* - projects for the K-6 classroom
- *Stay-at-Home Excel* - 50 home-based businesses to start with the help of Excel

Live – On Stage – In Person: The Power Excel Seminars

That poster from Hatch Show Print on my website sort of started out as a joke. I was flying through Nashville and saw a display of old country music letterpress posters on the wall. The little sign by the posters said they were produced on a 100-year-old hand-cranked press and that the company was still operating in Nashville. I called them and hired them to produce a "concert" poster for my live Excel seminars. They had to think I was a little nuts. The print shop manager, Jim Sherraden, often did an informative presentation about the history of Hatch, and he cited my poster as the first to list a website URL.

I do my half-day or 1-day seminar for accounting groups across the country. Every large city has a local chapter of the Institute of Managerial Accountants or the Institute of Internal Auditors. The people who belong to these groups usually need 20-30 hours of continuing education (CPE) each year. If you join the organization and go to 12 lunch meetings, half of your CPE is done. The organizations will often sponsor a 1- or 2-day event with speakers so their members can earn the remaining CPE at one time. I often am invited to speak at these events. The poster on the door lets people know that they are not in for the usual tax update. (I don't mean to offend the wonderful people going through the new tax laws…someone's got to do that.)

Excel is used on 750 million devices. I've met a lady in Appalachia who used Excel to design original quilt patterns. I've met people who have designed workbooks in Excel that train people how to fly 737 jets. From quilts to jets, Excel is used everywhere.

When you hand the world's most flexible software to 750 million people, everyone finds interesting things to do or interesting ways to use Excel. I love traveling to do the in-person Excel seminars because I get to meet these people. At every seminar, someone has an interesting story of how they are using Excel. At every seminar, I always learn a few new Excel tricks from the people in the seminar. I joke that my job is collecting the cool and obscure tricks in Excel from people along the road and passing them on to people further on up the road. Many of the amazing tricks in this book came from people in my live Excel seminars.

This is truly a win-win. I have fun doing the seminars. The audience get to take home a cool Excel book. Among the 75 tricks that I show in a day, hopefully everyone will find a few that they can take back to work to start becoming more efficient the next day. Plus, people earn the CPE hours without hearing about any tax updates. Even at the Association for Computers and Taxation, where their annual meeting is all about tax updates, they bring me in to do a 2-hour session to offer a little levity between the tax updates!

The Excel Master Pin

Do you own one of the highly-coveted Excel Master pins?

When I do my live Power Excel seminars, I always encourage the audience to "show me up." Someone in

that room is going to have a better way to do something in Excel. I used to offer a small prize to the first person to teach me something during the seminar. I would also predict that the first person to show me up that day walked into the room and sat in row 2.

I have no idea why they always go to row 2. But I noticed early on that the best Exceller always chooses a seat in row 2. They want to be close. But not front-row close. Almost every time, the first cool idea from the audience comes to row 2. (On the times when the first tip comes from another row, I quip, "Did you arrive late, and row 2 was already full?")

Over the years, the prize varied from an Excel function clock to a free book or a laminated tip card. But the most popular prize was a tiny enamel pin: "Excel Master. Ask me your Excel questions." I handed out a few of these at each seminar. When I go back to a city a few years later, it is cool to see someone showing up with that pin.

"I Just Got a Promotion Because of Your Website"

It is gratifying when I hear this. Once you pass the 40th percentile of Excel skills – once you move beyond AutoSum and start to tap into Excel's power – there is a clear path to dramatically better Excel skills.

In a lot of companies, Excel is used for entering data on a grid with maybe a total at the bottom. If you work at one of those companies and can add subtotals to your skill set, you can now do in a minute what someone else might spend an hour doing.

Learn how to create and customize a chart, and you can summarize data into information.

Take the steps to learn how to create and customize a pivot table, and you gain the ability to find truth in a sea of numbers.

Compared to your co-workers, you can now make Excel sing and dance and produce faster results than anyone else. Your manager's manager will often notice, and you will become a trusted resource – the person who can figure out how to get answers to questions.

It is really gratifying when someone comes up to me and says they picked up some knowledge from one of my videos or the message board and used that to get a new job.

One guy said he had a job delivering pizzas. As he drove, he had a laptop continuously streaming the YouTube channel from ExcelIsFun and my channel. When I met him, he was in row 2, stunning the audience with great Excel tricks.

The Excel Function Clock was Born on a Slow Friday Afternoon

It was a Friday afternoon at work and time was dragging. I would look at the clock, do some VLOOKUPs, then look back at the clock and barely a minute had passed.

it struck me that it would be funny if someone made a clock where the 3 was replaced with the Excel function =PI(). This simple function with no arguments returns 3.14. So, =PI() wouldn't be exactly at 3. It would have to be just a bit beyond the 3. The solution would be to use the INT function to return just the integer portion of PI(). =INT(PI()) returns just 3. Perfect! I am sure I pitched both of these ideas to Kevin Adkins, who probably didn't think it was a funny as I did. That never deters me, though.

Over a few evenings, I started collecting functions for the other numbers on the clock. I tried to go with things that were useful but a bit obscure. After, all what fun would it be to have =SUM(2,-1) for 1? Most people already know SUM. After writing all 12 functions, I actually found the graphic designer who designed the clocks for the old Signals mail order catalog. The Excel function clock was on Call For Help a few times. Once, Leo Laporte attached it to a lanyard and wore the clock as if he were rapper Flavor Flav. It was funny stuff.

Here are the 12 formulas:

1. =MIN(1,10). Min returns the minimum number. Since 1<10, the function returns 1.

2. =MONTH(23790). That is the serial number for my birthday, February 17, 1965. That is month number 2.

3. =INT(PI()). =PI() would've been 1/7 of the way past 3, so =INT returns the integer 3.

4. =LEN("FOUR"). I used LEN daily. =MID(A2,LEN(A2)-7,2) gets the last 2 characters. How long is FOUR? 4.

5. =SQRT(25). The square root of 25 is 5.

6. =FACT(3). Factorials are used to calculate lottery probability. The Factorial of 3 is 3x2x1 or 6.

7. =GCD(77,49). Middle school match is simpler with Excel. The greatest common divisor of 77 and 49 is 7

8. =2^3. The ^ raises 2 to the 3 power. =2*2*2 is 8.

9. =PMT(9%,9,-53.96). If you borrowed $53.96 from the bank to buy some MrExcel books and had to pay it back over 9 years with a 9% interest rate, each yearly payment would be $9.

10. =LCM(2,5). Another one for the 7th graders. The Lowest Common Multiple of 2 and 5 is 10.

11. =ROMAN(2). Hmm. My fascination with =ROMAN() began before my 40th book. The =ROMAN(2) is II, which looks sort of like 11. Just like XL sounds sort of like Excel.

12. =COLUMN(L1). tells you the column number of a cell. L is column number 12.

If you are thinking you need to get one of these for yourself, head over to http://mrx.cl/excelclock.

A Brilliant Idea - TrainerTage (Trainer Days)

In 2013 and 2014, I was invited to Lucerne Switzerland to speak at a conference called TrainerTage. The conference is in German, but they told me I would be fine if I spoke *slowly* in English.

But something odd happened: Mary Ellen Jelen and I flew to Switzerland. It was time for my first session. When I showed the Double-click the Fill handle trick, no one gasped. Every time that I do this trick for the IMA, a few people in the audience gasp. But here, in Switzerland, no one gasped.

At the end of my hour-long session (with my very best tricks), Tanja Kuhn explained they needed a higher level. As I came to realize, this conference was designed for people who did Microsoft Office training across Europe. Every one in the room also traveled every week to train others in Office. I was clearly out-matched.

Every January, trainers from Switzerland, Germany, and the Netherlands gather for very high-level sessions. Each member of Tanja's team researches a new feature in Office and presents it to their peers.

I became friends with many of the people there.

My Excel 2013 In Depth book was a 1200+ page book - over five pounds of Excel. In Germany, the equivalent book is written by Dietmar Gieringer. Dietmar and I hit it off. I would sit in his seminars, understanding very little German, but able to follow what Dietmar was doing in Excel and learning new tricks.

Clockwise from above: Dietmar Gieringer,
Andreas Thehos, Dominik Petri,
Tony DeJonker (AlwayExcel.com)
The TrainerTage trainers: Kai Schneider,
Dietmar Gieringer, Bea Lengyel , Tanja Kuhn, (Bill Jelen),
Pia Bork, Ute Simon, Dieter Schiecke, Marcus Hahner.

I Don't Have a Corner on Excel Knowledge

I've written 40 books about Excel, but there is so much more to learn. Every time I watch someone else do an Excel presentation, I learn new tricks.

Excel consultant Andrew Spain did a short five-trick session at my seminar in Huntsville, Alabama. Two of

those tricks were brand new to me. (My favorite: If you forget to hold down Ctrl while dragging the fill handle to extend 1 into 1, 2, 3, you can toggle Ctrl on and off at the end of the drag. While the tooltip does not update, the mouse cursor toggles a small + to indicate that you are filling instead of copying.) That's Andrew Spain and me on the left.

Thomas Fries does a training program for people who have been displaced in the job market. His seminar gives them a hand up so they can say they have Excel skills on their resume. I dropped into his class one day for five minutes and learned two new things.

During the days of the Call for Help TV show in Toronto, I discovered that you could buy group tickets for

the Toronto Blue Jays on Tuesdays for $2 each. (And that's $2 Canadian – about US$1.80!). I bought a bunch of tickets and invited anyone who used MrExcel.com to come to the baseball game. Duane Aubin, Freddy Fuentes and John Cockerill were there – you can ask them. No one from that night remembers the score because we sat in left field discussing the best way to do VLOOKUP!

Also in this photo - Tracy Syrstad from MrExcel Consulting. Duane Aubin in the back right helped me write *The Spreadsheet at 25*. In the white shirt towards the right is our dear departed friend Nate Oliver - NateO at MrExcel.com.

Photo credit: Freddy Fuentes

There were some people in the next section who overheard our conversation and started heckling that they used Lotus. It turns out that they were from a local accounting company and had also bought $2 group seats; I ended up sponsoring their company baseball team. (They even let me have one at-bat, where I hit the ball about one meter and managed to beat the throw to first base.) At the bar after the baseball game, we talked about Excel, and I picked up a few new tricks from the Toronto Excellers.

4

New in Excel 2016 - Waterfall Charts & More

For twelve years, I worked at a company doing data analysis. One of my regular tasks was to analyze the profit on sales proposals before they went out the door. I did this with a waterfall chart. For me, the waterfall chart never would have to dip below the zero axis. I used a few tricks to make the columns float and drew the connector lines in by hand using a ruler and a black pen.

Excel 2016 finally offers a built-in waterfall chart type. Select your range of data and create the chart. You need to choose which columns are Totals and need to touch the axis. It is very simple.

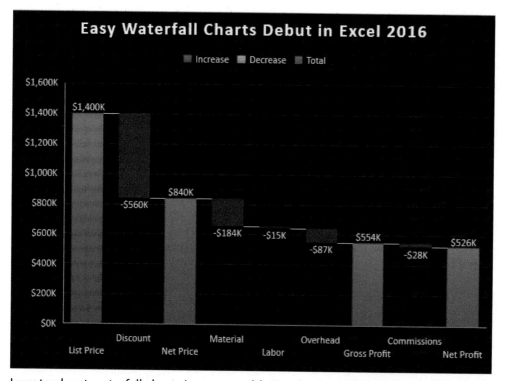

I wrote about waterfall charts in my monthly Excel column for *Strategic Finance* magazine. People wrote in saying that my method would not work for a cash flow analysis where the balance would dip below zero. They were right, you had to go through an insane amount of hoops to have a column dip below zero before Excel 2016. Now it all simply works with one click in Excel 2016.

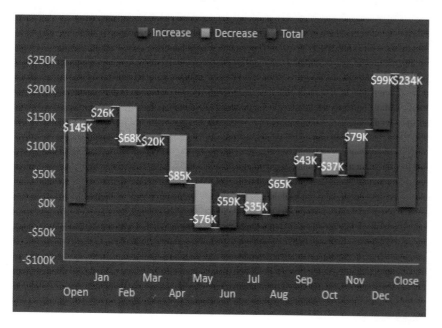

New in Excel 2016 - Forecast Sheets

Another great feature in Excel 2016 is the the Forecast Sheet function. Select a time series. Excel will look for seasonality and produce a forecast and a confidence interval.

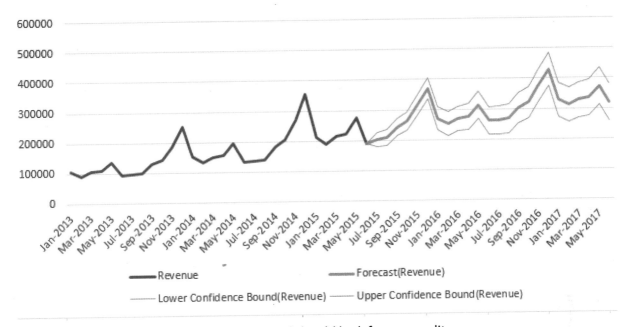

There are various settings to control how Excel should look for seasonality.

◢ Options

    Forecast Start   0

    ☑ Confidence Interval   95%

    Seasonality
    ◉ Detect Automatically
    ◯ Set Manually   0

    ☐ Include forecast statistics

Excel use new formulas to fill in the future months below your time series.

| | | f_x | =FORECAST.ETS(A54,$B$2:$B$31,$A$2:$A$31,1,1) |

Forecast(Revenue) ▾	Lower Confidence Bound(Revenue) ▾	Upper
334415.8178	275088.80	
372506.2078	311945.05	
319465.9705	257690.75	

=FORECAST.ETS(A55,$B$2:$B$31,$A$2:$A$31,1,1)
=C55-FORECAST.ETS.CONFINT(A55,$B$2:$B$31,$A$2:$A$31,0.95,1,1)

I Love Weird Excel Things

If you have a weird bug in Excel, I love to hear about that. If you have some brilliant idea that would make Excel better, I love to hear about that, too.

I recall working in 1990s. I used Excel every day. I had an arrow on the floor pointing to Redmond. I would face that way and probably use a few expletives whenever I would beat my head against the wall with something that could have been better in Excel.

"If Excel would just do *this*, it would make my life so much easier."

If you use Excel 20 hours a week, I am sure that you have thought of improvements that would make Excel easier for you.

When I ran across one of these ideas, all I could do was face northwest and wonder why the Excel team hadn't done this yet. The Internet was not prevalent. You couldn't bounce over to the Excel Team blog and leave a comment like you can today. By the way, the Excel team does read those comments: https://blogs.office.com/excel/.

I launched MrExcel.com and wrote my first Excel book before I ever met anyone from Redmond. When I finally made the call and was granted a two-hour meeting with David Gainer, I was shocked to see that my first book was on the conference room table. But it wasn't just there: It had dozens of sticky notes and highlighted sections.

"Uh oh," I thought, as my mind raced through all those places where I had criticized Excel for not doing what I wanted.

But David was awesome. Smart. He listened. He shared some of his ideas and vision for where Excel should be going. Before, they were just nameless people in Redmond. Now, I actually had a face and a name.

And here is what I've come to realize: I have great ideas about what should be in Excel. I know that I can pass my ideas on to the Excel team, and they get put on the big whiteboard of what should happen next. There are 100+ ideas on that board, and for each release of Excel, eight might make it to the product.

Each release of Excel might have a focus. For example, the calculation engine was improved in Excel 2007. If you had a great idea on the board in 2005-2006 and it was not calculation related, you weren't going to see your feature get added to Excel.

There are resource constraints. Excel has to ship the same day as the rest of Office. At some point, you have to pick and choose which features get added and which stay on the whiteboard for another time.

I first complained about the blank cells in the row fields of pivottables in my first book in 2002. That feature was not fixed in 2003 or in 2007. But I kept asking, and eventually it came. It was fixed in 2010 with the amazing Repeat All Item Labels. I was a little disappointed that the tooltip for the feature did not say, "We put this in so Bill Jelen will stop bugging us," but I knew that I had a small part in convincing the Excel team to put that feature in there.

So – one very cool thing about my job is having a conduit to pitch new Excel ideas to the people who can actually make it happen. I understand many won't happen and others won't happen for a few versions. But some do happen.

The next time you see me at a seminar, pass those ideas and frustrations along to me, and I will pass them on to the keeper of the great Excel idea whiteboard.

The People at the MrExcel Message Board Answers 800,000 Excel Questions

When I launched MrExcel.com in November 1998, I would get up every morning and answers yesterday's e-mailed questions before heading in to work. Initially, it was a question or two each weekday. But, by May 1999, I was getting more questions than I could answer in an hour. I was answering questions from 5 AM to 6 AM and then heading in to work. I either had to start getting up at 4 AM or find another way.

I downloaded WWWBoard from Matt's Script Archive. I asked people to post their question at the message board. And I asked that, after posting, they look at the last few questions to see if they could help someone else out. It was like the take-a-penny, leave-a-penny tray at a cash register. If you need help, post a question. If you can help someone else out, help them out. It worked. People started posting and answering questions.

In the early days, I noticed a few people would stop by almost every day and answer a question or two. Ivan F. Moala. Cecilia. The late Dave Hawley.

One day, at work. I was stumped. I went out to my own message board, and described my problem. An hour later, Ivan F. Moala from New Zealand had posted an amazing answer. I knew I had something.

The board transformed over the years, morphing into bigger platforms. I was on a $10-a-month hosting plan at Pair Networks in Pittsburgh. One day, I get a call from them wondering what I was doing. "You are on a $10-a-month plan, but you are using as much traffic as our $1,000-a-month plan!" Apparently, the MrExcel Message Board had taken on a life of its own.

Today, the amazing people at the MrExcel Message Board have answered 800,000 questions about Excel. We've attempted to keep every question live on the site. There are some massive competitors who have competing forums, but they have no problem wiping out their history. I run into people all the time who say they use my forum. I ask what their handle is. "Oh – I've never had to post – I just search. Every answer is already there."

The MrExcel community is staffed by volunteers. Over the years, various experts have worked tirelessly as moderators and administrators. My sincere thanks to Andew Poulsom, barry houdini, Colo, fairwinds, Ivan F Moala, Joe4, Jon von der Heyden, Juan Pablo Gonzalez, NateO, PaddyD, Peter_SSs, Richard Schollar, RoryA, Scott Huish, Smitty, Starl, SydneyGeek, VoG, Von Pookie, zenou, and Zack Barresse. Suat Ozgur and Scott Pierson handled the tech issues with the board.

As far as the people answering questions, over 30 people have answered more than 10,000 questions at the board. This is a staggering contribution to the Excel community. Thanks to Andrew Poulsom (below left) and Aladin Akyurek (below right) with over 70,000 posts each. Norie and Jonmo1 have over 60,000 posts. Joe4, Smitty, Peter_SSs, RoryA, Richard Schollar, Rick Rothstein and barry houdini have contributed more than 20,000 posts. Many of the experts ar MrExcel.com are awarded the MVP Award in Excel from Microsoft.

If you ask Google any Excel question, the odds are pretty good that one of the top answers will be from MrExcel or one of the pirates who have stolen questions from our site. If you can't find your answer on Google, it is free to post a new question. Make sure to give the post a title that describes what you are trying to do. Even in the middle of the night, someone will likely have an answer.

How Did You Get So Good with Spreadsheets? - Bill

As I look back, there are four main events that caused me to be really good with spreadsheets. I erroneously started calling myself MrExcel after only the first two had happened.

1. In 1985, two professors at Notre Dame were doing a research project to compare learning methods. Half of the MBA students were taught Lotus 1-2-3 using a traditional method. The other half watched a 4-hour program on interactive laser disk. All of the students then took a 25-question test about Lotus 1-2-3. As the teaching assistant for Dr. Khalil Matta, it was my job to grade the 25-question test. After grading many tests, I noticed that none of these MBA students would ever score higher than 66% on the test. After months of watching this, I thought to myself, if I sit down with the test at a computer running Lotus 1-2-3 and figure out the answer to all 25 questions, I would be better with spreadsheets than that year's graduating class of MBAs. So - thank you to Gary Kern and Khalil Matta.

2. After college, I got a job working in the M.I.S. department at Telxon in Akron, Ohio. I was writing COBOL programs to support the accounting and finance departments. Back then, if you could knock out a rush program in 8 hours to answer a question, you were a hero. I heard the Finance department was looking at a 4th generation query tool called EZIQ that would allow them to query mainframe data and run their own reports. This was a relief to me, as I would have to do less of their rush reporting. But then, the second bit of news. They were going to hire an analyst to run the reports for them. I interviewed. They lured me upstairs.

After moving to Finance, I discovered that EZIQ was not able to produce the reports that the CFO wanted. But there was another option in EZIQ - to take the mainframe data and download it to a spreadsheet. Even back in 1989, the most powerful button in this 4th generation reporting software was Export to Spreadsheet. I was creating reports out using all sorts of data analysis tricks in Lotus 1-2-3 from 1989 to 1994 and then in Excel from 1995 onward. Every day, I was running new reports. It was a great job - a lot of variety. I was running reports for Finance, Accounting, Operations, Order Entry, Sales, Marketing, and sometimes even the manufacturing plant. This is where I became really good with Data Consolidate, VLOOKUP, Subtotals, Pivot Tables. My thanks to Mark Hauser for hiring me out of the IT department.

I managed to get some budget for the *Inside Microsoft Excel* journal and absorbed that every month. I now learn that much of that was written by Excel MVP Bob Umlas, the same guy who tech edits my books. I've published two of Bob's books as well.

3. In 1998, my buddy Kevin Adkins started calling me MrExcel. He hatched this plan for me to write a book. Every day, Kevin was supposed to come in with a new Excel question. After 100 days, I would take all of those questions and write a book. It was a great plan, but Kevin did not come up with enough questions. After a month, we had only 3 questions. I needed a way to generate new questions.

At the same time, our hated competitor made a hostile takeover bid to buy Telxon. I was about to be out of a job. So, on Thanksgiving weekend in 1998, I launched MrExcel.com. The stated purpose: "Send me your Excel questions. I will send you the answers. The best question each week will appear on the website. The best questions will appear in a book." That was only partially true. In the back of my head, I thought, "If I can get 50 people who use Excel to send me an e-mail, I will have 50 places to send my resume when the takeover is complete."

The site went live on Friday. Somehow, I was picked up by the Excite.com search engine and appeared in their top 10 results for Excel. Wednesday morning, I woke up to find 2 Excel questions in my inbox. I eagerly opened the first one. It was from an engineer. He was asking about features of Excel that I had never used. I thought, "what a horrible way to start" and clicked Next to go to the other e-mail. This time, it was a scientist, and I had no clue what the answer was. My website is calling me MrExcel, and I am 0 for 2 on day one. What a mistake.

But over the next six months, I would wake up every day at 5AM and answer the e-mailed questions for an hour. If I did not know the answer, I would use Excel help to figure it out and send the answer back. While Telxon had trained me to be really good at transforming mainframe data into information, answering questions every morning taught me a lot about other facets of Excel.

Oh - and the suitor backed out of their bid to take over Telxon. I continued to work at Telxon during the day and was MrExcel at night.

MrExcel.com became my full-time gig in the year 2000. New management at Telxon were packaging the company for sale. They asked me to move to Cincinnati. We even found a house. But then they accidentally sent me the WARN letter saying my facility was closing and offering a six-month buyout. I took the buyout, figuring I could do Excel consulting for five months and then start looking for a job if it was not working. There was only one day that I woke up and did not have a project to do. I loved the 2-4 hour projects. I never wanted to move in to a company and work for weeks or months. I liked the quick hit of a macro to solve a problem and then move on.

When your day is comprised of doing two-hour consulting jobs, you get to meet a lot of interesting people and interesting companies. I've done VBA programs for stock day traders. I've done VBA programs for people who think they have a new way to beat the casino or race track. (As an aside, any gamblers should check out the *Excel Simulations* book by Dr. Gerard Verschuuren. This is a fun book that spans topics from gambling to genetics.). I've been lucky to get a gig with the Harlem Globetrotters. As a kid, I always hoped to play basketball for the Globetrotters. Several issues made that a dubious goal. (I scored a total of 4 points in an entire season of 5th grade basketball). But - I am thrilled to be creating pivot tables for them. My friend Jerry Kohl is always thinking of innovative ways to use Excel at his Brighton company. Today, I am often too busy writing or traveling to do VBA consulting, but I have a great team of consultants who build VBA macros to automate taks for clients around the world.

I started getting requests to do seminars around the Akron area. I would go in, show subtotals, pivot tables, and so on. High-level stuff. One day, while doing a seminar at the Greater Akron Chamber, someone asked me a really simple question. While I showed them =PROPER(A2&" "&B2) to join first and last names together, I noticed the people were more interested in this simple little formula. I started making the seminars very interactive. I invited people to "show me up" by surprising me with new tricks in Excel that I did not know. This became a fun part of the seminars. I always remember where some of the best tricks came from. Dave in row 1 in Columbus, Indiana, showed me the right-click, drag right, drag left menu. Derek in row 6 in Springfield, Missouri, showed me how to sort subtotals so the largest customer is at the top. Dan in row 2 in Philadelphia showed me the hack to AutoFilter a pivot table. Ctrl+Drag the Fill Handle to fill 1, 2, 3 came from the right side of the auditorium in Kent, Ohio, but I don't remember her name. The list goes on and on.

Excel Around the World

Clockwise from top left: Highclere Castle, London phone booth, Amsterdam MVP meeting, PASS BAC,
Brian Kamimoto aka Brian from Maui, Derek Fraley (from row 6!) and Olen Greer, Robert Jelen before my Daytona Beach seminar, Mary Ellen Jelen with a leatherback turtle hatchling in Trinidad, Areef Ali in Trinidad, Mark Rosenkrantz and Ernst Schuurman in Amsterdam, Mel, Bryony, Richard, Jon, and Russ in London, Bill with the Hatch Show Print poster at Stonehenge.

The Rock Bottom Brewery in Bellevue Washington

Once a year, Excel gurus from around the world descend on the Rock Bottom Brewery in Bellevue, Washington, for a week of Excel discussions. I've met many friends here. If you have a favorite Excel blog or author, I've probably met them at the Rock Bottom Brewery.

Now, the big problem that we have: The Rock Bottom Brewery closes each evening, and we have nothing to do during the day. Luckily, we found a few meetings over at Microsoft where we can hang out with the project managers who are working on the next version of Excel.

This is generally a horrible experience for new Excel project managers. They walk into a room with 24 Excel experts. They show the great feature that they've been working on. And then the people in the room proceed to tell them how much we love the feature by piling on twenty-seven ways to make it better. And we are passionate. We'll will make pitches about why our proposed features are the right features. I suspect most Excel PMs leave the room with some PTSD. The experienced Excel project managers don't present at the MVP Summit. They sit in the back of the room and watch. Because out of the hour-long discussion that erupts, a few good valuable nuggets make sense. They make it into the product. As a participant, it is easy to get frustrated that "the Excel team isn't listening to ME," but in fact, it is an honor to be in that room and to have some hope of making an impact on the vast sea of Excel ideas.

So the next time you use Flash Fill or create an Excel 2016 waterfall chart, hoist a pint to the Rock Bottom Brewery in Bellevue.

Photo credit: Allie Rutherford To protest that Power Pivot was not included in all editions of Office 2013, I ran over to the Microsoft Company Store and bought enough Pivot shirts to outfit all of the Excel MVPs attending the Summit. We showed up for the Meet the Excel Team wearing these shirts. I will note that soon after, Power Pivot was added to the stand-alone boxed edition of Excel 2013.

Index

Symbols

EXCEL FORMULAS

IF & Related

Pay a 2% bonus on revenue in F2 if the sale is $20K or higher: =IF(F2>=20000,.02*F2,0)

Pay the bonus if F2 over $20K and G2 > 50%: =IF(AND(F2>20000,G2>.5),.02*F2,0)

1% bonus for sales over 100 and 2% for sales over 400: =IF(F2>400,.02,IF(F2>100,.01,0))*F2

Count all numbers > 100: =COUNTIF(A2:A99,">100")

Sum all numbers > 100: =SUMIF(A2:A99,">100",A2:A99)

Sum all numbers over average: =SUMIF(A2:A99,">"&AVERAGE(A2:A99),A2:A99)

Sum all numbers where Region in B is East: =SUMIF(B2:B99,"East",A2:A99)

When testing for multiple conditions, use COUNTIFS, AVERAGEIFS, or SUMIFS. Add the numbers in A if B is East and C is Widgets: =SUMIFS(A2:A99,B2:B99,"East", C2:C99,"Widgets")

Avoid Errors

Use =IFERROR(Formula,Value if Error) to prevent a calculation from returning an error.

To prevent DIV/0 errors: =IFERROR(D2/C2,0)

To prevent #N/A from lookup: =IFERROR(VLOOKUP(...),"Not Found")

Use $ to Lock a Reference

Most cell references will change as you copy the formula. This is usually great, but sometimes you need a formula to always point to a particular cell (say, a tax rate stored in M1). Change M1 to $M$1 in the formula to lock the formula reference. To freeze only the row, use M$1 – the formula will change to other columns when copied left or right. To freeze only the column, use $M1 the row can change, but it will always point to M.

Tip: Press F4 while the insertion point is next to M1 in the formula bar to automatically add the dollar signs. Pressing F4 repeatedly will toggle through M1, $M$1, M$1, $M1, then back to M1.

VLOOKUP

Use the exact match version VLOOKUP to get a value from a lookup table. In the figure below, the original data had ItemID but no Item Description. Use VLOOKUP to return the description from a lookup table. Some guidelines:

- The ID that you are looking up has to be in the left column of the lookup table.
- Put four $ in the lookup table reference so the table doesn't shift as you copy the formula.
- The column # is the column within the lookup table. In the figure below, column G is the 2nd column in F3:G30.
- The final FALSE indicates you want an exact match. Always end with FALSE.

	A	B	C	D	E	F	G
	Item	Date	Qty	Description		Wa SKU	Description
2	W25-6	8/16/2009	878	18K Italian Gold Women's			
3	CR 50-4	8/16/2009	213				
4	CR 50-4	8/17/2009	744				
5	BR26-3	8/18/2009	169				
6	CR50-6	8/18/2009	822				
7	ER46-14	8/18/2009	740				
8	RG78-25	8/18/2009	638				

fx =VLOOKUP(A2,$F$3:$G$30,2,FALSE)

Troubleshooting: VLOOKUP does not pay attention to upper case. "ABC" will match "Abc". However, VLOOKUP will not find a match if one value has extra spaces. If VLOOKUP should be finding a match and you are getting #N/A, use F2 to put the cell in edit mode. See if the flashing insertion point is a few spaces away from the last character. To remove leading and trailing spaces, use =TRIM(). Also: a number stored as text will not match a cell with a true number. Select the entire column containing numbers stored as text and type Alt+D followed by E and F to convert text numbers to values.

Use the range lookup to find values within a range. When 12835 is not found in the bonus table, Excel returns the next smaller value. This is the only time the lookup table has to be sorted.

fx =VLOOKUP(C2,$F$2:$G$6,2)

C	D	E	F	G	H
Amount	Bonus		Sale	Bonus	
12835	12		0	0	
19634	12		5000	5	
5898	5		10000	12	
27995	100		20000	50	
6239	5		25000	100	
19957	12				

Spearing Through Sheets

Sum Cell C5 on worksheets Jan through Dec with =SUM(Jan:Dec!C5). If the worksheet name contains a space or other special character, use apostrophes: =SUM('Jan 14: Dec 14'!C5).

Text Formulas

Join A2 & B2 with space in between: =A2&" "&B2 (& is like CONCATENATE but shorter to spell!)

Proper Case: =PROPER(A2) (Doesn't work with McD names)

Upper Case: =UPPER(A2)

Lower Case =LOWER(A2)

Length of text: =LEN(A2)

Left 5 characters: =LEFT(A2,5)

Left all but right 2: =LEFT(A2,LEN(A2)-2)

Characters 3 through 7: =MID(A2,3,5)

Right 3 characters: =RIGHT(A2,3)

Location of first Dash: =FIND("-",A2)

Up to first dash: =LEFT(A2,FIND("-",A2)-1)

All after first dash:=MID(A2,FIND("-",A2)+1,999)

Note that FIND is case-sensitive. Use =SEARCH("*mart",A2) when case does not matter or when you need to include a wildcard.

To replace 2014 with 2015, use =SUBSTITUTE(B1,"2014","2015")

Summing Visible Rows

If you've hidden rows using a filter, switch from SUM to SUBTOTAL. =SUBTOTAL(9,A2:A99) will total only the visible rows. Caution: if you manually hid the rows, use =SUBTOTAL(109,...).

AGGREGATE is like SUBTOTAL, but with 19 functions instead of 11. You can choose to ignore hidden rows, error cells, and other SUBTOTAL/AGGREGATE functions.

Formula Auditing

See all formulas at once with Ctrl+` (in the USA, the ` and the ~ share a key just below Esc).

Which cells does the current cell rely on? Formulas, Trace Precedents.

Which cells use the current cell to calculate? Formulas, Trace Dependents.

If either Trace command shows an arrow pointing to a worksheet icon, double click the arrow for a list of off-sheet precedents.

You can click either Trace icon multiple times to see 2nd, 3rd level arrows.

Click Remove All Arrows to remove the arrows.

MREXCEL.COM

Formula Speed – Running Totals

Say you have numbers in A2:A10000. You want a running total in B. The simple method: =A2 in cell B2, then =A3+B2 in cells B3:B10000. The complex method is =SUM(A$2:A2). While the 2nd method seems easier, the first formula calculates faster. The first formula looks at 2 cells for each formula. The second method looks at thousands of cells for each formula. For more formula speed tips, see www.decisionmodels.com

Range Names

A named range can refer to a single cell, a range of cells, or a formula. To assign a name to a single cell, select the cell, then type a name in the Name Box to the left of the formula bar. Names can not contain spaces. Use GrossProfit or Gross_Profit instead of two words.

Once you have defined some names, you can use the names for navigation. Open the dropdown arrow in the Name Box and click a name to move to that cell. Names can also be used in a formula: =GrossProfit/Revenue.

For a fast way to create names, use Formulas, Create from Selection. In the figure below, 7 names will be created. Jan will refer to B2:B5. Dill will refer to B5:D5.

	A	B	C	D
1		Jan	Feb	Mar
2	Apple	1	2	4
3	Banana	8	16	32
4	Cherry	64	128	256
5	Dill	512	1024	2048

Create Names from Selection

Create names from values in the:
- ☑ Top row
- ☑ Left column
- ☐ Bottom row

=SUM(Jan,Feb) will add the values in B2:C5. =SUM(Feb Dill) will return the intersection of Feb and Dill or 1024. (The space between Feb and Dill is the intersection operator.) =SUM(Banana:Dill) will add B3:D5.

Implicit intersection: Type =Banana anywhere in columns B:D and Excel will return only the cell in the Banana range that falls in the same column as the formula.

Converting Formula Results to Values

To freeze formula results as values: in Excel 2010 or higher, use: Ctrl+C, followed by the Application key and then V. For earlier versions, use Ctrl+C, followed by Alt+E then SV.

Loan Payments

For monthly payments, divide the annual interest rate by 12. If you want the payment amount to be positive, use a negative amount for the principle. For $350,000 mortgage, 30 years, 4% interest:

=PMT(4%/12,360,-350000)

Exponents & Roots

Use ^ for exponents: =5^3 is 5*5*5 or 125

Raise to a fraction for a root: =256^(1/4) is fourth root of 256 or 4.

Compounded Growth Rate

Year 1 sales: 100K. Year 5 sales: 225K. Compounded Annual Growth Rate =(Year5/Year1)^(1/(Years-1))-1

=(225/100)^(1/4)-1 = 22.4745%

Rounding

Round to 2 decimals: =ROUND(A2,2)

Round to 100's: =ROUND(A2,-2)

Round to nearest 25: =MROUND(A2,25)

Round up next 1: =CEILING(A2,1)

Round up to next 100: =CEILING(A2,3)

Round down to next 10: =FLOOR(A2,2)

Strip off decimals: =INT(A2)

Keep only decimals =MOD(A2,1)

Ranking & Counting

Find the rank of an item with =RANK(A2,A$2:A$20). If two items are tied for 5th place, both will have a RANK of 5 and there will be nothing ranked 6. If you are using VLOOKUP to return the top 10 items from the RANK column and need every rank to appear once, use =RANK(A2,A$2:A$20)+COUNTIF(A$1:A1,A2).

To calculate the rank as a percentile between 0 and 100%, use =PERCENTRANK.INC(A$2:A$20,A2).

=COUNT(A2:A99) only counts numeric cells. To count text and numeric cells, use =COUNTA(A2:A99).

Date Functions

End of Month: =EOMONTH(A2,0)

End of Last Month: =EOMONTH(A2,-1)

First of Month: =EOMONTH(A2,-1)+1

First of Week: =TODAY()-WEEKDAY(TODAY(),3)

Today's Date: =TODAY()

Current Time: =NOW()-TODAY()

Year: =YEAR(A2)

Month (as 1-12): =MONTH(A2)

Month as "Jan": =TEXT(A2,"MMM")

15 Months after A2: =DATE(YEAR(A2), MONTH(A2)+15,DAY(A2))

To show 40 hours, use custom number format [h]:mm

Calculate work days when closed Weds & Sat: =NETWORKDAYS.INTL(A2,B2,"0010010")

Other Useful Functions

Metric conversions: =CONVERT(A2,"km","mi")

Largest Value: =MAX(A2:A99)

2nd Largest Value: =LARGE(A2:A99,2)

Smallest Value: =MIN(A2:A99)

3rd Smallest Value: =SMALL(A2:A99,3)

Random integer from 10 to 50: = RANDBETWEEN(10,50)

Roman numerals =ROMAN(2014)

Arabic numerals =ARABIC("MMIV") (2013 only)

Repeat | A2 times =REPT("|",A2)

To show the formula from A2, use =FORMULATEXT(A2) (New in 2013)

Create hyperlink with =HYPERLINK("http://"&A2,A2)

Worksheet name: =MID(CELL("filename"), FIND("]",CELL("filename"))+1,32)

To refer to a cell reference that is calculated on the fly, use =INDIRECT(TEXT(TODAY(), "MMM")&"!A2")

To change the size of the reference, use =OFFSET(A2,0,0,COUNTA(A:A)-1,1)

MREXCEL.COM © 2014 MrExcel.com

Follow Bill Jelen on Twitter @MrExcel

Fair use: If you **bought** this PDF, print up to 10 copies with my compliments. Beyond that, buy a license to print more copies; $1 per 10 copies via PayPal to Karma @ MrExcel.com. Need to make just 1 copy? Go ahead, but please tweet "#FF @MrExcel Thanks for the #Excel tips!"

$2.95 Print ISBN 978-1-61547-996-2
$1.00 PDF ISBN 978-1-61547-989-4

Excel Classifieds / Excel Resources

Excel
Learning Zone

Do you need to learn Microsoft Excel? We have dozens of **video tutorials** to teach you how to become an expert with Excel in no time.

Our lessons are presented by **Richard Rost**, a Microsoft

Complete Idiot's G

Use this special link to watch our Level 1 Excel lesson absolutely **FREE** of charge:
http://599cd.com/XMRXL

In addition to Excel, we also have lessons available for Windows, Word, our specialty, **Microsoft Access**, and lots more.

Acce ss
Learning Zone